THE
PORNOGRAPHY
CONTROVERSY

THE PORNOGRAPHY CONTROVERSY

**Changing Moral Standards
in
American Life**

Ray C. Rist

Transaction Books
New Brunswick, New Jersey

Library of Congress Catalog Number: 73-92813
ISBN: 0-87855-093-3 (cloth); 0-87855-587-0 (paper)

Printed in the United States of America

iv

CONTENTS

PORNOGRAPHY AND DILEMMAS OF MORALITY

PORNOGRAPHY AND SOCIAL SCIENCE RESEARCH

PREFACE

The United States is a complex and highly heterogeneous society. It is faced with such paramount issues as racism, poverty, environmental pollution, the nuclear arms race, corruption of government, and the decline of democratic institutions. Is it not then paradoxical that so much attention and energy is spent discussing and debating "what to do" about pornography? Considering the other problems that confront us, a discussion of action related to sexually explicit material may seem a frivolous luxury that American society can ill afford at this time. Those addressing themselves to saving the eco-system (and the human species) or those working for a new and more humane political system can rightly ask why even the most extreme sexual material should compete as an imminent social problem for the attention of citizens.

Objectively, of course, sexual material does not in any way compare with these conditions. Pornography is no more than a "pseudo" problem when any attempt is made, for example, to evaluate it in light of the possibility of nuclear warfare. Yet for many, the presence of pornography in American society is viewed as a threat to the "moral standards" of the country or as an omen of the decay and decline in the "moral fabric" of the society. The concern is sometimes expressed as follows: "If the moral climate of the country is polluted with pornography, it won't make any difference what the air is like." A polarity of views emerge when debating whether pornography constitutes a legitimate social problem. Those who express concern about such material hold the view that issues of public morality take precedence over issues related to objective social conditions. Others argue that the material conditions of the society are more important than any attempt to formulate public moral standards. Such opposing views often give evidence of differing perspectives on the appropriate role of the state and the means by which this civil society should be governed.

Were pornography amenable to empirical analysis—could it be analyzed, evaluated or measured for irrefutable conclusions as to its "goodness" or "badness," its "corruption" or "edification," its short- and long-term effects on human values and behavior—then there would be data upon which many of the present debates and dilemmas could be resolved—assuming all parties involved were agreeable to base conclusions on research findings. But sexual material does not appear to be accurately evaluated by measures now available; we have been, heretofore, unable to create measures of values which are themselves "value free." In other words, the very criteria by which one would wish to evaluate pornography, its "goodness" or "badness," are in themselves subjectively determined and represent normative decisions on the part of those defining the terms.

The current controversy over the presence of pornography in American society occurs simultaneously on two levels: one philosophical or theoretical; the other pragmatic or operational. The philosophical issues relate to notions of morality, to the parameters of civil democracy and to the rights of the individual as a member of both society and the state. The pragmatic or operational concerns are: enactment of law, the use of coercion to contain certain forms of cultural expression and defining what, in fact, constitutes pornography.

The essays in this volume address themselves to these two levels of the controversy. It should be evident that there is no consensus among the authors represented. Opposing points of view are presented with respect to theoretical as well as operational concerns. In this conection, one will find a myriad of views on what would constitute the "good society" as well as the "good state."

The fact that there is no single proper posture toward either morality or law means both the individual and the collectivity must continually scrutinize their operational positions as well as their theoretical assumptions. To assume an absolute—either with respect to what constitutes "pornography" or "what to do" about it—is to assume a static society, and, as we suggest in our subtitle, "Changing Moral Standards in American Life," social change in America is alive and well.

January 1974
Portland, Oregon

SOME
THEORETICAL
CONCERNS

1 Pornography as a Social Problem: Reflections on the Relation of Morality and the Law

Ray C. Rist

In American society, the use of law has become a major, if not the exclusive, instrument for the amelioration of what are believed to be pressing social problems.[1] With incessant and escalating pressures to "do something," the passage of legislation provides both the politician with a visible demonstration of his concern and his constituents with reassurance that something is indeed being done to resolve the problem.[2] Mandatory automobile-emission inspections, the hiring of women and minorities for other than their traditionally segregated and low-paying jobs, the banning of the pesticide DDT, and the refusal of cities to allow theaters to show live sexual acts are but a few of the situations in which behavior is being compelled or prohibited by law in response to a perceived problem. In the end, the law is being used to coerce people into being virtuous.

But things are not always as they appear. The passage of legislation does not necessarily imply the existence within a community of a consensus as to what precisely constitutes the "problem," or how most effectively to resolve it. On the contrary, there may be significant disagreement on the issue and the resultant law may be only the reflections of one segment of the population who were able to transform their particular position into law.[3] Using law to impose virtue implies a conception of what behavior is believed to be virtuous or moral or proper. When law is used in this

1

manner, it becomes a means of expressing the views of those who have the power to define the terms and have these terms become the ones on which the problem is approached. Though the reliance on law to respond to social problems in this society has taken on an aura of being both inevitable and desirable, it need not be either. Further, the attempt to solve problems through the instrumentality of law may not diminish the magnitude of the situation, but in fact enhance it. Thus the law comes to be placed in the paradoxical position of reinforcing what it theoretically intended to eradicate.

MORALITY AND LAW

John Stuart Mill has written what is perhaps the most frequently quoted libertarian position on the relation of the individual to the state. He noted in his essay, *On Liberty*:

the sole end for which mankind are warranted, individually or collectively, in interfering with the liberty or action of any of their number, is self protection. That the only purpose for which power can be rightfully exercised over any member of a civilized community, against his will, is to prevent harm to others. His own good, either physical or moral, is not sufficient warrant. He cannot rightfully be compelled to do or forebear because it will be better for him to do so, because it will make him happier, because, in the opinion of others, to do so would be wise, or even right. These are good reasons for remonstrating with him or reasoning with him, or entreating him, but not for compelling him, or visiting him with any evil in case he do otherwise.[4]

Mill is obviously opposed to the intervention of the state in the lives of individuals to decide for them what is right or wrong. In short, he rejects the notion of the state as paternalistic.

Yet, in Mill's statement lies the basis upon which one can justify the use of law—to "prevent harm to others." The conditions, however, by which one determines the presence of "harm," or even more fundamentally, how one defines "harm," are not spelled out by Mill and thus remain ambiguous. The cursory argument often made that Mill stands against the use of law to govern the actions of men falls apart upon close examination. Mill is not that unequivocal. The ambiguity in his stance arises both from leaving several key terms undefined and implying a need for "balancing" the rights and responsibilities of the individual and the state. The ambiguity of his position is further deepened by not distinguishing the state from the collectivity of persons who come together to form that state—the society. In the quote noted above, he writes of the "civilized community," but one is left to infer whether he meant the state or the society.

If Mill is correct in suggesting a need for the "balancing" standard between the society and the state, there emerges a series of complex issues and questions. A number of them relate to the situation previously alluded to where Mill does not define critical terms. If one is going to have to balance the various "harms" confronting him, it would be well to know what precisely it is that needs to be balanced, how to measure it, how to observe changes in its impact, and how to make informed evaluations as to its condition before and after the passage of law. If law is to be an instrument of preserving the "civilized community" through imposing virtue, then there needs to be some means by which to assay its effectiveness. Such assessment is nearly nonexistent. As Skolnick notes,

> the lack of even a rudimentary social scientific approach to the law-and-morals issue has resulted in deplorable unclarity. Issues are not joined, complexities are bypassed, and empirical evidence ignored—with a distressingly foggy outcome.[5]

I want to suggest that such is the current situation with respect to the debate over the presence of sexually explicit material in American society.[6] The debate has a "deplorable unclarity" and often ends in a "distressingly foggy outcome." In agreement with Skolnick, I will also suggest that the situation is the result of the lack of a "rudimentary social scientific approach" to the problem and the reliance, instead, on a collection of assumptions—untested and unexplicated.

There are at least two discernible theoretical perspectives upon which those who have sought to utilize law as a coercive agent to "prevent harm to others" have justified their case. The first holds that law is no more than a reflection of the most cherished values commonly held by members of the society. Thus, the social mores of the society are transformed into the laws of the state. William Graham Sumner held to this position and theorized that law represented a "crystallization of the mores combined with collective power to maintain the status quo."[7] But Sumner also noted the process by which mores are transformed into law is not always readily discernible. He posited the existence of both "public morals" and "positive law" and suggested the frequent shifts in the content of legal statutes resulted from a shifting of the boundaries between those values perceived as residing .in law and those perceived as residing in societal mores. Of further importance in Sumner's position is that he believes both could be effective means of insuring social control; that the pursuit of virtue could be other than the enactment of laws. Not all forms of societal control necessarily had to transform themselves into forms of state control.

From a different perspective, Durkheim stressed the distinctions between the state and its processes of legislation and the society with its "collective consciousness." For Durkheim, the former was the source of much that is rational and logical. It is deliberative and methodical, while the collective morality of the society may be swayed by irrationalities of passion, nationalism or religious fervor. Thus the state becomes the source of guidelines for the society which itself exists with obscure and indefinite myths and legends. He noted:

It is not accurate to say that the State embodies the collective consciousness, for that goes beyond the State at every point. In the main, that consciousness is diffused: there is at all times a vast number of social sentiments and social states of mind of all kinds, of which the State hears only a faint echo. The State is the center only of a particular kind of consciousness, of one that is limited but higher, clearer and with a more vivid sense of itself. There is nothing so obscure and so indefinite as those collective representations that are spread throughout all societies—myths, religious and moral legends, and so on. . . . The representations that derive from the State . . . are distinguished from the other collective representations by their higher degree of consciousness and reflection.[8]

Rather than law embodying the sentiments of the society, as suggested by Sumner, Durkheim posits law to be higher and more removed from these obscure impulses of the society. Law, for Durkheim, is reflective, not reflexive.

In the current controversy over the presence of sexually explicit material in American society, the two positions represented by Sumner and Durkheim appear nearly to merge in urging the use of law to repress such material. Criminal law statutes are suggested as the most rational and effective means of controlling the resultant "irrational" behavior likely to occur as a result of reading such material. Thus, law is necessary for the prevention of "harm." Likewise, the instrumental use of law becomes the goal of those who would wish for American society to convert its public morals into positive law. This latter position indicates the necessity of some formal statement by the state as to the unacceptability of such material—to define clearly the boundaries between acceptable and unacceptable social behavior. Such guidelines will give public expression to what is also presumed to be a public consensus on the matter. With the two positions converging in their perspective as to the use of law, with respect to sexually explicit material, there results both a push and a pull towards the creation of law to control such material.

IMMORALITY AND LAW

If the philosophical positions of Sumner and Durkheim have, in fact, coincided in regard to the "proper posture" of law toward sexually explicit material, the several components of that merger should be discernible. There are at least three distinct rationales for the control of such material through law. In the following pages, we shall focus upon each in turn.[9]

The first claim is simply that sexually explicit material causes harm: that it has a serious and deleterious impact upon individuals and upon the moral fabric of the society in general. The use of such material is also said to cause not only personal problems, but social ones, as well. This claim is ultimately empirical and raises issues of effects, causes, the interpretation of "facts," and even the methodology for gaining such facts.

In discussing the difficulties of ascertaining the presence or absence of effects in the general area of "crimes without victims," Skolnick has noted:

> A description of effects entails several difficulties, not the least of which is distinguishing independent from dependent variables. For instance, do repressive laws tend to eliminate social problems or simply aggravate them? "Nothing can be more certain," wrote Oliver Goldsmith, "than that numerous written laws are a sign of a degenerate community, and are frequently not the consequences of vicious morals in a state, but the causes." Goldsmith's puritan contemporaries in the United States held an opposite opinion. For them, numerous written proscriptive laws were a sign of a godly community and were an appropriate means for curbing vicious morals in a state.[10]

After a number of years of remaining noncommital on the subject and in opposition to a large body of data collected by the Commission on Obscenity and Pornography, the Supreme Court ruled, in five obscenity-related cases, on June 21, 1973, that, in the absence of contrary evidence, the courts in the United States can now assume negative effects of sexually explicit material and they need not be proved by scientific inquiry.[11] Until this ruling, the Supreme Court had been guided by the landmark *Roth* decision of 1957 where it held that the protections of the First and Fourteenth Amendments—requiring that harm, or an immediate danger of harm, be shown in justification of a governmental prohibition—did not apply to the dissemination of the "obscene."[12] But with the recent ruling, it is now permissible for legislatures to act against sexually explicit material on the basis of unprovable assumptions of harm (ignoring contrary evidence) with respect to the effects issue. Relevant excerpts from one of the majority opinions written by Chief Justice Warren Burger are as follows:

> But it is argued, there is no scientific data which conclusively demonstrates that exposure to obscene materials adversely affects men and women or their society. It is urged on behalf of the petitioner that, absent such a demonstration, any kind of state regulation is "impermissible."

We regret this argument. Although there is no conclusive proof of a connection between antisocial behavior and obscene materials, the legislature of Georgia could quite reasonably determine that such a connection does or might exist.

From the beginning of civilized societies, legislatures and judges have acted on various unprovable assumptions. Such assumptions underlie much lawful state regulation of commercial and business affairs.

If we accept the unprovable assumption that a complete education requires certain books, and the well nigh universal belief that good books, plays, and art lift the spirit, improve the mind, enrich the human personality and develop character, can we then say that a state legislature may not act on the corollary assumption that commerce in obscene books, or public exhibitions focused on obscene conduct, have a tendency to exert a corrupting and degrading impact leading to antisocial behavior?[13]

This position of the Chief Justice, couched in such ambiguous terms as "might exist," "various unprovable assumptions," or "tendency" clearly comes down on the side of social control, even in the absence of empirical verification. In fact, it might be asked whether the stance of the majority justices would have changed had twice the data been amassed indicating an absence of a clear correlation between such material and behavior. I doubt it. The decision was ultimately one for which social science data was irrelevant; it was one based on a philosophical assumption, not an empirical statement.

Parenthetically, this decision began to have an impact almost from the day it was announced. For example, the sheriff of a county in Virginia (proudly identified by the sheriff as the birthplace of James Madison and the home of Thomas Jefferson) ordered all copies of *Playboy* and similar men's magazines to be removed from all retail outlets in the county. The sheriff, after stating that "anything with pubic hair showing, we think, is objectionable," supported his argument with the following comments: "I think they have a tendency to bring about violations of our state laws. We've had several rape cases here in the past years and magazines like this could lead to things like that. I have arrested rapists here and they've had pictures of naked women in their rooms."[14]

There is a key sociological problem inherent in this first claim of the harm of sexually explicit material: it is the means by which reality is socially constructed; the means by which definitions of situations are offered as the appropriate definitions. This is crucial for any number of authorities, ranging from the president of the United States to the chief justice of the Supreme Court to the sheriff of that county in Virginia. They have all made assumptions about such material, acted upon those assumptions and justified them with a particular value system as opposed to empirical evidence. Such constructions of reality result in a, situation where there is no possibility of refuting the presuppositions—for they do not allow for verification. The most social science may hope to accomplish in this situation is, at least, to force a wedge into these constructions of reality by presenting alternative and competing definitions of the phenomena.[15] A corollary to this position is the necessity also to study those who create the definitions, to analyze their values and judgements, for, ultimately, such definitions may find themselves incorporated into the administration of law.

Beyond contending such material is the cause of harmful effects, a second claim emerges from the synthesis of the positions of Sumner and Durkheim that there is a general societal consensus that such material is distasteful and should therefore be forbidden. In short, law is claimed to coincide with consensus. Immorality is what everyone knows to be immoral and, consequently, there is no need for individual discretion in deciding what is or is not to be acceptable. From Sumner's perspective would come the argument that all "right-thinking citizens" would wish to preserve their society and its conventional morality. Sexually explicit material threatens that societal consensus and should therefore be suppressed. For those who, on the other hand, see the state as the embodiment of rationality and reason, the position would be that the law is an instrument which teaches—guiding, nurturing and sustaining an impulsive society. Therefore, to bring the society to an awareness of the harmful effects of sexually explicit material, it is necessary to make use of the law in its teaching capacity so that the citizens can become enlightened. One finds hints of the Sumner and the Durkheim positions in these two passages from Devlin:

Society is entitled by means of its laws to protect itself from dangers, whether from within or without . . . . The justification for this is that established government is necessary for the existence of society and, therefore, its safety against violent overthrow must be secured. But an established morality is as necessary as good government to the welfare of the society. Societies disintegrate from within more frequently than they are broken up by external pressures. There is disintegration when no common morality is observed and history shows that the loosening of moral bonds is often the first stage of disintegration, so that society is justified in taking steps to preserve its moral code as it does to preserve its government and other essential institutions.

And again, he writes:

Society cannot live without morals. Its morals are those standard of conduct which the reasonable man approves. A rational man, who is also a good man, may have other standards. If he has no standards at all he is not a good man and need not be further considered.[16]

With this proposition, as with the first, there are difficulties. For example, there is the assumption that, in as heterogeneous a society as the United States, a body of values and norms exists which is acceptable throughout the society, regardless of social class, ethnicity, region, race or religion. At one level, this assumption is quite correct. There is little debate over the undesirability of such behavior as incest or child-beating. But when one moves to such behavior as the use of alcohol, tobacco, drugs, or sexually explicit material, there is little credence in maintaining that all members of the society agree on how such behavior is to be evaluated. In the past history of this country, one finds situations where a small group of individuals, who were highly organized in support of a particular position, succeeded in having that position become the dominant community standard through the legislation of law.[17] Howard Becker refers to those who seek to transform a particular moral position into law and thus create a criminal classification for the negation of that position as "moral entrepreneurs."[18] In an earlier time, the prohibitionist served as an excellent representative of this type. Out of fervor to save people from the immorality of drinking, the Eighteenth Amendment was passed prohibiting everyone from drinking. A convincing parallel can be drawn to the activities of many organizations currently attempting to have sexually explicit material repressed.[19] Common to both is an attempt to have one set of norms, one set of values, for the dominant and public standards of the whole society. An irony apparent in some aspects of this struggle of one group for moral ascendancy is the very reality of the struggle itself which belies the claim of consensus. In the end, it is not so much consensus as dominance and not so much morality as status which motivates many of the participants in the struggle.

Of the recommendations of the Commission on Obscenity and Pornography, which released its report in September of 1970, none gained the attention or was the subject of more controversy than the one which read: "The Commission recommends that federal, state, and local legislation prohibiting the sale, exhibition, or distribution of sexual materials to consenting adults should be repealed."[20] By recommending this repeal action, the commission went counter to what is a third proposition congruent with the two theoretical perspectives previously mentioned. This proposition is that the principal result of the enforcement of the criminal law, with respect to the use of sexually explicit material, will be a deterrant to the use of such material. With the sanction of law as a formal codification of societal mores, it is argued there would be a strong inhibiting factor restraining persons from using the material. Any measure less than law—relying on informal social controls, for example—is held to be ineffective and would only lead to flouting disregard of the dominant consensus. The corollary to this position is that the greater the penalty for both the use and distribution of such material, the less the presence of the material in the society. Succinctly, if the pain outweighs the pleasure, the behavior will cease.[21]

Skolnick terms this perspective on the use of law as "enforcement theory" and notes:

There are a variety of difficulties with that easy assumption. First, all potential defenders will not calculate the threat of sanctions with the same precision . . . . Secondly, potential offenders may use different yardsticks. The subjective meaning of a period of imprisonment may well differ, depending upon the types of crime. Third, even assuming a process of rational calculation, the size of a penalty constitutes only one part of the equation. Equally important is the probability that enforcement will take place. If a potential offender is to make a rational calculation, how is he to weigh the size of the penalty against the probability of enforcement? Is a penalty of one year, with a chance of one in one hundred of being caught, a greater or lesser deterrent than a penalty of five years with a chance of one in one thousand of being caught?[22]

If threats or sanctions are to be successful in deterring the use of sexually explicit material, there would have to be a perception among its potential users of the rationality of such restrictions. To legitimate such sanctions, it is generally argued that the material has negative and anti-social effects on individuals and that it causes general societal harm through its corrupting influences on social morals. But when that law is perceived to lack a legitimate rationality or justification for its repressive measures, through a comparison to personal experience, then that law tends to lose its desired effect to guide and curb the proscribed behavior. In the absence of consent, those who would enforce the law have only coercion and threat of sanction to employ in seeking compliance. Ultimately, law is only possible in a democratic society when those who submit to it do so because they believe it to be legitimate and possessing a sanctioned authority.

With sexual material, there appears to have been a gradual lessening of support for restrictive legislation, not only because of increased concern with the First Amendment guarantees of freedom to read and see what one desires, but, perhaps more profoundly, because, in the test against personal experience, the claims of harm and degeneracy do not hold up. In a national survey conducted for the Commission on Obscenity and Pornography, several pertinent questions were asked.[23] One was whether reading sexually explicit material "provided entertainment." Forty-eight percent of the total sample thought it did and 18 percent said it did for them personally. Asked if such material "provided information about sex," 61 percent agreed it did and 24 percent said it had for them personally. On the other hand, when asked if sexual materials "lead to breakdown of morals," 56 percent agreed it did, but only 1 percent said it had that effect on themselves, 13 percent said it had such an effect on someone they knew, and 38 percent said they personally knew no one who had been so affected. Asked if sexual material "makes people sex crazy," 37 percent agreed it did, but less than half of 1 percent said it had done it to them personally, 9 percent said it was done to someone they knew, and 27 percent said it was done to none they knew. The last two questions suggest some gap between the values and the actual experience of the respondents, but the nearly total absence of personally experienced negative effects may be the basis for an emergent skepticism about presumed societal effects.

VIRTUE WITHOUT LAW?

The major premises advocated by those who seek to employ criminal law to restrict and control sexually explicit material all use coercion to enforce virtue. The first premise, suggesting that sexually explicit material causes individual as well as societal harm, is extremely difficult to measure "objectively." Empirical conclusions are thus tenuous at best. There is also the further difficulty of agreeing on the definition of key terms one would use for measurement. The second premise—a general societal consensus as to the undesirability of such material—is difficult to substantiate. What is often argued as representative of a general view is more often that of a small, but highly organized and articulate, group that has been successful in promoting its conception of the social order as the most appropriate and legitimate one. The final permise—enforcement being the most effective means of dealing with such material and diminishing its presence in the society—is yet to be verified. As in other situations where there is no demonstrable "victim," enforcement is often sporadic, arbitrary and subject to the whims of the enforcers.

When law becomes a vehicle to enforce a particular moral philosophy, there is the continual danger of its abuse, since the law does not reflect a consensus as to the appropriate social policy for the society, but the power of a particular group engaged in status politics. In the arena of law, the issue of sexually explicit material is not one of some moral absolute, but one of priorities. To operationalize a program of repression against sexual material has very real social costs. Not only are the energies of enforcement officials diverted from other possible areas of concern, but there is a significant outlay of community funds for such enforcement. In 1970, the Commission on Obscenity and Pornography conservatively estimated the cost of enforcing state and local statutes against sexually explicit material at between $5 and $10 million dollars annually. In addition, there were additional federal costs of between $3 and $5 million more each year.[24] In a very pragmatic way, the question can be posed as to whether American citizens believe that this is a good way to spend a sum of between $8 and $15 million dollars each year, particularly if the alternative were increased aid to libraries, hospitals, prisons, or simply lower taxes.

When a single definition of what is correct, proper, and moral becomes ascendant, those who do not hold such views or conform to such behavior patterns are subject to being labelled "deviant" or "criminal."[25] It is assumed such labelling will deter others and induce the labelled to refrain in the future. In this manner, the dominant mores and values of the group in a position to transform their values into law will be maintained. Yet, definitions of reality are always tenuous, being continually constructed and reconstructed. Value systems do not escape this state of flux. Thus, an irony of exclusive reliance on law to ensure virtue is that, as value systems change, the legitimacy of a particular morality in the guise of law becomes weakened. There is less inhibition to explore the new and taboo. The forbidden is enticing. Those who seek a dominant position for their moral position are inadvertently laying the seeds for the eventual overthrow of that position. The law then finds itself in the untenable position of reinforcing what it was designed to eradicate. Such, I suspect, will be the case with sexually explicit material in the United States—at least until that time when we have more adequately reflected on the ends of liberal democracy and the needs of civil society.

NOTES

1. The theoretical framework used in this article is, in large part, derived from that developed by Jerome Skolnick in his piece, "Coercion to Virtue: The Enforcement of Morals," *Southern California Law Review*, vol. 41, no. 3 (1968).

2. For two insightful discussions on the process by which certain social conditions become defined as "social problems," and the variously ensuing political responses, c.f. Robert Ross, and Graham Staines, "The Politics of Analyzing Social Problems," *Social Problems*, vol. 20, no. 1 (Summer 1972); and Thomas Schwartz, "Social Problems Awareness Manifested Through Sociological Research, Newspapers and Creative Literature," *The Sociological Quarterly*, vol. 14, no. 1 (Winter, 1973).

3. The work by Joseph Gusfield, *Symbolic Crusade* (Urbana, Illinois: University of Illinois Press, 1963), is perhaps the landmark study in the relation of status politics and perceptions of the moral order. His work details the activities of the Woman's Christian Temperance Movement and the passage of the Eighteenth Amendment.

4. John Stuart Mill, *On Liberty* (New York: Appleton-Century-Crofts, 1943), pp 84-85.

5. Skolnick, "Coercion to Virtue," pp. 590-91.

6. Following the Commission on Obscenity and Pornography, the term "sexually explicit material" or "sexual material" will be used throughout the remainder of this paper in lieu of such terms as "pornography," "pornographic," "obscene," and "erotica." As the commission suggests, these latter terms have lost any precise meaning and often represent no more than subjective disapproval of certain materials.

7. Cf. Harry Ball, George Simpson, and Kiyoshi Ikeda, "Law and Social Change: Sumner Reconsidered," *American Journal of Sociology*, vol. 67 (1962): 532-40, for a general discussion of Sumner's views presented here.

8. Emile Durkheim, *Professional Ethics and Civic Morals* (New York: The Free Press 1958), p. 50.

9. Skolnick, "Coercion to Virtue," pp. 593-639, has elaborated upon these at great length. What is presented in the following discussion is an attempt to transpose that analysis to the issue of sexually explicit material, which Skolnick himself does not do.

10. Ibid., pp. 594-95.

11. For a summary of many of the rulings of the Supreme Court, prior to the mid-1960s and an analysis of their implications, cf. R. Kuh, *Foolish Figleaves?* (New York: MacMillan), 1967.

12. *Roth* vs. *United States*, 354 U.S. 476 (1957).

13. Quoted from the *New York Times*, June 22, 1973, 42-c.

14. Quoted from the *Washington Star-News*, July 5, 1973, 1.

15. The impact of the *Report of the Commission on Obscenity* in doing precisely this—creating a gap in purely political definitions of situations—is examined at some length in R. Rist, "Policy, Politics, and Social Research: A Study in the Relationship of Federal Commissions and Social Science," *Social Problems*, vol. 21, no. 1 (Summer 1973). This article is also reprinted in this volume.

16. Patrick Devlin, *The Enforcement of Morals* (London: Oxford University Press, 1965), pp. 13-14 and 24-25.

17. Cf. Gusfield, *Symbolic Crusade*.

18. Howard S. Becker, *The Outsiders* (New York: The Free Press 1963), pp. 147-65. He notes, "Rules are the products of someone's initiative and we can think of the people who exhibit such enterprise as *moral entrepreneurs*" (emphasis in the original), p. 147.

19. Cf. Louis Zurcher, and Charles Bowman, "The Natural History of an ad hoc anti-Pornography Organization in Southtown, U.S.A." and Louis Zurcher, and Robert Kirkpatrick, "The Natural History of an ad hoc anti-Pornography Organization in Midville, U.S.A." Technical Reports submitted to the Commission on Obscenity and Pornography, vol. 5 (Washington, D.C.: U.S. Government Printing Office, 1970).

20. *Report of the Commission on Obscenity and Pornography* (Washington, D.C.: U.S. Government Printing Office, 1970), p. 51.

21. This clearly appears to be the assumptions behind the drug laws enacted in New York State (in effect September 1973) where distribution and possession both can result in mandatory death penalties.

22. Skolnick, "Coercion to Virtue," p. 623.

23. *Report of the Commission on Obscenity and Pornography*, p. 159.

24. Ibid., p. 38.

25. There is the functionalist position that such labelling is a necessary ingredient to maintain social cohesion in any group through a definition of boundaries. This position is elaborated in Kai Erickson, *Wayward Puritans* (New York: John Wiley, 1966).

2 Obscenity as an Esthetic Category

Abraham Kaplan

My problem is not what to do about obscenity, but what to make of it. Control over the arts in this country—whether by official power or by unofficial influence—rests largely on allegations of obscenity. But patterns of social control cannot reasonably be appraised without some conception of what it is that is being controlled. Accordingly, I ask what constitutes obscenity in relation to the arts. Can a work of art be obscene and still be esthetic in status and function? What part, if any, does the obscene play in the esthetic experience? What characteristics of the art object mark its occurrence?

These questions belong to the philosophy of art, not to its psychology or sociology. To answer them is not to assert matters of fact, but to clarify relations of ideas. Such a clarification must take facts into account, of course—but its outcome, if successful, is a clear conception rather than a true proposition. Still less does an answer to these questions comprise a social policy or a procedure for implementing policy. Nor do I pretend that the distinctions to be drawn in this essay can be directly applied in a court of law. I shall

Reprinted, with permission, from a symposium, Obscenity and the Arts, appearing in *Law and Contemporary Problems*, vol. 20, no. 4 (Autumn, 1955). Published by the Duke University School of Law, Durham, North Carolina. Copright © 1955 by Duke University Press.

be content if they throw light on the problem of obscenity for the artist, his audience and the critic who interprets each to the other.

I

Many people, anxious to defend freedom of expression in the arts, attack the suppression of obscenity on the grounds that obscenity has no objective existence, but is to be found only in the mind of the censor. I share the conclusion which this argument is intended to bolster—namely, that censorship should be condemned; but the argument itself appears to me to be fallacious. Its premise is the undeniable proposition that judgments of the obscene vary with time and place. But from this true premise, the invalid inference is made to a subjectivist conclusion: all that can be common to such varying judgments is a subjective emotion of disapproval. "Obscenity exists only in the minds and emotions of those who believe in it, and is not a quality of a book or picture."[1] To think otherwise, so this logic runs, is to be guilty of a superstition which is "the modern counterpart of ancient witchcraft."[2]

Those exercised over obscenity do perhaps resemble the old prosecutors of witchcraft in their fanaticism and irrationality.[3] The emphasis on the relativism of obscenity thus exposes the narrowness and rigidity of traditionalist morality. But the belief in witchcraft was simply false. The belief in obscenity is false only if its relational character is overlooked. What is superstitious is an absolutist conception,[4] alleged to apply universally whether it be recognized or not. The alternative to absolutism is not subjectivism, but an insistence on objectivity *relative to a specified context*. The rationality of a belief is similarly relative to the evidence available for it. But this relation is not only compatible with objectivity, but even defines it. Such a standpoint has come to be known as *objective relativism* or *contextualism*.[5]

Judgments of obscenity vary because they are contextual. I mean more than that "dirt" is misplaced matter, i.e., that propriety varies with circumstances. I mean that obscenity is to be found in words or pictures only insofar as these can be interpreted to have a certain meaning; and meaning itself is contextual. D.H. Lawrence has protested against objectivism in that "it is the mind which is the

Augean stables, not language."[6] But language has no content at all, obscene or otherwise, without mind. It means what it does only because it is interpreted in definite contexts, and it is in just such contexts of interpretation that its obscenity is to be localized. So far as the facts of relativity are concerned, obscenity is no more subjective than is any esthetic quality.

What is sound in the relativist position is preserved in the recognition of the difference between an art *object* and the *work* of art which results when the object is responded to in an esthetic context. The art experience is not a passive one, but requires the active participation of the respondent. And obscenity is a property of the resultant work, not of the object itself, out of context. When people disagree about whether or not something is obscene, they are likely to be judging different works of art (constructed, as it were, from the same object), rather than reacting differently to the same work. The important problem posed by relativism is, then, *which* work we are to judge when confronted with a particular art object: it is the problem of interpretation. Of course, standards of propriety may differ, just as there are differences in, say, what would amuse us versus the ancient Greeks. But when we read the comedies of Aristophanes, these differences either enter into the interpretation we give to the plays (the art objects), and so give rise to different works of art for us than for his contemporaries, or else the differences are not esthetically relevant at all. Once such differences are explicitly brought into the context, the relativism is objectified.

All art is essentially ambiguous, in the sense that the interpretation it calls for is an imaginative one. The object cannot be so fully specified as to leave no room in its reading for our own creative activity.[7] But what allows for an imaginative reading also makes possible a reading which is wholly our own projection. It is this danger, and not subjectivism, which is the point of the truism that, "to the pure, all things are pure." But not all interpretations *are* merely projective. The qualifications of the reader may make all the difference. A pure mind is just as likely to miss a double entendre in Shakespeare as an ignorant one is to misread his Elizabethan usages. A proper judgment of obscenity in the arts can only be made by an informed and sensitive reader—not necessarily because only he can decide whether a work *is* obscene, but because only he can decide *what* work it is that is being judged.

I say a "proper" judgment, but the more accurate is: a judgment made in the *ideal* context—ideal, that is, from the standpoint of esthetic appreciation and criticism. But there are other sorts of contexts in which a judgment might be made. There is the *personal* context, constituted by the judger himself. And there are various *standard* contexts (specified statistically, or in other ways) which also have their uses. Which context is to be chosen depends on the purpose for which the judgment is being made. I know of no principle of selection or evaluation apart from such purposes. To the question, "Who is to judge whether a work is obscene?" we can reply only with the counter-questions, "What is to be done with the judgment when it is made? And why is it being made at all?"

Yet, I do not mean to pretend that the principle of contextualism leaves us with no difficulties in practice. On the contrary, it allows us to become clearly aware of just how serious the difficulties are. Competent critics disagree sharply among themselves. The ideal context is as difficult to achieve as ideals usually are. But it is not true that, from the nature of the case, the ideal is a hopeless one. Beauty and obscenity alike are in the eye of the beholder. But if—as artists, critics and lovers of the arts, not as censors—we are prepared to enter into interpretation and evaluation in the one case, why not in the other?

II

Contextualism has brought us to the position that obscenity may be an objective property of a work of art, provided that the work itself is recognized as being relative to some context of response to the art object. Many people deny that obscenity is an attribute even of the work of art, localizing it instead in the mind of the artist, by way of his "intention." But what are we to understand by artistic "intention"? Are there not different *sorts* of answers appropriate to the question of why a particular art object was created?

We may answer, first, in terms of the artist's *motive*: money or glory or whatever ends external to his efforts he expected to be served by them. The legal judgment of obscenity sometimes considers motive—apparently, a work is more likely to be obscene if the artist expected to make money from his labors. But plainly, motive as such is completely irrelevant esthetically. A poet may write to pay for his mother's funeral (Johnson's *Rasselas*) or to seduce a woman who reminds him of his mother, but neither motive has much to do with *what* he writes.

Second, artistic "intention" may be construed as *purpose*: a specification in terms of the artist's medium of how his motive is expressed. The purpose may be to satirize the clergy, to expose the madness of chivalric romance, or to proclaim the rights of woman. Unquestionably, purpose must be conceded an esthetic relevance—it is what the artist tried to do *in* his work, not *by* it. Many artists accused of obscenity have defended themselves by insisting on their moral purpose.

But more important than what the artist tried to do is what in fact he *did* do, and this may be taken as a third sense of "intention"—namely, the *intent* of the work itself. A specification of purpose may define an esthetic genre, but never a particular work of art. Every work has its own unique intent: the purpose as embodied in its own specific substance. When Judge Woolsey speaks of Joyce's not "exploiting" obscenity, he is referring to Joyce's artistic purpose, perhaps also to his lack of a monetary motive.[8] But when he refers to the absence of "the leer of the sensualist," it is intent which is involved.[9] What is at question is as much an experienced quality of the work as is the "ring" of sincerity, which is to be contrasted with sincerity itself—the latter being a matter of motive and purpose, but not of intent.

Motive, then, helps localize obscenity only insofar as it determines purpose, and the latter, in turn, only as it is embodied in intent. But this brings us back once more from the mind of the artist to the perceived characteristics of the work of art itself.

The alternative remains to be considered of localizing obscenity in the mind of the audience—i.e., in the *effect* of the work. The obscene, in the classic legal conception, is what tends to corrupt. This criterion is thought to be more "objective" than reference to the artist's intention. But such reference, at least in the sense of intent, is inescapably involved in the criterion. For the effect might otherwise have been the result of a purely projective interpretation, in which case it is not *that* work which is being judged to be obscene. To resort to the effect of the work is to commit oneself to distinguishing between its causal agency and its operation as a trigger mechanism—as providing an occasion for projecting onto itself a corruption already present in the reader.

Plainly, the matter of which context is selected becomes crucial. The courts may choose as standard context Judge Woolsey's "*l'homme moyen sensuel*,"[10] but unless this standard is carefully specified (by Dr. Kinsey?), there is the serious danger that it will be replaced unwittingly by the personal context of the man passing judgment. To compare it with the standard of "the reasonable man" in the law of torts is to overlook the fact that "reasonableness" can, at least in principle, be intersubjectively specified—in terms of probabilities and their logical consequences. But where is the logic of sexual sensitivity that corresponds to the "reasonableness" of inductive and deductive inference? This question is especially embarrassing in view of the claim sometimes made that "familiarity with obscenity blunts the sensibilities,"[11] so that on the criterion of effect, the standard context invites a circular argument: the work is obscene because it *would* produce the effect if only it were not such familiar obscenity!

In the ideal context, the test of effect is wholly inapplicable. For the esthetic experience requires a kind of disinterest or detachment —if you will, a "psychic distance"—which is incompatible with the corruption in question. Only when we hold the work of art at arm's length is it artistic at all. The work brings emotions to mind or presents them for contemplation. When they are actually felt, we have overstepped the bounds of art. Sad music does not make us literally sad. On the contrary, the more vividly and clearly we apprehend the specific quality of "sadness" of the music, the less sorrowful our own emotions. Of course, art evokes feelings; but it is *imagined* feeling, not what is actually felt as a quality of what we do and undergo. Art also works against the translation of imagined feeling into action. It does so partly by providing us insight into feeling, and so allowing us to subject passion to the control of the understanding, as was urged by Spinoza;[12] and partly by providing a catharsis or sublimation of feeling, as in the conceptions of Aristotle and Freud.[13] In short, "there is a high breathlessness about beauty that cancels lust," as Santayana put it.[14] To be sure, the extreme of psychic distance is also incompatible with esthetic experience, as in the case of the intellectual or—what is more to the point—the Philistine. But to ignore altogether the role of distance is to confuse art with promotion—advertising or propaganda.

Pornography is promotional: it is the obscene responded to with minimal psychic distance. Fundamentally, therefore, it is a category of effect. To say that a work is pornographic is to say something about the feelings and actions which it produces in its respondents. We may, of course, identify it by its purpose, rather than by direct observation of effect. Its motive—monetary, sexual or whatever—is likely to be shared with most art. But its esthetic intent is lacking altogether, insofar as the object is being read as pornographic. For, in this case, it is not itself the *object* of an experience, esthetic or any other, but rather a stimulus *to* an experience not focused on it. It serves to elicit, not the imaginative contemplation of an expressive substance, but rather the release in fantasy of a compelling impulse.

Pornography as such, therefore, is no more esthetic than is an object of sentiment, which has no intrinsic interest but is responded to by way of associations external to its own substance, though not external to the references it contains (like the words "Souvenir of San Francisco" on the bottom of a tasteless ashtray). But, though the pornographic as such is never artistic, contextualism warns us that an art object in a particular context—like that of the schoolboy with Venus—may serve pornographically, rather than as a basis for cooperation with the artist in creating a work of art. Indeed, the converse is also possible: a Pompeian wall painting or a Central American sculpture may have been deliberately produced as pornographic, but may constitute, for us, a work of art. In our culture, pornography masquerades as art with sufficient frequency to deserve a special designation—I suggest *erotica*. It is a species of what artists call "kitsch": the vulgarities that hide behind a label of Art with a capital "A." Erotica consists of works that lack even the decency of being *honestly* pornographic.

The distinctions among these categories, however, have been made here on only the conceptual level. As a matter of fact, little is known concerning the actual effects—either of stimulation or sublimation—which can be produced by words and pictures. But when obscenity is distinguished from pornography by reference to effect, it follows that art as such is never pornographic (though it may be obscene, and in several senses is very likely to be). The effect of art on life is not so specific and immediate as is comprised in the concept of pornography. Action flows from impulses, habits and predispositions which are not so easily changed as puritans both fear and hope. At most, an art object might trigger a process already primed. But, insofar as this is its manner of working, it ceases to be art.

Obscenity, then, so far as it relates to art, can be localized neither in intention nor in effect, but only in the expressive substance of the work of art itself. Ultimately, to be sure, the content of a work of art, as of any vehicle of communication, is an abstraction from both intention and effect. Whether or not a word is insulting depends, at bottom, on its being used in order to convey an insult and its being responded to as conveying one. Yet, when this usage is established, the word is insulting even when spoken in innocence or to an insensible hearer; it has been misused or misunderstood, that is all. The question is one of the ideal context of its occurrence, not the personal context, nor yet a standard context selected to serve some extraneous interest.

I do not mean to say that obscenity is a matter of the occurrence of "dirty words." On the contrary; it is the work as a whole which must be considered. For it is an important characteristic of a work of art that it cannot be interpreted piecemeal. Each element affects the content of all the others. The work is an integrated, coherent whole whose expressive quality cannot be additively constructed from what is expressed by its isolated parts. Judge Woolsey's position is esthetically unassailable when he says of *Ulysses* that, although it contains "many words usually considered dirty . . . [each] word of the book contributes like a bit of mosaic to the detail of the picture which Joyce is seeking to construct for his readers."[15] Indeed, isolated words may easily lose their expressiveness by mechanical repetition, to be restored to artistic potency only by skillful exploitation of a fresh setting in a complex work. The obscenity that occurs in a work of art may be as shocking to some as locker room talk; but it is wholly different in quality. The one is expressive; the other marks both the failure of expression and the lack of something to express.

It is a further consequence of this conception that obscenity in art not only does not lie in baldness of sexual references, but is, in fact, incompatible with wholly explicit statements. Explicitness may

be pornographic, but it has no place in art. Where nothing is left to
the imagination, the reading of the art object may stimulate an
experience, but does not itself constitute one. No opportunity is
provided for that sharing in the act of creation which alone makes an
experience esthetic. Nothing is a work of art for *me* unless I have
been able to put something of my deeper self into it. The art object
invites me to express something of that self and guides me in my
efforts to do so; but the effort must be mine. Hence the popularity
of the merely pornographic: it makes so few demands, replacing
genuine expression with a spurious consummation.

As an esthetic category, obscenity, by contrast, is made of the
very stuff of imagination. In one etymology, "obscene" is from
"obscurus"—what is concealed. Expression is concealment, as well as
revelation. Art speaks in symbols, and at the core of every symbol is
a secret which only imagination can fathom. The symbol itself thus
takes on the mysterious quality of what it hides. It is experienced as
charged with feeling and produces tension by at once inviting and
resisting penetration. Both art and obscenity have a single genetic
root: the infantile capacity to endow a mere sign with the affect that
belongs properly to what it signifies.[16] A creature incapable of
obscenity is also incapable of art. Magic, too, avails itself of this
capacity: words themselves become things, imbued with mysterious
powers over other things. Psychologically, obscenity stands between
art and magic—neither wholly make-believe, like the one; nor yet
wholly believing, like the other. In many cultures, obscenity has an
important role in magical rituals. In our own, its magical character is
betrayed in the puritan's supposition that words alone can work evil,
and that evil will be averted if only the words are not uttered.

III

Because there is, after all, a difference between a symbol and
what it symbolizes, obscenity is a matter, not of what the work
refers to, but rather of the *expressive* substance of the work.
Puritans may condemn a work for presenting certain aspects of life;
artists may defend it because what is presented are certain aspects of
life. Truth is used, both as a mark of obscenity and as a mark of its
absence. In fact, it can serve as neither. The question of whether the

world *is* as art (referentially) presents it to be is irrelevant to esthetic quality in general, and to the quality of obscenity in particular. Art is not obscene by virtue, merely, of its subject, nor does it cease to be obscene merely because its subject is virtuous. A verse attributed to D.H. Lawrence complains, "Tell me what's wrong with words or with you, that the thing is all right but the word is taboo!" But there is nothing wrong with recognizing that words and things are different, and that properties of the one cannot necessarily be imputed to the other. Words are public, for instance, and easy to produce, and can occur in contexts where the things they refer to would not be appropriate and could not occur. The Stoics argued that, "there being nothing dishonest in the conjugal duty, it could not be denoted by any dishonest word, and that therefore the word used by clowns to denote it is as good as any other."[17] The question is, however, whether clowing is not different from conjugal life as the Stoics themselves conceived it, and whether the language used is not in fact part of the clowning.

In short, obscenity, like art itself, is not a matter of referential, but of expressive meanings. What is relevant is not subject, but substance; not an isolable message, but an embodied content. The artist does not bodily translate a subject into the work, but transforms it—he selects from it and gives it form. Thereby, the work becomes more than merely an instrument of communication; it commands intrinsic interest because of its own inherent qualities. No subject as such can be obscene. To be sure, the subject of a work of art contributes to its substance—reference enters into the service of expression—and so has an indirect relevance.[18] But the indirectness is crucial. A sexual subject (or similar reference) is a necessary condition for obscenity, but not a sufficient one; only for pornography and for propaganda, does the referential message suffice.

Thus, though censorship may extend to themes as well as treatments, obscenity does not. The immorality of the actual characters and their conduct, which provide the novelist with his material, are alike irrelevant to the charge of obscenity and to the defense against it. For words are not the things they mean; art is not life. Art supplements life and does not merely duplicate it. The question of obscenity is a question of what the novelist is bringing onto the scene, and the first answer to that question must be "a novel"; a sequence of incidents *with form and expression*. The qualities of the work are not determined by the traits of its subject matter. Truth, therefore, in the sense of depicting life as it is, neither produces nor precludes obscenity.

IV

Obscenity, then, is an experienced quality of the work of art and can no more be localized in the subject matter of the work than in its intent or effect. But *what* quality is it? There are, in fact, several species of the obscene, which must be distinguished from one another because they differ so widely in their esthetic status and function.

First, is what I call *conventional obscenity*: the quality of any work which attacks established sexual patterns and practices in any given society. In essence, it is the presentation of a sexual heterodoxy, a rejection of accepted standards of sexual behavior. Zola, Ibsen and Shaw provide familiar examples of this quality. The accusations of obscenity directed against them can be seen clearly—in retrospect—to have been social, rather than moral. The guilt with which they were charged was not sin, but a violation of good taste and, even more, of sound judgment. For sexual heterodoxy is frequently generalized, by both the writer and his readers, to an overall radicalism. To attack established morality in any respect is to undermine the authority of every established pattern. It surprises no one that the same authors wrote *Nana* and *J'Accuse*; or *Ghosts*, and *An Enemy of the People*; or *Mrs. Warren's Profession*, and *Saint Joan*. It is a commonplace that mores tend everywhere to be moralized, so that unconventionality of any kind is condemned as immoral and, if sexual, as obscene.

The dual vocabulary for sexual subject matters, to be found in many cultures besides our own, is a device to preserve the conventions. The four-letter word is a scapegoat which allows the rest of the language to be free of sin.[19] The use of a foreign language (especially Latin) for questionable passages conveys a detached point of view which leaves the conventions undisturbed. More important, the foreignness restricts the work to a well-educated elite, whose conformity is not in doubt or who may, indeed, feel privileged to stand above the mores altogether. Conventional obscenity is not too good for the masses; it is too dangerous for them. If they begin by attacking accepted standards of sexual behavior, so the theory runs, they will end by rejecting all social constraints in an orgy of anarchic egoism.

Accordingly, it is conventional obscenity which is the main concern of the censor—not, say, the pornography of night club entertainment. From the viewpoint of the censor, the tired businessman may call "time out," but he mustn't change the rules of the game. It is one thing for him to declare a moratorium on his debt to society, but quite another for him to repudiate his honorable obligations. In short, he may be wicked, but not scandalous; and scandal consists of open revolt against sexual constraints, rather than covert evasion of them. Pope Paul IV was consistent in expurgating Boccaccio by retaining the episodes, but transforming the erring nuns and monks into laymen:[20] thus scandal was averted.

It might appear that conventional obscenity has nothing to do with art, as such, but only with propaganda—for a work is usually identified as conventionally obscene on the basis of its message, not its expressive content; and art does not convey messages. As Sidney long ago pointed out in his defense of poesy,[21] the poet does not lie, because he asserts nothing. He therefore does not assert that sexual conventions must be changed, but, at most, presents for imaginative contemplation the workings of our or other conventions. Some artists, however, consciously adopt a propagandistic stance. Yet, conventional obscenity does not depend upon a literalistic approach to art by way of subject, reference and message, rather than substance, expression and embodied meaning. Both puritan and propagandist overlook the more subtle morality in the content of a work of art, in terms of which conventional obscenity is not limited to a reformist purpose, but plays an important role in all artistic intent.

The artist's integrity requires that he present the world as he sees it; his creativity, that he see it afresh, in his own terms. The new vision is bound to be different, and as different, is judged to be wicked by the conformist morality of the old. The Hays motion picture production code requires that "correct standards of life" be presented, "subject only to the requirements of drama and entertainment"! But if they are subjected also to the requirements of honest and creative art, their "correctness" is likely to be challenged. Again and again in the history of art, the creative artist has had to take his stand against the Academy, as the repository of tradition, not merely in art, but in life as well.

Clive Bell is scarcely exaggerating when he warns that, "of all the enemies of art, culture is perhaps the most dangerous."[22] The academic artist is likely to be free of conventional obscenity, but also to be innocent of esthetic quality. The artist who creates new forms and exploits new techniques—who develops, in a word, a new style—does so because he has something new to say; and in art, whatever is said needs its own language. The very newness is then felt as an attack on established patterns. The hostility to "modern art" evinced by the pillars of church, state and society is not a product of insensitivity. On the contrary, it displays a realistic awareness of the threat which art has always posed to sheer conformity. The charge of obscenity directed against the arts is strictly comparable to the moral depravity regularly ascribed to heretical religious sects. "Thou shalt have no other gods before me!" A new vision of God—so says the priesthood—can only be a visitation of the Devil.

Art, in short, is a matter of inspiration as well as of skill. And inspiration—from the standpoint of the conventional—is a demonic corruption of the old, rather than a new revelation of the divine. The "genius" is one who is possessed, and hence dangerous. Mann's *Faustus* embodies a recurrent myth of the artist: he has sold his soul to the Devil to enjoy the fruits of the sin of *hubris* committed in imitating the Creator. A vicious circle is thus engendered. The Philistine distrust of the artist leads to his rejection by established society, which provokes a counterattack that, in turn, is taken to justify the initial reaction. It is not true, then, that we can generalize from sexual heterodoxy to wholesale radicalism. Rather, we can particularize from the artist's rejection of convention—because, for him, it is stale, flat and unprofitable—to a sexual heterodoxy, and thus to conventional obscenity. The representation of pubic hair, for instance, is commonly regarded as obscene. But this is largely because it did not appear in the classic nude; and it did not appear there because the prevailing custom was to remove the pubic hair from the body.[23] This is not our custom; but it is the custom in our art, and to depart from it, therefore, is to be obscene.

It is easy to exaggerate the danger to established patterns posed by art. We have already seen that there is no ground for supposing the effect of art on life to be immediate and direct. On the other hand, it is also easy to exaggerate the contribution to society which conventional obscenity makes. Traditional morality may be sound even if it is conformist, and, in many respects, it surely *is* sound. Society needs stability as well as change; some changes *are* for the worse. Stability cannot be identified with stagnation and death, as Herbert Read has rashly claimed in defense of the artists as *advocati diaboli*.[24] The part of reason, it seems to me, is to reject both the sterile conformism which condemns art for its conventional obscenity and the destructive individualism which takes pride in standing above "the law of the herd."

V

A second type of obscenity I call *Dionysian obscenity*. It consists of what society regards as "excessive" sexualism. Familiar examples are provided by Aristophanes, Boccaccio, Rabelais and the Elizabethans. As a quality of the work of art, it is an expression of an exuberant delight in life. Dionysian obscenity is present in its clearest form in the old Greek comedy, where its connection with fertility rites and phallic ceremonies is obvious. It has played a part in such rites and ceremonies in many other cultures, as well.

Its occurrence in art forms is equally widespread. For art rests above all on a delight in color, sound, texture and shape. The appeal of art is first sensuous; and the difference between the sensuous and the sensual is only in the suffix, not the root. The art object presents for enjoyment an esthetic surface in which formal and expressive values are present, to be sure, but only as fused with an immediate sensory appeal. The work of art may lead us, as Plato and Plotinus hoped,[25] to the world beyond sense; but it can do so only *through* sense. And sense must delight us in the passage. This fact was at the bottom of the iconoclastic controversy and has led some strict puritans to condemn all art as essentially immoral. The premise from which the condemnation springs is a sound one, even if the conclusion is not. We cannot consistently worship beauty and despise the pleasures which the bodily senses can afford. Matthew Arnold was distressed at the "vulgarity" of some of Keats' letters to Fanny Brawne; but more realistic critics have recognized that, if he were incapable of such letters, he would not have written *The Eve of St. Agnes.*[26] Dionysian obscenity in art is of a piece with the enthusiasm which the artist displays over the delightful qualities of his medium.

But the artist is not merely celebrating the joys of esthetic perception. He is also providing a symbolic consummation for the entire range of human desire. It is the artist who can truly say that, being human, nothing human is alien to him. He is forever drawing the circle which takes in what man and nature reject. He himself is wounded by such rejection, and, in comforting himself, he pleases everyone.

It is scarcely accidental that so much art, in all cultures and in all media, has to do with love. The human interest of love, in all its phases and manifestations, is the inexhaustible lode from which art unceasingly draws beauty. Can anyone doubt that if the human mammal gave birth in litters, painters and sculptors would find in multiple breasts the exquisite forms that the female nude now provides them? Whatever art touches it transfigures. But, though the poet makes of love the divine passion, it remains *passion.* And when he presents that passion for what it is, in its full-bodied vigor, we call him obscene.

Whatever else art may be, it is an intensification of emotion. And when the emotion is a sexual one, the result is Dionysian obscenity. We cannot pretend that the poetry, painting, sculpture and even the music of love owe nothing and repay nothing to our sexuality. We may recognize this without reducing beauty altogether to an effusion of sex. But art is not confined to the bare surface of human feeling. It enriches experiences only because its roots penetrate to the depths of feeling and so bring our emotional life to flower.

The consummations of art, however, are symbolic. It is for this reason that "excessive" sexuality so often finds a place in art: there is no other place for it to go. The symbol is possible when the reality is not. Dionysian obscenity is a symbolic release of impulses thwarted in fact. It compensates us for the frustrations imposed by rigid conventions. It is not merely a device to elude external repression; it is a mechanism whereby we can admit our feelings to ourselves. Sex becomes permissible when it is esthetically symbolized. We condemn it as obscene only when, being brought face to face with our own impulses, it overwhelms us with anxiety and guilt.

On this basis, Dionysian obscenity not only need not be immoral, but it may even serve as a moral agent. By providing a catharsis or sublimation, art may act as a safety valve without which libidinal pressures may become explosive. This is especially suggested by the comic quality so characteristic of Dionysian obscenity. Modern burlesque, from a historical viewpoint, is a pathetic attempt to recapture this quality. Comedy releases, in laughter, tensions which might otherwise prove no laughing matter. The comic spirit detaches us from our impulses and their frustration, allowing satisfaction on another level.

It is for this reason, too, that Dionysian obscenity is so seldom pornographic. Pornography is grim and earnest and feeds only on frustration. In art, sexual energies are not gathered up for a desperate assault on social restraints, but are canalized so as to structure an esthetic experience which is, in itself, deeply satisfying.

The protest against Dionysian obscenity is essentially a protest against sexuality as such. It is a denunciation of the innate depravity of human nature, which finds satisfaction in "the lure of the senses and the evils of the flesh." The Dionysian, on the other hand, refuses to regard the act of love as inherently sinful. On the contrary, for him it is the supreme manifestation of what is good in life: the indomitable creative impulse. This same impulse finds expression in art. In Dionysian obscenity, art and life join in vigorous, unrestrained laughter.

VI

A third kind of obscenity, which I call *the obscenity of the perverse*, is completely different in quality. Unlike conventional obscenity, it is not an attack on accepted standards; nor is it, like Dionysian obscenity, an affirmation of impulse, despite restraints. It is, rather, a rebellion against convention—which at the same time acknowledges the authority of received standards. In the obscenity of the perverse, the artist "accepts the common code only to flout it; conscious of sin, he makes sin attractive; his theme is 'the flowers of evil.' "[27] Baudelaire himself, by his own admission, makes sin hideous. The truly perverse (e.g., Huysmans, de Sade) finds sin attractive *because* it is sin. His obscenity lacks the naïveté of the Dionysian; it is likely to be lewd in a sophisticated fashion. The effect is that of calculated indecency.

Dionysian obscenity celebrates sex; conventional obscenity is neutral towards sex, being concerned primarily with the social evils of particular sex patterns. With perverse obscenity, sex is dirty, and it occupies itself with sex for the sake of the dirt. In viewing all obscenity as "smut" and "filth," the puritan only betrays his own perversion. There is here a profound ambivalence, a rebellion which is also a submission. Satan is not a free spirit, but a rebel divided against himself. In freedom, there is a vigor and forthrightness, an enlargement of the soul, which is the antithesis of evil. In perverse obscenity, we have the pathetic spectacle of the Black Mass—worshippers without a god, seeking in hatred and rejection what they are incapable of accepting in love.

At bottom, the obscenity of the perverse is sheer hypocrisy: it is not so black as it paints itself. While pretending to rise above morality, it abjectly submits to it and thereby becomes truly immoral. It plays false to its own dignity and freedom. While pretending to delight in sex, in fact it abhors sexuality, being convinced of its sinfulness and seeking it out only for the sin. For the perverse, sex is desirable only because it is forbidden; it remains in the end a bitter fruit. Paradoxically, it is the puritan who creates such obscenity; its foundation is secrecy and shame. The obscene is what is off the scene—hidden, covered. And shame, as ethnologists have long recognized, is not merely the cause of covering, but also the effect.[28] The secret becomes shameful because of its secrecy. To be perverse is to uncover it, merely because it is hidden. This is the obscenity of the leer and the innuendo. The asterisks and dashes of the supposed puritan serve in fact to convey the perverse content unambiguously.

Basically, what perverse obscenity expresses is fear—fear of the great power of the sexual impulses. It is because of this power that prohibitions and constraints have been imposed upon it in all societies. But just because it is hidden, it looms larger and more threatening. What is perverse is not the concern with being overwhelmed by brute desire; it is the role of reason to look to the defenses of rationality. The perversion consists in purchasing freedom from anxiety by assuming a burden of guilt, selling one's soul to the Devil for fear of being rejected by God. Perverse obscenity tries to cope with the forces of sexuality by a symbolic denial of their potency. It plays with fire in a childish effort to convince itself it cannot be burned. But what is manifest in it is only the futility and the fear. By contrast, Dionysian obscenity triumphs over impulse by freely yielding to it, while conventional obscenity resolutely sets itself to canalize impulse more effectively than custom permits.

There is thus a close connection between the obscenity of the perverse and blasphemy. Historically, indeed, the early strictures against obscenity were based on this single connection.[29] The obscenity of the perverse simultaneously makes too much and too little of sex; just as the blasphemer acknowledges God by denying Him, profanes the holy to damn himself. Diabolism, after all, is just another religion. Perverse obscenity does not wish to profane love in order to remove the taboo from it. Just the contrary: it pretends to ignore the taboo so as to destroy what is, for it, the fearful holiness of love. It is perverse obscenity, not the Dionysian, which is likely to be exploited in pornography; for pornography, as D.H. Lawrence has noted, is "the attempt to insult sex, to do dirt on it."[30] In the obscenity of the perverse, sex is no more than a disgusting necessity; the perversion lies in finding pleasure in the disgust.

Such an attitude is plainly foreign to art and could enter into esthetic experience only to drain it completely of esthetic quality. It is approximated, however, by a type of obscenity which lies between the Dionysian and the perverse—what might be called *romantic obscenity*. This is the category, exemplified in Swinburne and the "fleshly" school, which preserves the sense of sin, yet celebrates sexuality in spite of it. It lacks the pagan innocence of the Dionysian, but also the lust for evil of the perverse. It is romantic, as expressing a felt need to cover the nakedness of sex with sentiment and estheticism. This need is nowhere more apparent than in the strident insistence on being unashamedly sensual. The art in which romantic obscenity is to be found has something of the pathos of adolescent bravado.

VII

In another of its etymologies, the word "obscene" is given the sense of inauspicious and ill-omened.[31] This is the sense appropriate to the obscenity of the perverse, for its content is hate, not love. It seeks in sexuality only what is life-denying, finding in sinfulness the great Nay which it struggles to express. Its impulse is to destroy itself, though it contents itself with a stylized gesture towards the self-castration which some fathers of the church performed in fact. Obscenity may thus become linked with symbols of violence.

Aggression is as much repressed and controlled by society as are libidinal impulses. Murder is as universally condemned as incest, hostility as rigidly patterned as sexuality. Aggressive impulses, therefore, also seek expression in the symbols of art. Corresponding to the sexuality of Dionysian comedy is the violence of Greek tragedy. The impulses of love and hate may become confused and intertwined and sex may be patterned into sadomasochistic perversion. In the expression of this content, psychic distance can no longer be maintained, but is submerged in empathic identifications both with brutality and with its victims. A new category of the obscene emerges: the *pornography of violence*.

In this type of obscenity, sexual desires find symbolic release only as they are transformed into acts of aggression.[32] Countless popular novels have been constructed according to a rigid pattern of alternation of violence and sex which coincide only at the climax, when the virile hero is allowed to shoot the wicked beauty. More sophisticated in style and structure, but essentially the same in substance, is the work of the "realistic" school, sometimes associated with the name of Hemingway. Death in the afternoon prepares for love at midnight. There is no question that writing of this genre is effective; the question is only whether the effect is esthetic—an abattoir can provide a moving experience. Esthetic or not, this genre is enormously successful; including as it does the "detective" story and the crime "comic," the pornography of violence is more widespread in our culture than all the other categories of obscenity put together.

It is, perhaps, banal to associate this fact with the role of violence in our culture, as a source even of recreation for the spectator. Yet Henry Miller's denunciation must be taken seriously: "Fear, guilt and murder—these constitute the real triumvirate which rules our lives. *What is obscene then?* The whole fabric of life as we know it today."[33] It is easy to dismiss so sweeping a judgment. Yet it remains true that the pornography of violence enjoys an immunity denied altogether not only to Dionysian obscenity, but even to the fundamentally respectable conventional obscenity. A noteworthy exception is the action of the British Board of Film Censors in prohibiting the showing of Disney's *Snow White* to children, on the ground that it might frighten them, at a time when all the children in London were being taught how to wear gasmasks.[34]

VIII

Moral issues, as such, fall outside the scope of this essay. Yet esthetics cannot ignore the moral content of art, and the esthetics of obscenity must finally face the question of how obscenity, in its various species, affects that content.

The moral content of art is plainly not a matter of doctrinaire messages, but rather of something more fundamental. As I conceive it, it is nothing less than the affirmation of life, a great yea-saying to the human condition. In mastering its medium and imposing form on its materials, art creates a microcosm in which everything is significant and everything is of value, the perfection of what experience in the macrocosm might be made to provide. In this capacity, art may serve as the voice of prophecy and, like all prophets, go unheard or be stoned when its teaching is at variance with a law no longer alive to the demands of life. If human life itself is the subject to be artistically transformed, art insists on seeing it whole, for only thus can it understand and revitalize it; but when art uncovers what men wish to keep hidden, it is despised and condemned. And always, art remains a challenge to evil and death, forcing enduring human values out of the sadly deficient and evanescent material of experience.

In this conception, conventional and Dionysian obscenity, and perhaps also romantic obscenity, all play their part in the performance of the esthetic function; but not pornography, not the obscenity of the perverse, and especially not the pornography of violence. For these are in the service of death, not of life. They belong to that monstrous morality and taste of the burial ground where death is glorified and the sculpture of Michelangelo is given a fig leaf. The god of such obscenity is not Eros, but Thanatos. Not the wages of sin, but sin itself, is death.

NOTES

1. Theodore Schroeder, *Freedom of the Press and "Obscene" Literature* (Printed by the author, Coscob, Conn., 1906), p. 42; and *"Obscene" Literature and Constitutional Law* (Coscob, Conn.: privately printed, 1911), pp. 13-14.

2. Morris Ernst and William Seagle, *To the Pure: A Study of Obscenity and the Censor* (New York: Viking Press, 1928).

3. See Vilfredo Pareto, *The Mind and Society*, vol. 2. trans. A. Bongiorno and A. Livingston (New York: Harcourt, 1935), p. 1010.

4. Mortimore Adler, *Art and Prudence* (Pittsburgh: Duquesne University Press, 1937), p. 126.

5. John Dewey, *Art as Experience* (New York: Capricorn Books, 1934).

6. D.H. Lawrence, *Sex Literature and Censorship* (New York: The Viking Press, 1953), p. 59.

7. See Abraham Kaplan and Ernest Kris, "Esthetic Ambiguity," in Ernest Kris, ed., *Psychoanalytic Explorations in Art* (New York: Schocken, 1952).

8. United States v. One Book Called "Ulysses," 5 F. Supp. 182, 183 (S.D.N.Y. 1933) *aff'd*, 72 F. 2d (2nd Cir. 1934).

9. Ibid., p. 183.

10. Ibid., p. 184.

11. United States v. Harmon, 45 Fed. 414, 423 (D. Kansas, 1891).

12. Benedictus Spinoza, *Ethics*.

13. Aristotle, *Poetics* (Cambridge, Mass.: Harvard University Press, 1965); and Sigmund Freud, *General Introduction to Psychoanalysis* (London: Allen & Unwin, 1922), pp. 327-28.

14. George Santayana, *Reason in Art* (New York: MacMillan, 1934), p. 171.

15. United States v. One Book Called "Ulysses." See also James Farrell, "Testimony on Censorship," in *Reflections at Fifty* (New York: Avon, 1954), p. 212.

16. Sandor Ferenczi, "On Obscene Words," in *Sex in Psychoanalysis* (New York: Dover, 1950).

17. Pierre Bayle, *The Dictionary Historical and Critical* (Indianapolis: Bobbs-Merrill, 1837, reprinted 1965), p. 850.

18. Abraham Kaplan, "Referential Meaning in the Arts," *Journal of Aesthetics and Art Criticism*, 12 (1954): 457.

19. H. Read, "An Obscenity Symbol," *American Speech*, 9 (1934): 264-67.

20. A.L. Haight, *Banned Books* (New York: Bowker, 1935), p. 8.

21. Philip Sidney, *The Defense of Poesie* (New York: Oxford University Press, 1951).

22. Clive Bell, *Art* (New York: Capricorn Books, 1927), p. 267.

23. Havelock Ellis, *Studies in the Psychology of Sex*, vol. 4 (New York: New American Library, 1936), p. 94.

24. Marjorie Bowen, *Ethics in Modern Art* (New York: Penguin, 1939), p. ix.

25. Plotinus, *On The One and Good Being, The Treatise of the Sixth Ennead*.

26. Clive Bell, *Art*, p. 271-72.

27. Albert Guerard, *Art for Art's Sake* (New York: Schocken, 1936), pp. 189-90.

28. Edward Westermarck, *The History of the Human Marriage*, 3rd ed. (New York: Finch Press, 1901), p. 211.

29. D. Alpert, "Judicial Censorship of Obscene Literature," *Harvard Law Review*, vol. 52, no. 4 (1938): 43-44.

30. D.H. Lawrence, *Sex Literature and Censorship*, p. 74.

31. Havelock Ellis, "The Revaluation of Obscenity," *Essays of Love and Virtue* (Garden City, New York: Garden City Publishing, 1933), p. 99.

32. Gershon Legman, *Love and Death* (New York: Hacker, 1949); George Orwell, "Raffles and Miss Blandish," in *Critical Essays* (New York: Harcourt and Brace, 1946).

33. Henry Miller, "Obscenity and the Law of Reflection," in Henry Miller, *The Air-Conditioned Nightmare* (New York: New Directions, 1947).

34. H.L. Mencken, *The American Language Supplement One* (New York: Random House, 1948), p. 644.

PORNOGRAPHY
AND
DILEMMAS OF LAW

3 Beyond the (Garbage) Pale, or Democracy, Censorship and the Arts

Walter Berns

The case against censorship is very old and very familiar. Almost anyone can formulate it without difficulty. One has merely to set the venerable Milton's *Areopagitica* in modern prose, using modern spelling, punctuation and examples. This is essentially what the civil libertarians did in their successful struggle, during the past century, with the censors. The unenlightened holder of the bishop's imprimatur, Milton's "unleasur'd licencer" who has never known "the labour of book-writing," became the ignorant policeman or the bigoted school board member who is offended by "Mrs. Warren's Profession," or the benighted librarian who refuses to shelf *The Scarlet Letter*, or the insensitive customs official who seizes *Ulysses* in the name of an outrageous law, or the Comstockian vigilante who glues together the pages of every copy of *A Farewell to Arms* she can find in the bookstore. The industrious learned Milton, insulted by being asked to "appear in Print like a punie with his guardian and his censors hand on the back of his title to be his bayle and surety," was replaced by Shaw, Hawthorne, Joyce or Hemingway, and those who followed in their wake, all victims of the mean-spirited and

Reprinted with permission from Harry M. Clor, editor, *Censorship and Freedom of Expression* (Chicago: Rand McNally & Company, 1971). Copyright © 1970 by the Public Affairs Conference Center, Kenyon College, Gamblier, Ohio.

narrow-minded officials who were appointed, or in some cases took it upon themselves, to judge what others should read, or at least not read. The presumed advantage of truth when it grapples with falsehood became the inevitable victory of "enduring ideas" in the free competition of the market. With these updated versions of old and familiar arguments, the civil libertarians have prevailed.

They prevailed partly because of the absurdity of some of their opposition, and also because of a difficulty inherent in the task their opponents set for themselves. The censors would proscribe the obscene and, even assuming, as our law did, that obscene speech is no part of the speech protected by the First Amendment to the Constitution, it is not easy to formulate a rule of law that distinguishes the non-obscene from the obscene. Is it the presence of four-letter words? But many a literary masterpiece contains four-letter words. Detailed descriptions of sexual acts? James Joyce provides these. Words tending to corrupt those into whose hands they are likely to fall? But who is to say what corrupts or, for that matter, whether anything corrupts or, again, what is meant by corruption? Is it an appeal to a "prurient interest" or is it a work that is "patently offensive"? If that is what is meant by the obscene, many a "socially important work," many a book, play or film with "redeeming social value," would be lost to us. The college professors said so, and if college professors do not know what is socially important, who does? Be that as it may, they succeeded in convincing the Supreme Court, and the result was the complete rout of the "forces of reaction." To the college professors, therefore, as well as to the "courageous" publishers and the "public-spirited" attorneys who had selflessly fought the cases through the courts, a debt of gratitude is owed by the lovers of Shaw, Hawthorne, Joyce and Hemingway—and others too numerous to detail here. In the same spirit, one might say that never has there been such a flourishing of the arts in this country.

Astonishingly, the editors of the *New York Times* disagree, and in an editorial printed on April 1, 1969, under the heading "Beyond the (Garbage) Pale," they expressed their disagreement in language that we have been accustomed to read only in the journals of the "reactionary right."

The explicit portrayal on the stage of sexual intercourse is the final step in the erosion of taste and subtlety in the theater. It reduces actors to mere exhibitionists, turns audiences into voyeurs and debases sexual relationships almost to the level of prostitution.

It is difficult to see any great principle of civil liberties involved when persons indulging themselves onstage in this kind of peep-show activity are arrested for "public lewdness and obscenity"—as were the actors and staff of a recently opened New York production that, in displaying sodomy and other sexual aberrations, reached the *reductio ad obscenum* of the theatrical art. While there may be no difference in principle between pornography on the stage, on the screen and on the printed page, there is a difference in immediacy and in direct visual impact when it is carried out by live actors before a (presumably) live audience.

The fact that the legally enforceable standards of public decency have been interpreted away by the courts almost to the point of no return does not absolve artists, producers or publishers from all responsibility or restraint in pandering to the lowest possible public taste in quest of the largest possible monetary reward. Nor does the fact that a play, film, article or book attacks the so-called "establishment," revels in gutter language or drools over every known or unknown form of erotica justify the suspension of sophisticated critical judgment.

Yet this does seem to be just what has been suspended in the case of many recent works, viz. one current best-seller hailed as a "masterpiece," which, wallowing in a self-indulgent public psychoanalysis, drowns its literary merits in revolting excesses of masturbation and copulation.

The utter degradation of taste in pursuit of the dollar is perhaps best observed in films, both domestic and foreign such as one of the more notorious Swedish imports, refreshingly described by one reviewer unafraid of being called a "square" as "pseudo-pornography at its ugliest and least titillating and pseudo-sociology at its lowest point of technical ineptitude."

Far from providing a measure of cultural emancipation, such descents into degeneracy represent caricatures of art, deserving no exemption from the laws of common decency merely because they masquerade as drama or literature. It is preposterous to banish topless waitresses when there is no bottom to voyeurism on the stage or in the movie houses.

In the end, however, there may be an even more effective answer. The insensate pursuit of the urge to shock, carried from one excess to a more abysmal one, is bound to achieve its own antidote in total boredom. When there is no lower depth to descend to, ennui will erase the problem.

This must be reckoned an astonishing statement because, in the liberal world for which the *Times* speaks, it has not been customary—to put it mildly—to cast any doubt on the wisdom of an anti-censorship policy. Now suddenly, the *Times*, contrary to what its readers might expect, and contrary even to the general tenor of its own drama and literary pages, registers its misgivings. This is not what they wanted to happen. In their struggle against the censor they did not mean to defend "the explicit portrayal of sexual intercourse" on the stage or in films; they did not have in mind "sodomy and other sexual aberrations." They intended to protect the freedom of the arts from bigoted censors; they were defending *Ulysses* when the customs laws would have excluded it from the country, and sensitive foreign films, such as "Les Amants," from Ohio's laws; but they certainly did not intend to establish a place for "revolting excesses of masturbation and copulation."

A TRULY INVISIBLE HAND

Nine months later, one of the country's principal foes of censorship checked in with the same disclaimer. *Ulysses*, yes, said Morris Ernst, but "sodomy on the stage or masturbation in the public area," no! Although the fact had never appeared with any prominence in the arguments that had made him one of the foremost civil liberties lawyers in the country, Ernst now insists that he had always made it clear that he "would hate to live in a world with utter freedom." He deeply resents "the idea that the lowest common denominator, the most tawdry magazine, pandering for profit ... should be able to compete in the marketplace with no restraints." The free market place has become the dirty marketplace, and Ernst wants no part in it and no responsibility for it.[1]

But surely this was inevitable. Pornography and the taste for it are not new phenomena. What is new is the fact that it can display itself openly in the marketplace, so to speak, whereas in the past it had been confined by the laws to the back alleys, or to the underworld, where its sales were limited, not by a weakness of the potential demand, but rather by the comparative inaccessibility of the market. Prodded by the civil libertarians, the Supreme Court made pornography a growth industry by giving it a license to operate in the accessible and legitimate market, thereby bringing buyer and seller closer together. True, the Court did not directly license "Oh! Calcutta!" or "Che!"; but so long as the court is consistent, these works are certain to benefit from the licenses given to "Les Amants," *Fanny Hill* and the others. Consider the state of the law developed on their behalf. So long as a work is not *"utterly* without redeeming social value" (the emphasis is the Supreme Court's), it cannot be proscribed, even if it is "patently offensive" and is found by a jury to appeal to a "prurient interest." All that is needed to save any work from the censor, or the police, is some college professor willing to testify as to its "social value" or "social importance," and there is no shortage of such professors with such testimony. Indeed, the work has not been written, staged, or filmed that cannot find its champions somewhere among the professors.[2]

It was not supposed to turn out this way. Some invisible and benign hand was supposed to operate in this market too, and guarantee the triumph of the true and the beautiful. People, said Justice William O. Douglas in a recent obscenity case, "are mature enough to pick and choose, to recognize trash when they see it, to be attracted to the literature that satisfies their deepest need, and . . . to move from plateau to plateau and finally reach the world of enduring ideas." This is the liberal faith. The *Times* shared it, and it is worth noting that even in its distress it refuses to foresake it altogether. The editors express their disgust with what has happened, but they must know that this will be unavailing with those who are themselves disgusting. Certainly the "artists, producers [and] publishers . . . pandering to the lowest public taste in quest of the largest possible monetary reward" are not going to forego this reward simply because some fainthearted libertarians, even on the *Times,* look upon their work as disgusting. "I paid to see filth and I want filth," said the woman from Connecticut, to protest the showing of an expurgated "I Am Curious (Yellow)." If she is willing to pay to see filth, then, no matter what the *Times* says, there will always be "artists, producers [and] publishers" to see to it that she gets her money's worth. That is why there used to be laws against filth—because the legislators who wrote these laws knew full well the fruitlessness of relying on admonitions or expressions of disgust. The *Times* does not call for the refurbishment of these laws, but appeals instead to the "laws of common decency," as if these so-called laws had not passed into desuetude with the demise of the legislation that constituted their foundation. So, in the end, we return to the old liberal faith in an invisible hand that will provide our salvation: "When there is no lower depth to descend to, ennui will erase the problem."

Such a conclusion is pitifully inadequate, but it is an accurate reflection of the way thinking has gone on this issue during our time. Neither the *Times* nor Morris Ernst has a grasp of the principle with which—or even a suitable vocabulary in which—to challenge the powerful orthodoxy that has long governed the public discussion of censorship and the arts. To be a liberal is to be against censorship, or it is to be nothing—or so it has been thought—and, after a career spent arguing against censorship, it is not easy to formulate an argument in its favor. But the *Times* and Mr. Ernst deserve our gratitude nevertheless, for, although they leave it undefined, their disclaimers do have the merit of acknowledging that there is something wrong with things as they are, that there *is* a problem. The respectability attached to their names makes it easier to re-examine this problem.

Just as it is difficult to formulate a law that distinguishes the non-obscene from the obscene, it is still more difficult to distinguish the obscene from the work of genuine literary merit. In fact, it is impossible—and our failure to understand this may be said to be a condition, if not a cause, of our present situation. Our laws proscribe obscenity as such and by name, and we are unwilling to admit that great literary and dramatic works can be, and frequently are, obscene. In combination these two facts explain how we came to have, with the sanction of the law, what is probably the most vulgar theatre and literature in history. The paradox is readily explained. The various statutes making up the law have made obscenity a criminal thing, and our judges assume that if a work of art is really a work of art, and not vulgar rubbish, it cannot be obscene. Thus, Judge Woolsey, in his celebrated opinion in the *Ulysses* case, recounts how he had asked two literary friends whether the book was obscene within the legal definition, which he had explained to them, and how they had both agreed with him that it was not. But of course *Ulysses* is obscene. It is not so obscene as Aristophanes' "Assembly of Women," for example, an undoubted masterpiece which would not be a masterpiece—or anything else—if its obscenity were removed, but it is obscene nevertheless.

The trouble stems from the fact that the Tariff Act of 1930 set out to exclude "obscene" books from the country, and Judge Woolsey, being a sensible man, did not want this to happen to *Ulysses*. So he fashioned a rule to protect it. But the same rule of law protects *The Tropic of Cancer* because, according to the rule's necessarily clumsy categories, the latter is no more obscene than the former, however it compares on another scale and whatever the esthetic distances separating its author, Henry Miller, and James Joyce as writers. Eventually, and for the same reason, the protection of the law was extended to *Trim, MANual* and *Grecian Guild Pictorial*, the homosexual magazines involved in a case before the Supreme Court in 1962, and then to *Fanny Hill*. At this point, if one ignores the Ginzburg aberration and the recent children's cases,[3] the censors seem to have given up, and we have—well, anything that anyone will pay to see or read. Thus, having begun by exempting the work of art from the censorship laws, we have effectively arrived at the civil libertarian's destination: the case where the Supreme Court throws up its hand and concludes that there is no such thing as obscenity.

Underlying this unfortunate development is the familiar liberal idea of progress. Rather than attempting to inhibit artists and scientists, the good polity will grant them complete freedom of expression and of inquiry, and will benefit collectively by so doing. What is good for the arts and sciences is good for the polity: this proposition has gone largely unquestioned among us for 200 years. The case for censorship rests on its denial, and can be made only by separately examining its parts. What is good for the arts and sciences? What is good for the polity? The case for censorship arises initially out of a consideration of the second question.

The case for censorship is at least as old as the case against it, and, contrary to what is usually thought today, it has been made under decent and even democratic auspices by intelligent men. To the extent that it is known today, however, it is thought to be pernicious or, at best, irrelevant to the enlightened conditions of the twentieth century. It starts from the premise that the laws cannot remain indifferent to the manner in which men amuse themselves, or to the kinds of amusement offered them. "The object of art," as Lessing put the case, "is pleasure, and pleasure is not indispensable. What kind and what degree of pleasure shall be permitted may justly depend on the law-giver."[4] Such a view, especially in this uncompromising form, appears excessively Spartan and illiberal to us; yet Lessing was one of the greatest lovers of art who ever lived and wrote.

We turn to the arts—to literature, films, and the theatre, as well as to the graphic arts which were the special concern of Lessing—for the pleasure to be derived from them, which pleasure has the capacity to form our tastes and thereby to affect our lives. It helps determine the kind of men we become, and helps shape the lives of those with whom and among whom we live. So one can properly ask: is it politically uninteresting whether men derive pleasure from performing their duties as citizens, fathers and husbands or, on the other hand, from watching their laws and customs and institutions being ridiculed on the stage? Whether the passions are excited by, and the affections drawn to, what is noble or what is base? Whether the relations between men and women are depicted in terms of an eroticism wholly divorced from love and calculated to destroy the capacity for love and the institutions, such as the family, that depend on love? Whether a dramatist uses pleasure to attach men to what is beautiful or to what is ugly? We may not be accustomed to thinking of these things in this manner, but it is not strange that so much of the obscenity from which so many of us derive our pleasure today has an avowed political purpose.[5] The pornographers seem to know intuitively what liberals have forgotten, namely, that there is indeed a "causal relationship ... between word or pictures and human behavior." At least they are not waiting for behavioral science to discover this fact.

Pornography's purpose is sometimes directly political and sometimes political in the sense that it will have political consequences, intended or not. This latter purpose is to make us shameless, and it seems to be succeeding with astonishing speed. Activities that were once confined to the private scene—to the "obscene," to make an etymological assumption—are now presented for our delectation and emulation at center stage. Nothing that is appropriate to one place is inappropriate to any other place. No act, we are to infer, no human possibility, no possible physical combination or connection, is shameful. Even our lawmakers now so declare. "However plebian my tastes may be," Justice Douglas asked somewhat disingenuously in the *Ginzburg* case, "who am I to say that others' tastes must be so limited and that others' tastes have no 'social importance'?" By extension, we might say that nothing prevents a dog from enjoying sexual intercourse in the marketplace, and it is unnatural to deprive men of the same pleasure, either actively or as voyeurs in the theatre. Shame itself is unnatural, a convention devised by hypocrites to inhibit the pleasures of the body. We must get rid of our "hangups."

THE IMPORTANCE OF SHAME

But what if, contrary to what is now so generally assumed, shame is natural to man, in the sense of being an original feature of human existence? What if it is shamelessness that is unnatural, in the sense of having to be acquired? What if the beauty that men are capable of knowing and achieving in their living with each other derives from the fact that man is naturally the only creature capable of blushing? Consider the case of voyeurism, a case that, under the circumstances, comes quickly to mind. Some of us—I have even known students to confess to it—experience discomfort watching others on the stage or screen performing sexual acts, or even the acts preparatory to sexual acts, such as the disrobing of a woman by a man. This discomfort is caused by shame, or is akin to shame. True, it could derive from the fear of being discovered enjoying what society still sees as a forbidden game. The voyeur who experiences shame in this sense is judging himself by the conventions of his society and, according to the usual modern account, the greater the distance separating him from his society in space or time, the less he will experience this kind of shame. This shame, which we may term *concealing shame*, is a function of the fear of discovery by one's own group. The group may have its reasons for forbidding a particular act, thereby leading those who engage in that act to conceal it—to be ashamed of it—but these reasons have nothing to do with the nature of man. Voyeurism, according to this account, is a perversion only because society says it is, and a man guided only by nature would not be ashamed of it.

According to another view, however, not to be ashamed—to be a shameless voyeur—is more likely to require explanation, for voyeurism is by nature a perversion.

Anyone who draws his sexual gratification from looking at another lives continuously at a distance. If it is normal to approach and unite with the partner, then it is precisely characteristic of the voyeur that he remains alone, without a partner, an outsider who acts in a stealthy and furtive manner. To keep his distance when it is essential to draw near is one of the paradoxes of his perversion. The looking of the voyeur is of course also a looking at and, as such, is as different from the looks exchanged by lovers as medical palpation from a gentle caress of the hand.[6]

From this point of view, voyeurism is perversion, not merely because it is contrary to convention, but because it is contrary to nature. Convention here follows nature. Whereas sexual attraction brings man and woman together seeking a unity that culminates in the living being they create together, the voyeur maintains a distance; and because he maintains a distance he looks at, he does not communicate; and because he looks at he objectifies, he makes an object of that with which it is natural to join; objectifying, he is incapable of uniting and is therefore incapable of love. The need to conceal voyeurism--the concealing shame—is a corollary of the *protective shame*, the shame that impels lovers to search for privacy and for an experience protected from the profane and the eyes of the stranger. The stranger is "at odds with the shared unity of the [erotic couple], and his mere presence tends to introduce some objectification into every immediate relationship."[7] Shame, both concealing and protective, protects lovers and therefore love. And a polity without love—without the tenderness and the poetry and the beauty—without, in a word, the uniquely human things that depend on it and derive from it—a polity without love would be an unnatural monstrosity.[8]

THE FORGOTTEN ARGUMENT

To speak in a more obviously political manner, there is a connection between self-restraint and shame, and therefore a connection between shame and self-government or democracy. Thus there is a political danger in promoting shamelessness and the fullest self-expression or indulgence. To live together requires rules and a governing of the passions, and those who are without shame will be unruly and unrulable; having lost the ability to restrain themselves by observing the rules they collectively give themselves, they will have to be ruled by others. Tyranny is the natural and inevitable mode of government for the shameless and self-indulgent who have carried liberty beyond any restraint, natural or conventional.

Such, indeed, was the argument made by political philosophers prior to the twentieth century, when it was generally understood that democracy, more than any other form of government, required self-restraint, which it would inculcate through moral education and impose on itself through laws, including laws governing the manner of public amusements. It was the tyrant who could usually allow the people to indulge themselves. Indulgence of the sort we are now witnessing did not threaten his rule, because his rule did not depend on a citizenry of good character. Anyone can be ruled by a tyrant, and the more debased his subjects the safer his rule. A case can be made for complete freedom of the arts among such people, whose pleasures are derived from activities divorced from their labors and any duties associated with citizenship. Among them, a theatre, for example, can serve to divert the search for pleasure from what the tyrant regards as dangerous or pernicious pursuits.[9]

Such an argument was not unknown among thoughtful men at the time modern democracies were being constituted. It is to be found in Jean-Jacques Rousseau's *Letter to M. d'Alembert on the Theatre*. Its principles were known by Washington and Jefferson, to say nothing of the anti-federalists, and later on by Lincoln, all of whom insisted that democracy would not work without citizens of good character. And, until ecently, no justice of the Supreme Court and no man in public life doubted the necessity for the law to make at least a modest effort to promote that good character, if only by protecting the effort of other institutions, such as the church and the family, to nourish and maintain it. The case for censorship, at first glance, was made wholly with a view to the political good, and it had as its premise that what was good for the arts and sciences was *not* necessarily good for the polity.

There was no illusion among these thinkers that censorship laws would be easy to administer; they also recognized the danger these laws represented. One obvious danger was that the lawmakers will demand too much, that the Anthony Comstocks who are always with us will become the agents of the law and demand not merely decency but sanctity. Macaulay stated the problem in his essay on Restoration Comedy (mild fare compared to that regularly exhibited in our day):

> It must, indeed, be acknowledged, in justice to the writers of whom we have spoken thus severely, that they were to a great extent the creatures of their age. And if it be asked why that age encouraged immorality which no other age would have tolerated, we have no hesitation in answering that this great depravation of the national taste was the effect of the prevalence of Puritanism under the Commonwealth.
>
> To punish public outrages on morals and religion is unquestionably within the competence of rulers. But when a government, not content with requiring decency, requires sanctity, it oversteps the bounds which mark its proper functions. And it may be laid down as a universal rule that a government which attempts more than it ought will perform less . . . . And so a government which, not content with repressing scandalous excesses, demands from its subjects fervent and austere piety, will soon discover that, while attempting to render an impossible service to the cause of virtue, it has in truth only promoted vice.

The truth of this was amply demonstrated in the United States during the Prohibition era, when the attempt was made to enforce abstemiousness and not, labels to the contrary, temperance. In a word, the principle should be not to attempt to eradicate vice—the means by which that might conceivably be accomplished are incompatible with free government—but rather, to make vice difficult, knowing that while it will continue to flourish covertly, at least it will not be openly exhibited. And that was considered important.

We must remember that this old and largely forgotten case for censorship was made by men who were not insensitive to the beauty of the arts and the noble role they can play in men's lives. Rousseau admitted that he never willingly missed a performance of any of Molière's plays, and did so in the very context of arguing that all theatrical productions should be banned in the decent and self-governing polity. Like Plato, he would banish the poets, even though he was himself a poet—also a musician, opera composer and novelist—who demonstrated his love for and knowledge of poetry— or, as we would say, the arts—in his works and in his life. But he was above all a thinker of the highest rank, and as such he knew that the basic premise of the later liberalism is false. A century later, John Stuart Mill could no longer conceive of a conflict between the intrinsic and therefore legitimate demands of the sciences and the intrinsic and therefore legitimate demands of the polity. Rousseau had argued that the "restoration" of the arts and sciences did not tend to purify morals, but that, on the contrary, their restoration and popularization would destroy the possibility of a good civil society. His contemporaries were shocked and angered by this teaching and excluded Rousseau from their company; and, taught by them and more directly by Mill and his followers—Justice Douglas, for example—we might tend to dismiss it as the teaching of a madman or a fool. Are we, however, still prepared to stand with Mill and his predecessors against Rousseau, to argue that what is good for science is necessarily also good for civil society? Or have certain terrible events and conditions prepared us to reconsider that issue? If so, and especially in the light of certain literary and theatrical events, we might be prepared to reconsider the issue of whether what is good for the arts is necessarily good for civil society.

In practice, censors have acted out of an unsophisticated concern for public morality, with no love for the arts, and with no appreciation of what would be sacrificed if their policy were to be adopted. Their opponents have resisted them out of a sophisticated concern for the freedom of expression, often with a true love for the arts, but with no concern for the effect of this freedom on public morality. Thus, it appears that concern for public morality requires censorship, while concern for the arts requires the abolition of censorship.

The law developed by our courts is an attempt to avoid this dilemma by denying that it exists. But with what results? Rousseau predicted there would be, not only a corruption of public morality, but a degradation of the arts. His case for censorship appears at first glance to be made wholly with a view to protecting the simple and decent political order from corruption at the hands of sophisticated literature and the theatre; in fact his case was also made with a view to preventing the corruption of the arts themselves. Their popularization would be their degradation. To deny the tension between politics and the arts is to assume that the relation between them requires no governing, that what is produced by writers and dramatists may be ignored by the law in the same manner that the production of economic goods and services was once said to be of no legitimate concern of the law. The free market will be permitted to operate, with the result that what appears in print and on the stage will be determined by the tastes operating in that market, which in a democracy will be a mass market. The law will no longer attempt to influence this market; having denied the distinction between the non-obscene and the obscene; it will, in fact, come to deny the distinction between art and trash. This is what has happened. Justice Douglas, who told us that the "ideal of the Free Society written into our Constitution ... is that people are mature enough ... to recognize trash when they see it," also denies that anyone, mature or immature, can define the difference between art and trash. "Some like Chopin, others like 'rock and roll.' Some are 'normal,' some are masochistic, some deviant in other respects .... But why is freedom of the press and expression denied them? When the Court today speaks of 'social value' does it mean a 'value' to the majority? ... If a publication caters to the idiosyncracies of a minority, why does it not have 'social importance'?[10] To him, the question of whether or not a publication has "social value" is answered by whether anyone wants to read it—thus, *any* publication may have "social value." It is all a question of idiosyncratic taste: some like Chopin, some like rock and roll; some are normal—or, as he writes it, "normal"—and some masochistic or deviant—or, as he ought to have written it, "deviant." These statements, of course, make nonsense of Douglas' business of ascending "from plateau to plateau and finally reach[ing] the world of enduring ideas"; because if everything has value, and if there is no standard by which to judge among them, then there is no upward or downward, no "plateau" higher than another "plateau," no art or trash and, of course, no problem. Art is now defined as the "socially important," and this, in turn, is defined by Douglas as anything anyone has a taste for.

DISTINGUISHING ART FROM TRASH

It is true that Douglas is uniquely vulgar for a Supreme Court justice, but his colleagues have not been far behind him on the substantive issue. In principle, they acknowledge the category of socially "important" publications and productions, but they do not depend on an educated critical judgment to define it. They simply accept the judgment of any literary hack willing to testify, which amounts to transferring the mass market to the courtroom. It was solemnly said in testimony that *Fanny Hill* is a work of social importance, which was then rephrased as "literary merit" and "historical value," just the sort of thing to be taught in the classroom (and, as Douglas argued, in sermons from the pulpit). Another "expert witness" described it as a work of art that "asks for and receives a literary response." Its style was said to be "literary" and its central character, in addition to being a whore, was an "intellectual," which is probably considered the highest praise within the power of these experts to bestow. An intellectual, the court was then told, is one who is "extremely curious about life and who seeks . . . to record with accuracy the details of the external world"—in Fanny's case, such "external details" as her "physical sensations."

Censorship, undertaken in the name of the public necessity to maintain the distinction between the non-obscene and the obscene, has the secondary effect of lending some support to the distinction between art and trash. At least, it requires a judgment on what is proper and what is improper, which is to say a judgment on what is worthy of being enjoyed and what is unworthy, and this has the effect of supporting the idea that there is a distinction to be made, and that the distinction is important. Our law, as announced by the judges of our highest court, now denies this, explicitly in the case of Douglas and implicitly in the case of his colleagues making up the rest of the Court's majority. The law has resigned in favor of the free mass market, and it has done so, not because the free market is seen as a mechanism best calculated to bring about a particular result (for example, the material wealth desired by the *laissez-faire* economists), but because it attaches no significance to the decisions the market will make. The popularization of the arts will not lead to their degradation, because there is no such thing as degradation.

The *New York Times* does not agree with this when it calls for "sophisticated critical judgment" to save us from the pile of muck that now constitutionally passes for art. But the "sophisticated critical judgment" of its own drama and book pages praised the very works condemned in the editorial; besides, much of this market is impervious to "sophisticated critical judgment." This is confirmed in the *Times* itself, in a piece printed a few months later on the first page of the Sunday drama section: "Nobody yet knows how to control the effect of nudity for a production's purposes, but producers encourage it anyhow. Why? The explanation, I should think, is obvious: sex, as always, is good box office."[11] Exactly. It was the law, not the critics, that kept the strip tease and the "skin flick" confined to the illegitimate theatre, and it is foolish to think, or to have thought, that the critics alone will be able to keep them there, or to keep them from flourishing in the legitimate theatre. That game is caught, as Lincoln would have said. The question remains unanswered, whether or not "sophisticated critical judgment" can preserve artistic tastes in another part of the same theatre, or whether there will *be* any "sophisticated critical judgment." To ask this is to wonder whether the public taste—or at least, a part of the public's taste—can be educated, and educated with no assistance from the law. This is an old question; to ask it is to return to Rousseau's quarrel with Voltaire and the Enlightenment, and to Tocqueville and John Stuart Mill—in short, to the beginnings of modern democracy, where, in political philosophy, the question received thematic treatment.

A ROLE FOR THE UNIVERSITY?

The principle of modern democracy is the natural equality of all men, and the problem was to find some way of preventing this principle from becoming all-pervasive, and especially from invading the arts and sciences themselves. Stated otherwise, the problem was to find a substitute for the aristocratic class which had formerly sustained the arts and sciences—some basis on which, or some citadel from which, the arts and sciences could resist public opinion. The constitutional principle of freedom of speech and of the press would, perhaps, protect them from hostile political passions, but this institutional device would not protect them from the much more subtle danger of coming to share the public's taste and of doing the public's work according to the public's standards. One solution, championed by some, was the modern university—which, as Allan Bloom has recently written, was to be "a center for reflection and education independent of the regime and the pervasive influence of its principles, free of the overwhelming effect of public opinion in its crude and subtle forms, devoted to the dispassionate quest for the important and comprehensive truths."[1][2] Tenure and academic freedom would protect the professors of the arts and sciences, and thereby protect the arts and sciences themselves, and the students would be educated in the principles of the arts and sciences and their tastes formed accordingly. The education of the public's taste in the arts, which will prevent the popularization of the arts from becoming the cause of their degradation, must take place in the universities if it is to take place at all.

But the so-called expert witnesses who testified in the obscenity cases came from these very universities. *Fanny Hill's* champions were university professors, and not from minor institutions. To rely on the professors to provide the "sophisticated critical judgment," or to educate the tastes of the mass market, or of any part of it, is to ignore what is going on in the universities. Several years ago Cornell paid $800 to a man to conduct a "happening" on campus as part of a Festival of Contemporary Art. This happening consisted of the following: a group of students was led to the city dump where they selected the charred remains of an old automobile, spread it with several hundred pounds of strawberry jam, removed their shirts and blouses, and then danced around it, stopping occasionally to lick the jam. By 1970 standards this is not especially offensive; it is silly, as so many "college boy" antics have been silly. What distinguishes it from goldfish swallowing and panty raids is that it was conducted under official university auspices, with the support and participation of professors.

The call for a "sophisticated critical judgment" is merely a variation on the general call for education, which libertarians have customarily offered as an alternative to the policy of forbidding or punishing speech. It is an attractive alternative, attractive because of its consistency with liberal principles, as well as for its avoidance of the difficulties accompanying a policy of censorship; unfortunately, given the present intellectual climate, education in this area is almost impossible. Consider the case of the parent who wants to convince his children of the impropriety of the use of the four-letter verb meaning to copulate. At the present time, the task confronting him is only slightly less formidable than that faced by the parent who would teach his children that the world is flat. Just as the latter will have to overcome a body of scientific evidence to the contrary, the former will have to overcome the power of common usage and the idea of propriety it implies. Until recently, propriety required the use of the verb "to make love,"[13] and this delicacy was not without purpose. It was meant to remind us—to teach us, or at least to allow us to be taught—that, whereas human copulation can be physically indistinguishable from animal copulation generally, it ought to be marked by the presence of a passion of which other animals are incapable. Now, to a quickly increasing extent, the four-letter verb—more "honest," in the opinion of its devotees—is being used openly and therefore without impropriety. The parent will fail in his effort to educate, because he will be on his own, trying to teach a lesson his society no longer wants taught—by the law, by the language or by the schools—especially by the schools. In 1964, when the administrators of the University of California at Berkeley could not find a reason to censure the students for whom "free speech" meant the brandishing of that four-letter verb on placards, it not only made legitimate what had been illegitimate, but announced that from that time forward it would not attempt to teach its students anything contrary to their passions—sexual, political or, with reference to drug use, physiological. What became true then at Berkeley is now true generally. The professors have nothing to teach their students. The younger ones have joined the students and have come to share their tastes and their political passions; the older ones are silent, and together they are in the process of abdicating to the students their authority to govern the universities, to enforce parietals, to prescribe the curriculum and even their right to teach. Critical judgment is being replaced by "doing your own thing," which is what Justice Douglas was talking about; this being so, it is doubtful, to say the least, whether the universities will be able to educate the tastes of anyone. And, if this is not done in the universities, where can it be done?[14] Where in the midst of all the vulgarity and this incessant clamor for doing one's own thing can we find a refuge for the arts—without which there can be no "sophisticated critical judgment."

Anyone who undertakes to defend censorship in the name of the arts is obliged to acknowledge that he has not exhausted his subject when he has completed that defense. What is missing is a defense of obscenity. What is missing is a defense of the obscenity employed by the greatest of our poets—Aristophanes and Chaucer, Shakespeare and Swift—because it is impossible to believe, it is unreasonable to believe, that what they did is indefensible; and what they did, among other things, was to write a good deal of obscenity.

They employed it mainly in comedy, but their purpose was not simply to make us laugh. Comedy, according to Aristotle,[15] makes us laugh at what is ludicrous in its ugliness, and its purpose is to teach, just as tragedy teaches by making us cry before what is destructive in nobility. The latter imitates what is higher, the former what is lower, but they are equally serious; Aristotle discussed both, and Shakespeare, for example, was a comic as well as a tragic poet.

Those aspects of his soul that make man truly human and distinguish him from all other beings—higher or lower in the natural order of things—require political life. No great poet ever denied this. Man's very virtues, as well as their counterparts, his vices, require him to be governed and to govern; they initiate demands that can be met only in political life—but the poet knows, with Rousseau, that the demands of human virtue cannot be fully met in political life because they transcend political life. The poet knows the beauty of that order beyond the polity; he reminds us that there is an order outside the conventional, and that we are part of that natural order, as well as of the conventional. Shakespeare knows, with Rousseau, that there is a tension between this natural order and the conventional or legal order, and his purpose is to resolve it, at least for some men, at the highest possible level. These men must first be shown that this world of convention is not the only world, and here is where obscenity may play a part—that beyond Venice there is Portia's Belmont, the utopia where the problems that plague Venice do not exist.[16] Obscenity can be used to ridicule the conventional. But it is used in the name of the natural, that order outside the conventional according to which the conventional may be criticized and, perhaps, if only to a limited extent, reformed. Obscenity in the hands of such a poet can serve to *elevate* men, some few of them, above the conventional order in which all of us are forced to live our mundane lives. Its purpose is to teach what is truly beautiful—not what convention holds to be beautiful—and to do so by means of pleasure, for obscenity can be pleasurable.

Shakespeare expresses this conflict between nature and law in Edmund's soliloquy at the beginning of Act I, Scene 2, of *King Lear*:

> Thou, Nature, art my goddess; to thy law
> My services are bound. Wherefore should I
> Stand in the plague of custom, and permit
> The curiosity of nations to deprive me,
> For that I am some twelve or fourteen moonshines
> Lag of a brother? Why bastard? wherefore base?
> When my dimensions are as well compact,
> My mind as generous, and my shape as true,
> As honest madam's issue? Why brand they us
> With base? with baseness? bastardy? base, base?
> Who, in the lusty stealth of nature, take
> More composition and fierce quality
> Than doth, within a dull, stale, tired bed,
> Go to th' creating a whole tribe of fops,
> Got 'tween asleep and wake?—Well, then,
> Legitimate Edgar, I must have your land:
> Our father's love is to the bastard Edmund

As to th' legitimate: fine word—*legitimate*!
Well, my legitimate, if this letter speed,
And my invention thrive, Edmund the base
Shall top th' legitimate. I grow; I prosper:—
Now, gods, stand up for bastards!

This serves to illustrate one of the themes to which great poets address themselves—what is right by law and what is right by nature—in the development of which the use of obscenity in comedy has a legitimate and perhaps even a noble role. When it is so used, it is fully justified, especially because great poetry, even when it is obscene, is of interest only to a few—those who read it primarily for what is beyond its obscenity, that towards which obscenity points. But when obscenity is employed as it is today, merely in an effort to capture an audience, or to shock without elevating, or in the effort to set loose idiosyncratic "selfs" doing their own things, or to bring down the constitutional order, it is not justified, for it lacks the ground on which to claim exemption from the law. The modern advocates of obscenity do not seem to be aware of this consequence of their advocacy. They have obliterated the distinction between art and trash, and in so doing they have deprived themselves of the ground on which they might protest the law. What possible argument could have been used against the police, had they decided to arrest the participants in the Cornell "happening" for indecent exposure, or against a law forbidding these festivals of contemporary "art?" In this generous world the police must also be accorded a right to do their "own thing," and they would probably be able to do it with the support of the majority, and therefore, of the law. In a world where everyone does his own thing, the majority not only rules but can do no wrong, because there is no standard of right and wrong. Justice Douglas sees his job as protecting the right of these contemporary "artists" to do their own thing, but a thoughtful judge is likely to ask how an artistic judgment that is wholly idiosyncratic can be capable of supporting an objection to the law. The objection, "*I* like it," is sufficiently rebutted by, "*we* don't."

How to express in a rule of law this distinction between the justified and the unjustified employment of obscenity is no simple task. That I have willingly admitted. I have also argued that it cannot be done at all on the premise from which our law has proceeded.

Finally, I have tried to indicate the consequences of a failure to maintain this distinction in the law: not only will we no longer be able to teach the distinction between the proper and the improper, but we will no longer be able to teach—and will therefore come to forget—the distinction between art and trash. Stated otherwise, censorship, because it inhibits self-indulgence and supports the idea of propriety and impropriety, protects political democracy; paradoxically, when it faces the problem of the justified and unjustified use of obscenity, censorship also serves to maintain the distinction between art and trash and, therefore, to protect art, thereby enhancing the quality of this democracy. This is something that we forgot. We began with a proper distrust of the capacities of juries and judges to make sound judgments in an area that lies outside their professional competence; but, led by the Supreme Court, we went on improperly to conclude that these judgments should not be made at all, because they cannot be made, since there is nothing for anyone to judge. No doubt the law used to err on occasion; but democracy can live without "Mrs. Warren's Profession," if it must, as well as without *Fanny Hill*—or, to speak more precisely, it can live with the error that consigns "Mrs. Warren's Profession" to under-the-counter custom, along with *Fanny Hill*. It remains to be seen whether the true friend of democracy will want to live in the world without the under-the-counter custom, the world that does not know the difference between "Mrs. Warren's Profession" and *Fanny Hill.*

NOTES

1. *New York Times*, January 5, 1970, p. 32. Whatever Ernst now says he used to say, or meant all along, what we remember from him is recorded on the printed page, and there he said that "censorship of the theater is truly an anomaly." He also scoffed at the idea that a book, any book, could be "corrupting (whatever that may mean)"; and insisted that censorship could be justified only if it could be demonstrated that a "causal relationship" existed "between word or picture and human behavior," emphasizing the fact that such a relationship had never been demonstrated "in the field of obscenity"! In fact, he added, "the indications seem to be to the contrary." Morris L. Ernst and Alan U. Schwartz, *Censorship: The Search for the Obscene* (New York: Macmillan, 1964), pp. 142, 200, 250-251.

2. Long Beach, California, January 13 [1970] (AP)—Four nude models—two male, two female—postured before the coeducational sociology class of 250 persons.

On movie screens, lesbian and heterosexual couples went through acts of lovemaking.

Sound systems blared recordings by the Beatles and from the rock musical 'Hair.'

Two hours after the class ended yesterday, California State College suspended its teachers, Marion Steele, 31 years old, and Dr. Donald Robertson, 29, for 30 days without pay. Further action was threatened.

Mr. Steele and Dr. Robertson said they had staged the show to ridicule what they called America's prudishness about sex, as contrasted with its toleration of what they considered such 'glaring obscenities' as the Vietnam War, violence on television and pollution of air and water.

'This produces hangups and keeps millions from enjoying genuine sexual pleasure and makes our entire world obscene,' Dr. Robertson told the class.

—New York Times, January 14, 1970, p. 11.

3. In *Ginzburg v. United States*, 383 U.S. 463 (1966), the Supreme Court upheld the conviction, because Ginzburg had employed "pandering" in the advertising of his obscene wares, a rule never applied in the past and inapplicable in the future. The next year the Court resumed its habit of reversing obscenity convictions, although the publications involved were at least as offensive as anything Ginzburg had published. *Redrup v. New York*, 386 U.S. 767 (1967). States have been permitted to prohibit the sale of obscenity to minors, *Ginsberg v. New York*, 390 U.S. 629 (1968), but, on the other hand, they have not been allowed to classify films with a view to protecting minors—not, at least, with a "vague" ordinance. *Interstate Circuit, Inc. v. Dallas*, 390 U.S. 676 (1968). Mr. Justice Douglas would not prohibit the sale of obscenity even to children; he says, and he ought to know, that most juvenile delinquents are over 50.

4. *Laocoön*, (New York: Noonday Press, 1914) ch. 1, p. 10.

5. "Chè!" and "Hair," for example, are political plays. See also note 2.

6. Erwin W. Straus, *Phenomenological Psychology* (New York: Basic Books, 1966), p. 219. I have no doubt that it is possible to want to observe sexual acts for reasons unrelated to voyeurism. Just as a physician has a clinical interest in the parts of the body, philosophers will have an interest in the parts of the soul, or in the varieties of human things which are manifestations of the body and the soul. Such a "looking" would not be voyeurism and would be unaccompanied by shame; or, the desire to see and to understand would require the "seer" to overcome shame. Plato, *Republic*, 439e. In any event, the case of the philosopher is politically irrelevant, and esthetically irrelevant as well.

7. Ibid., p. 221.

8. It is easy to prove that shamefulness is not the only principle governing the question of what may properly be presented on the stage; shamefulness would not, for example, govern the case of a scene showing the copulating of a married couple who love each other very much. That is not intrinsically shameful—on the contrary—yet it still ought not to be shown. The principle here is, I think, an esthetic one: such a scene is dramatically weak, because the response of the audience would be characterized by prurience and not by a

sympathy with what the scene is intended to portray—namely, a beautiful love. This statement can be tested by joining a college town movie audience; it is confirmed unintentionally by a defender of nudity on the stage; see note 11.

9. The modern tyrant does not encourage passivity among his subjects; on the contrary, they are expected by him to be public-spirited: to work for the State, to exceed production schedules, to be citizen soldiers in the huge armies, and to love Big Brother. Indeed, in Nazi Germany and the Soviet Union alike, the citizens' private lives were and are discouraged, along with erotic love and the private attachments it fosters. Censorship in a modern tyrannical state is designed to abolish the private life to the extent that this is possible. George Orwell understood this perfectly. The strict censorship that characterizes modern tyranny, and distinguishes it sharply from pre-modern tyranny, derives from the basis of modern tyrannical rule: both Nazism and Communism have their roots in theory—more precisely, a kind of utopian theory. The modern tyrant parades as a political philosopher, the heir of Nietzsche or Marx, with a historical mission to perform. Therefore, he cannot leave his subjects alone.

10. *Ginzburg v. United States*, 383 U.S. 463, 489-490 (1966). Dissenting opinion.

11. *New York Times*, January 18, 1970. The author of this piece, Martin Gottfried, presumably a man of "sophisticated critical judgment"—since the *Times* printed him—defends "Chè!" and other similar plays, ending with a very sophisticated defense of a homosexual rape scene from a production entitled "Fortune and Men's Eyes," done, of course, in the nude and apparently leaving nothing to the imagination. His basic principle is that "no climactic scene, in any play, should happen offstage . . . . "

12. "The Democratization of the University," in Robert A. Goldwin, ed., *How Democratic is America?* (Chicago: Rand McNally, 1972).

13. That this is not merely the product of English or American "Puritanism" is proved, for example, by the French *faire d'amour* and the Italian *fare-all'amore*, as well as the fastidious German phrase, *mit einem lieben*.

14. In a number of universities, students are permitted to receive course credit for "courses" taught by themselves to themselves. Not surprisingly, it was left to Cornell to carry this to its absurd extreme. In May 1970, the Educational Policy Committee of the College of Arts and Sciences voted 5-2 to grant "three credit hours to ten students who had 'taught' themselves a course in children's literature"—including not only *Alice in Wonderland*, but *Pinocchio, Where the Wild Things Are*, and *Now We Are Six*. "The students claimed that they had not read the books before taking their course." This implies that it is one of the jobs of a university to remedy deficiencies in kindergarten education. In any case, as one of the two dissenters later reported to the full faculty, "whether the books had ever been read to them remains unclear." Cornell *Chronicle*, June 4, 1970.

15. Aristotle, *Poetics* (Cambridge, Mass.: Harvard University Press, 1965).

16. See the chapter on "The Merchant of Venice" in Allan Bloom and Harry V. Jaffa, *Shakespeare's Politics* (New York: Basic Books, 1964).

4 Legislative Recommendations

Report of the Committee on Obscenity and Pornography

On the basis of its findings, the Commission makes the following legislative recommendations. The disagreements of particular Commissioners with aspects of the Commission's legislative recommendations are noted below, where the recommendations are discussed in detail. Commissioners Link, Hill and Keating have filed a joint dissenting statement. In addition, Commissioners Keating and Link have submitted separate remarks. Commissioners Larsen and Wolfgang have filed statements explaining their dissent from certain Commission recommendations. A number of other Commissioners have filed short separate statements.[1]

In general outline, the Commission recommends that federal, state and local legislation should not seek to interfere with the right of adults who wish to do so to read, obtain or view explicit sexual materials.[2] On the other hand, we recommend legislative regulations upon the sale of sexual materials to young persons who do not have the consent of their parents, and we also recommend legislation to protect persons from having sexual materials thrust upon them

Reprinted from *The Report of the Commission on Obscenity and Pornography* (Washington, D.C.: U.S. Government Printing Office 1970), pp. 51-64.

without their consent through the mails or through open public display.

The Commission's specific legislative recommendations and the reasons underlying these recommendations are as follows:

STATUTES RELATING TO ADULTS

The Commission recommends that federal, state and local legislation prohibiting the sale, exhibition or distribution of sexual materials to consenting adults should be repealed. Twelve of the 17 participating members[3] of the Commission join in this recommendation.[4] Two additional Commissioners[5] subscribe to the bulk of the Commission's Report, but do not believe that the evidence presented at this time is sufficient to warrant the repeal of all prohibitions upon what adults may obtain. Three Commissioners dissent from the recommendation to repeal adult legislation and would retain existing laws prohibiting the dissemination of obscene materials to adults.[6]

The Commission believes that there is no warrant for continued governmental interference with the full freedom of adults to read, obtain or view whatever such material they wish. Our conclusion is based upon the following considerations:

1. Extensive empirical investigation, both by the Commission and by others, provides no evidence that exposure to or use of explicit sexual materials plays a significant role in the causation of social or individual harms such as crime, delinquency, sexual or nonsexual deviancy or severe emotional disturbances.[7] This research and its results are described in detail in the Report of the Effects Panel of the Commission. Empirical investigation thus supports the opinion of a substantial majority of persons professionally engaged in the treatment of deviancy, delinquency and antisocial behavior, that exposure to sexually explicit materials has no harmful causal role in these areas.

Studies show that a number of factors, such as disorganized family relationships and unfavorable peer influences, are intimately related to harmful sexual behavior or adverse character development. Exposure to sexually explicit materials, however, cannot be counted as among these determinative factors. Despite the existence of widespread legal prohibitions upon the dissemination of such materials, exposure to them appears to be a usual and harmless part of the process of growing up in our society and a frequent and nondamaging occurrence among adults. Indeed, a few Commission studies indicate that a possible distinction between sexual offenders and other people, with regard to experience with explicit sexual materials, is that sex offenders have seen markedly *less* of such materials while maturing.

This is not to say that exposure to explicit sexual materials has no effect upon human behavior. A prominent effect of exposure to sexual materials is that persons tend to talk more about sex as a result of seeing such materials. In addition, many persons become temporarily sexually aroused upon viewing explicit sexual materials and the frequency of their sexual activity may, in consequence, increase for short periods. Such behavior, however, is the type of sexual activity already established as usual activity for the particular individual.

In sum, empirical research designed to clarify the question has found no evidence to date that exposure to explicit sexual materials plays a significant role in the causation of delinquent or criminal behavior among youth or adults.[8]

2. On the positive side, explicit sexual materials are sought as a source of entertainment and information by substantial numbers of American adults. At times, these materials also appear to serve to increase and facilitate constructive communication about sexual matters within marriage. The most frequent purchaser of explicit sexual materials is a college-educated, married male, in his thirties or forties, who is of above average socioeconomic status. Even where materials are legally available to them, young adults and older adolescents do not constitute an important portion of the purchasers of such materials.

3. Society's attempts to legislate for adults in the area of obscenity have not been successful. Present laws prohibiting the consensual sale or distribution of explicit sexual materials to adults are extremely unsatisfactory in their practical application. The Constitution permits material to be deemed "obscene" for adults only if, as a whole, it appeals to the "prurient" interest of the average person, is "patently offensive" in light of "community standards," and lacks "redeeming social value." These vague and highly subjective esthetic, psychological and moral tests do not

provide meaningful guidance for law enforcement officials, juries or courts. As a result, law is inconsistently and sometimes erroneously applied and the distinctions made by courts between prohibited and permissible materials often appear indefensible. Errors in the application of the law and uncertainty about its scope also cause interference with the communication of constitutionally protected materials.

4. Public opinion in America does not support the imposition of legal prohibitions upon the right of adults to read or see explicit sexual materials. While a minority of Americans favor such prohibitions, a majority of the American people presently are of the view that adults should be legally able to read or see explicit sexual materials if they wish to do so.

5. The lack of consensus among Americans concerning whether explicit sexual materials should be available to adults in our society, and the significant number of adults who wish to have access to such materials, pose serious problems regarding the enforcement of legal prohibitions upon adults, even aside from the vagueness and subjectivity of present law. Consistent enforcement of even the clearest prohibitions upon consensual adult exposure to explicit sexual materials would require the expenditure of considerable law enforcement resources. In the absence of a persuasive demonstration of damage flowing from consensual exposure to such materials, there seems no justification for thus adding to the overwhelming tasks already placed upon the law enforcement system. Inconsistent enforcement of prohibitions, on the other hand, invites discrim-inatory action based upon considerations not directly relevant to the policy of the law. The latter alternative also breeds public disrespect for the legal process.

6. The foregoing considerations take on added significance because of the fact that adult obscenity laws deal in the realm of speech and communication. Americans deeply value the right of each individual to determine for himself what books he wishes to read and what pictures or films he wishes to see. Our traditions of free speech and press also value and protect the right of writers, publishers and booksellers to serve the diverse interests of the public. The spirit and letter of our Constitution tell us that government should not seek to interfere with these rights unless a clear threat of harm makes that course imperative. Moreover, the possibility of the

misuse of general obscenity statutes prohibiting distribution of books and films to adults constitutes a continuing threat to the free communication of ideas among Americans—one of the most important foundations of our liberties.

7. In reaching its recommendation that government should not seek to prohibit consensual distributions of sexual materials to adults, the Commission discussed several arguments which are often advanced in support of such legislation. The Commission carefully considered the view that adult legislation should be retained in order to aid in the protection of young persons from exposure to explicit sexual materials. We do not believe that the objective of protecting youth may justifiably be achieved at the expense of denying adults materials of their choice. It seems to us wholly inappropriate to adjust the level of adult communication to that considered suitable for children. Indeed, the Supreme Court has unanimously held that adult legislation premised on this basis is a clearly unconstitutional interference with liberty.

8. There is no reason to suppose that elimination of governmental prohibitions upon the sexual materials which may be made available to adults would adversely affect the availability to the public of other books, magazines, and films. At the present time, a large range of very explicit textual and pictorial materials are available to adults without legal restrictions in many areas of the country. The size of this industry is small when compared with the overall industry in books, magazines and motion pictures, and the business in explicit sexual materials is insignificant in comparison with other national economic enterprises. Nor is the business an especially profitable one; profit levels are, on the average, either normal as compared with other businesses or distinctly below average. The typical business entity is a relatively small entrepreneurial enterprise. The long-term consumer interest in such materials has remained relatively stable in the context of the economic growth of the nation generally, and of the media industries in particular.

9. The Commission has also taken cognizance of the concern of many people that the lawful distribution of explicit sexual materials to adults may have a deleterious effect upon the individual morality of American citizens and upon the moral climate in America as a whole. This concern appears to flow from a belief that exposure to explicit materials may cause moral confusion which, in turn, may

induce antisocial or criminal behavior. As noted above, the Commission has found no evidence to support such a contention. Nor is there evidence that exposure to explicit sexual materials adversely affects character or moral attitudes regarding sex and sexual conduct.[9]

The concern about the effect of obscenity upon morality is also expressed as a concern about the impact of sexual materials upon American values and standards. Such values and standards are currently in a process of complex change, in both sexual and nonsexual areas. The open availability of increasingly explicit sexual materials is only one of these changes. The current flux in sexual values is related to a number of powerful influences, among which are the ready availability of effective methods of contraception, changes of the role of women in our society and the increased education and mobility of our citizens. The availability of explicit sexual materials is, the Commission believes, not one of the important influences on sexual morality.

The Commission is of the view that it is exceedingly unwise for government to attempt to legislate individual moral values and standards independent of behavior, especially by restrictions upon consensual communication. This is certainly true in the absence of a clear public mandate to do so, and our studies have revealed no such mandate in the area of obscenity.

The Commission recognizes and believes that the existence of sound moral standards is of vital importance to individuals and to society. To be effective and meaningful, however, these standards must be based upon deep personal commitment flowing from values instilled in the home, in educational and religious training and through individual resolutions of personal confrontations with human experience. Governmental regulation of moral choice can deprive the individual of the responsibility for personal decision which is essential to the formation of genuine moral standards. Such regulation would also tend to establish an official moral orthodoxy, contrary to our most fundamental constitutional traditions.[10]

Therefore, the Commission recommends the repeal of existing federal legislation which prohibits or interferes with consensual distribution of "obscene" materials to adults. These statutes are: 18 U.S.C. Section 1461, 1462, 1464 and 1465; 19 U.S.C. Section 1305; and 39 U.S.C. Section 3006.[11] The Commission also

:ommends the repeal of existing state and local legislation which
iay similarly prohibit the consensual sale, exhibition, or the
distribution of sexual materials to adults.

STATUTES RELATING TO YOUNG PERSONS

The Commission recommends the adoption by the states of
legislation set forth in the Drafts of Proposed Statutes in Section III
of this Part of the Commission's Report prohibiting the commercial
distribution or display for sale of certain sexual materials to young
persons. Similar legislation might also be adopted, where appropriate, by local governments and by the federal government for
application in areas, such as the District of Columbia, where it has
primary jurisdiction over distributional conduct.

The Commission's recommendation of juvenile legislation is
joined by 14 members of the Commission. Two of these[12] feel the
legislation should be drawn so as to include appropriate descriptions
identifying the material as being unlawful for sale to children. Three
members disagree.[13] Other members of the Commission, who
generally join in its recommendation for juvenile legislation, disagree
with various detailed aspects of the Commission's legislative
proposal. These disagreements are noted in the following discussion.

The Commission's recommendation of juvenile legislation flows
from these findings and considerations:

A primary basis for the Commission's recommendation for repeal
of adult legislation is the fact that extensive empirical investigations
do not indicate any causal relationship between exposure to or use
of explicit sexual materials and such social or individual harms such
as crime, delinquency, sexual or nonsexual deviancy or severe
emotional disturbances. The absence of empirical evidence supporting such a causal relationship also applies to the exposure of children
to erotic materials. However, insufficient research is presently
available on the effect of the exposure of children to sexually
explicit materials to enable us to reach conclusions with the same
degree of confidence as for adult exposure. Strong ethical feelings
against experimentally exposing children to sexually explicit
materials considerably reduced the possibility of gathering the
necessary data and information regarding young persons.

In view of the limited amount of information concerning the effects of sexually explicit materials on children, other considerations have assumed primary importance in the Commission's deliberations. The Commission has been influenced, to a considerable degree, by its finding that a large majority of Americans believe that children should not be exposed to certain sexual materials. In addition, the Commission takes the view that parents should be free to make their own conclusions regarding the suitability of explicit sexual materials for their children and that it is appropriate for legislation to aid parents in controlling the access of their children to such materials during their formative years. The Commission recognizes that legislation cannot possibly isolate children from such materials entirely; it also recognizes that exposure of children to sexual materials may not only do no harm but may, in certain instances, actually facilitate much needed communication between parent and child over sexual matters. The Commission is aware, as well, of the considerable danger of creating an unnatural attraction or an enhanced interest in certain materials by making them "forbidden fruit" for young persons. The Commission believes, however, that these considerations can and should be weighed by individual parents in determining their attitudes toward the exposure of their children to sexual materials, and that legislation should aid, rather than undermine, such parental choice.

Taking account of the above considerations, the model juvenile legislation recommended by the Commission applies only to distributions to children made without parental consent. The recommended legislation applies only to commercial distributions and exhibitions; in the very few instances where noncommercial conduct in this area creates a problem, it can be dealt with under existing legal principles for the protection of young persons, such as prohibitions upon contributing to the delinquency of minors. The model legislation also prohibits displaying certain sexual materials for sale in a manner which permits children to view materials which cannot be sold to them. Two members of the Commission,[14] who recommend legislation prohibiting sales to juveniles, do not join in recommending this regulation upon display; one member of the Commission[15] recommends only this display provision, and does not recommend a special statute prohibiting sales to young persons.

The Commission, pursuant to Congressional direction, has given close attention to the definitions of prohibited material included in its recommended model legislation for young persons. A paramount consideration in the Commission's deliberations has been that definitions of prohibited materials be as specific and explicit as possible. Such specificity aids law enforcement and facilitates and encourages voluntary adherence to law on the part of retail dealers and exhibitors, while causing as little interference as possible with the proper distribution of materials to children and adults. The Commission's recommended legislation seeks to eliminate subjective definitional criteria insofar as that is possible and goes further in that regard than existing state legislation.

The Commission believes that only pictorial material should fall within prohibitions upon sale or commercial display to young persons. An attempt to define prohibited textual materials for young persons with the same degree of specificity as pictorial materials would, the Commission believes, not be advisable. Many worthwhile textual works, containing considerable value for young persons, treat sex in an explicit manner and are presently available to young persons. There appears to be no satisfactory way to distinguish, through a workable legal definition, between these works and those which may be deemed inappropriate by some persons for commercial distribution to young persons. As a result, the inclusion of textual material within juvenile legislative prohibitions would pose considerable risks for dealers and distributors in determining what books might legally be sold or displayed to young persons and would thus inhibit the entire distribution of verbal materials by those dealers who do not wish to expose themselves to such risks. The speculative risk of harm to juveniles from some textual material does not justify these dangers. The Commission believes, in addition, that parental concern over the material commercially available to children most often applies to pictorial matter.

The definition recommended by the Commission for inclusion in juvenile legislation covers a range of explicit pictorial and three-dimensional depictions of sexual activity. It does not, however, apply to depictions of nudity alone, unless genital areas are exposed and emphasized. The definition is applicable only if the explicit pictorial material constitutes a dominant part of a work. An exception is provided for works of artistic or anthropological significance.

Seven Commissioners would include verbal materials within the definition of materials prohibited for sale to young persons.[16] They would, however, also include a broad exception for such textual materials when they bear literary, historical, scientific, educational or other similar social value for young persons.

Because of changing standards as to what material, if any, is inappropriate for sale or display to children, the Commission's model statute contains a provision requiring legislative reconsideration of the need for, and scope of, such legislation at six-year intervals.

The model statute also exempts broadcast or telecast activity from its scope. Industry self-regulation in the past has resulted in little need for governmental intervention. If a need for governmental regulation should arise, the Commission believes that such regulations would be most appropriately prepared in this specialized area through the regulating power of the Federal Communications Commission, rather than through diverse state laws.

The Commission has not fixed upon a precise age limit for inclusion in its recommended juvenile legislation, believing that such a determination is most appropriately made by the states and localities which enact such provisions in light of local standards. All states now fix the age in juvenile obscenity statutes at under 17 or 18 years. The recommended model statute also excludes married persons, whatever their age, from the category of juveniles protected by the legislation.

The Commission considered the possibility of recommending the enactment of uniform federal legislation requiring a notice or label to be affixed to materials by their publishers, importers or manufacturers, when such materials fall within a definitional provision identical to that included within the recommended state or local model juvenile statute. Under such legislation, the required notice might be used by retail dealers and exhibitors, in jurisdictions which adopt the recommended juvenile legislation, as a guide to what material could not be sold or displayed to young persons. The Commission concluded, however, that such a federal notice or labelling provision would be unwise.[17] So long as definitional provisions are drafted to be as specific as possible, and especially if they include only pictorial material, the Commission believes that the establishment of a federal regulatory notice system is probably unnecessary; specific definitions of pictorial material, such as the Commission recommends, should themselves enable retail dealers and exhibitors to make accurate judgments regarding the status of particular magazines and films. The Commission is also extremely reluctant to recommend imposing any federal system for labelling reading or viewing matter on the basis of its quality or content. The precedent of such required labelling would pose a serious potential threat to First Amendment liberties in other areas of communication. Labels indicating sexual content might also be used artificially to enhance the appeal of certain materials. Two Commissioners[18] favor federally imposed labelling in order to advise dealers as clearly and accurately as possible about what material is forbidden for sale to young persons, placing the responsibility for judging whether material falls within the statute on the publisher or producer who is completely aware of its contents and who is in a position to examine each item individually.

Finally, the Commission considered, but does not affirmatively recommend, the enactment by the federal government of juvenile legislation which would prohibit the sale of certain explicit materials to juveniles through the mails. Such federal legislation would, the Commission believes, be virtually unenforceable since the constitutional requirement of proving the defendant's guilty knowledge means that a prosecution could be successful only if proof were available that the vendor knew that the purchaser was a minor. Except in circumstances which have not been found to be prevalent, as where a sale might be solicited through a mailing list composed of young persons, mail order purchases are made without any knowledge by the vendor of the purchaser's age. Certificates of age by the purchaser would be futile as an enforcement device and to require notarized affidavits to make a purchase through the mails would unduly interfere with purchase by adults. The Commission has found, moreover, that at present juveniles rarely purchase sexually explicit materials through the mail, making federal legislative machinery in this area apparently unnecessary.

PUBLIC DISPLAY AND UNSOLICITED MAILING

The Commission recommends enactment of state and local

legislation prohibiting public displays of sexually explicit pictorial materials, and approves in principle of the federal legislation, enacted as part of the 1970 Postal Reorganization Act, regarding the mailing of unsolicited advertisements of a sexually explicit nature. The Commission's recommendations in this area are based upon its finding, through its research, that certain explicit sexual materials are capable of causing considerable offense to numerous Americans when thrust upon them without their consent. The Commission believes that these unwanted intrusions upon individual sensibilities warrant legislative regulation and it further believes that such intrusions can be regulated effectively without any significant interference with consensual communication of sexual material among adults.

Public Display

The Commission's recommendations in the public display area have been formulated into a model state public display statute which is reproduced in the Drafts of Proposed Statutes in Section III of this Part of the Commission Report. Three Commissioners dissent from this recommendation.[19]

The model state statute recommended by the Commission (which would also be suitable for enactment in appropriate instances by local government units and by the federal government for areas where it has general legislative jurisdiction) prohibits the display of certain potentially offensive sexually explicit pictorial materials in places easily visible from public thoroughfares or the property of others.[20] Verbal materials are not included within the recommended prohibition. There appears to be no satisfactory way to define "offensive" words in legislation in order to make the parameters of prohibition upon their display both clear and sufficiently limited so as not to endanger the communication of messages of serious social concern. In addition, the fact that there are few, if any, "dirty" words which do not already appear fairly often in conversation among many Americans and in some very widely distributed books and films indicates that such words are no longer capable of causing the very high degree of offense to a large number of persons which would justify legislative interference. Five Commissioners disagree,[21] and would include verbal materials in the display prohibition because they believe certain words cause sufficient offense to warrant their inclusion in display prohibitions.

Telecasts are exempted from the coverage of the statute for the same reasons set forth above in connection with discussion of the Commission's recommendation of juvenile legislation.

The recommended model legislation defines in specific terms the explicit sexual pictorial materials which the Commission believes are capable of causing offense to a substantial number of persons. The definition covers a range of explicit pictorial and three-dimensional depictions of sexual activity. It does not apply to depictions of nudity alone, unless genital areas are exposed and emphasized. An exception is provided for works of artistic or anthropological significance. The Commission emphasizes that this legislation does not prohibit the sale or advertisement of any materials, but does prohibit the public display of potentially offensive pictorial matter. While such displays have not been found by the Commission to be a serious problem at the present time, increasing commercial distribution of explicit materials to adults may cause considerable offense to others in the future unless specific regulations governing public displays are adopted.

Unsolicited Mailing

The Commission, with three dissents,[22] also approves of federal legislation to prevent unsolicited advertisements containing potentially offensive sexual material from being communicated through the mails to persons who do not wish to receive such advertisements. The Federal Anti-Pandering Act, which went into effect in 1968, imposes some regulation in this area, but it permits a mail recipient to protect himself against such mail only after he has received at least one such advertisement and it protects him only against mail emanating from that particular source. The Commission believes it more appropriate to permit mail recipients to protect themselves against all such unwanted mail advertisements from any source. Federal legislation in this area was enacted just prior to the date of this report as part of the 1970 Postal Reorganization Act (Public Law 91-375, 91st Cong., 2nd sess., 39 U.S.C. Sections 3010-3011; 18 U.S.C. Sections 1735-1737).

The Commission considered two possible methods by which

persons might be broadly insulated from unsolicited sexual advertisements which they do not wish to receive. One approach, contained in the 1970 Postal Reorganization Act, authorizes the Post Office to compile and maintain current lists of persons who have stated that they do not wish to receive certain defined materials, makes these lists available at cost to mailers of unsolicited advertisements, and prohibits sending the defined material to persons whose names appear on the Post Office lists. A second approach, described in detail in the Commission's Progress Report of July, 1969, would require all mailers of unsolicited advertisements falling within the statutory definition to place a label or code on the envelope. Mail patrons would then be authorized to direct local postal authorities not to deliver coded mail to their homes or offices.

In principle, the Commission favors the first of these approaches employed by Congress in the 1970 Postal Reorganization Act. The Commission takes this view because it believes that the primary burden of regulating the flow of potentially offensive unsolicited mail should appropriately fall upon the mailers of such materials and because of its reluctance to initiate required federal labelling of reading or viewing matter because of its sexual content. The Commission believes, however, that under current mail order practices it may prove financially unfeasible for many smaller mailers to conform their mailing lists to those compiled by the Post Office. Use of computers to organize and search mailing lists will apparently be required by the new law; few, if any, small mailers utilize computers in this way today. If the current lists maintained by the Post Office came to contain a very large number of names—perhaps one million or more—even a computer search of these names, to discover any that were also present on a mailing list sought to be used by a mailer, might be prohibitively expensive. If such were the case, the Commission would believe the second possible approach to regulation to be more consistent with constitutional rights. This approach, however, might place serious burdens upon Post Office personnel. The Commission was not able to evaluate the practical significance of these burdens.

In considering the definition appropriate to legislation regulating unsolicited sexual advertisements, the Commission examined a large range of unsolicited material which has given rise to complaints to the Post Office Department in recent years. A definition was then formulated which quite specifically describes material which has been deemed offensive by substantial numbers of postal patrons. This definition is set forth in the footnote.[23] The Commission prefers this definitional provision to the less precise definitional provision in the 1970 Postal Reorganization Act.

DECLARATORY JUDGMENT LEGISLATION

The Commission recommends the enactment, in all jurisdictions which enact or retain provisions prohibiting the dissemination of sexual materials to adults or young persons, of legislation authorizing prosecutors to obtain declaratory judgments as to whether particular materials fall within existing legal prohibitions and appropriate injunctive relief. A model statute embodying this recommendation is presented in the Drafts of Proposed Statutes in Section III of this Part of the Commission Report. All but two[24] of the Commissioners concur in the substance of this recommendation. The Commission recognizes that the particular details governing the institution and appeal of declaratory judgment actions will necessarily vary from state to state depending upon local jurisdictional and procedural provisions. The Commission is about evenly divided with regard to whether local prosecutors should have authority to institute such actions directly, or whether the approval of an official with state-wide jurisdiction, such as the State Attorney General, should be required before an action for declaratory judgment is instituted.

A declaratory judgment procedure such as the Commission recommends would permit prosecutors to proceed civilly, rather than through the criminal process, against suspected violations of obscenity prohibition. If such civil procedures are utilized, penalties would be imposed for violation of the law only with respect to conduct occurring after a civil declaration is obtained. The Commission believes this course of action to be appropriate whenever there is any existing doubt regarding the legal status of materials; where other alternatives are available, the criminal process should not ordinarily be invoked against persons who might have reasonably believed, in good faith, that the books or films they distributed were entitled to constitutional protection, for the threat of criminal sanctions might otherwise deter the free distribution of constitutionally protected material. The Commission's recommended legislation would not only make a declaratory judgment procedure available, but would require prosecutors to utilize this process instead of immediate criminal prosecution in all cases except those where the materials in issue are unquestionably within the applicable statutory definitional provisions.

Withdrawal of Appellate Jurisdiction

The Commission recommends against the adoption of any legislation which would limit or abolish the jurisdiction of the Supreme Court of the United States or of other federal judges and courts in obscenity cases. Two Commissioners[25] favor such legislation, one[26] deems it inappropriate for the Commission to take a position on this issue.

Proposals to limit federal judicial jurisdiction over obscenity cases arise from disagreement over resolution by federal judges on the question of obscenity in litigation. The Commission believes that these disagreements flow in largest measure from the vague and subjective character of the legal tests for obscenity utilized in the past; under existing legal definitions, courts are required to engage in subjective decision making and their results may well be contrary to the subjective analyses of many citizens. Adoption of specific and explicit definitional provisions in prohibitory and regulatory legislation, as the Commission recommends, should eliminate most or all serious disagreements over the application of these definitions and thus eliminate the major source of concern which has motivated proposals to limit federal judicial jurisdiction.

More fundamentally, the Commission believes that it would be exceedingly unwise to adopt the suggested proposal from the point of view of protection of constitutional rights. The Commission believes that disagreements with court results in particular obscenity cases, even if these disagreements are soundly based in some instances, are not sufficiently important to justify tampering with existing judicial institutions which are often required to protect constitutional rights. Experience shows that, while courts may sometimes reverse convictions on a questionable basis, juries and lower courts also on occasion find guilt in cases involving books and films which are entitled to constitutional protection, and state appeals courts often uphold such findings. These violations of First Amendment rights would go uncorrected if such decisions could not be reversed at a higher court level.

The Commission also recommends against the creation of a precedent in the obscenity area for the elimination by Congress of federal judicial jurisdiction in other areas whenever a vocal majority or minority of citizens disagrees strongly with the results of the exercise of that jurisdiction. Freedom in many vital areas frequently depends upon the ability of the judiciary to follow the Constitution rather than strong popular sentiment. The problem of obscenity, in the absence of any indication that sexual materials cause societal harm, is not an appropriate social phenomenon upon which to base a precedent for removing federal judicial jurisdiction to protect fundamental rights guaranteed by the Bill of Rights.

NOTES

1. Commissioners Joseph T. Klapper, Morris A. Lipton, G. William Jones, Edward D. Greenwood and Irving Lehrman.

2. The phrase "explicit sexual materials" is used here and elsewhere in these recommendations to refer to the entire range of explicit sexual depictions or descriptions in books, magazines, photographs, films, statuary and other media. It includes the most explicit depictions, or what is often referred to as "hard-core pornography." The term, however, refers only to sexual materials, and not to "live" sex shows, such as strip tease or on-stage sexual activity or simulated sexual activity. The Commission did not study this phenomenon in detail and makes no recommendations in this area. See Preface to this Report.

3. Commissioner Charles H. Keating, Jr., chose not to participate in the deliberation and formulation of any of the Commission's recommendations.

4. Commissioner Edward E. Elson joins in this recommendation only on the understanding that there will be prior enactment of legislation prohibiting the public display of offensive sexual materials both pictorial and verbal, that there will be prior enactment of legislation restricting the sales of explicit sexual materials to juveniles, and that there be prior public and governmental support for the Commission's nonlegislative recommendations before such repeal is enacted.

5. Commissioners Irving Lehrman and Cathryn A. Spelts.

6. Commissioners Morton A. Hill, S.J., Winfrey C. Link and Thomas C. Lynch.

7. See footnote 4 in the Overview of Effects. [Commissioners G. William Jones, Joseph T. Klapper, and Morris A. Lipton believe "that in the interest of precision a distinction should be made between two types of statements which occur in this Report. One type, to which we subscribe, is that research to date

does not indicate that a causal relationship exists between exposure to erotica and the various social ills to which the research has been addressed. There are, however, also statements to the effect that 'no evidence' exists, and we believe these should more accurately read 'no reliable evidence.' Occasional aberrant findings, some of very doubtful validity, are noted and discussed in the Report of the Effects Panel. In our opinion, none of these, either individually or in sum, are of sufficient merit to constitute reliable evidence or to alter the summary conclusion that the research to date does not indicate a causal relationship."] *Report*, p. 27.

8. Ibid.

9. Ibid.

10. Commissioner Thomas D. Gill has amplified his position with reference to this finding as follows: legislation primarily motivated by an intent to establish or defend standards of public morality has not always been, as the Report of the Commission would have it, inappropriate, unsound and contrary to "our most fundamental constitutional traditions."

In fact, for at least 140 years after its adoption, the Constitution never appears to have been considered a barrier to the perpetuation of the belief held in the 13 original colonies that there was not only a right but a duty to codify in law the community's moral and social convictions. Granted homogeneous communities and granted the ensuing moral and social cohesiveness implied in such uniformity of interest, the right of these solid and massive majorities to protect their own values by legislation they deemed appropriate went unchallenged, so long as it did not impinge upon the individual's right to worship and speak as he pleased.

Only in the twentieth century has an increasingly pluralistic society begun to question both the wisdom and the validity of encasing its moral and social convictions in legal armor, and properly so, for if all laws to be effective must carry into their implementation the approval of a majority, this is peculiarly and all importantly the case with laws addressed to standards of morality, which speedily become exercises in community hypocrisy if they do not embody the wishes and convictions of a truly dominant majority of the people.

The Commission's studies have established that, on a national level, no more than 35 percent of our people favor adult controls in the field of obscenity, in the absence of some demonstrable social evil related to its presence and use.

The extensive survey of the prosecutorial offices of this country gives added affirmation of the principle that acceptable enforcement of obscenity legislation depends upon a solid undergirding of community support, such as may be and is found in the smaller, more homogeneous communities, but which is increasingly difficult to command in the largest urban areas where the divisiveness of life leads to splintered moral and social concepts. In effect, this report tells us that where you have substantial community concern you don't require the law, but lacking such concern, the law is a substitute of uncertain effectiveness.

If, then, legal rules controlling human conduct are designed to emphasize and reinforce society's moral convictions only in those areas where the pressures for transgression are the greatest and the resulting social consequences the most serious, there is a notable lack of justification for such intervention in the Commission's findings as to the magnitude of the public's concern and the efficacy of the enforcement of current obscenity laws. As has so often occurred, an approach which was both defendable and workable in one era has become vulnerable and suspect in another.

Fairness, however, requires that, despite these formidable considerations, something more be said—and therein is to be found the primary reason for this individual statement. It is by no means certain that the Commission's national study, accurate as it has every reason to be in presenting a national consensus, has an equal validity in depicting the group thinking of a given geographical area, state or community. It is believable, therefore, that notwithstanding the findings in the national reports, and quite consistent with them, there well may be found geographical pockets of homogeneous conviction, various regional, state and local units where the requisite massive majority support essential for the legal codification of community standards does exist. My concurrence in the recommendation for the abolition of obscenity controls for consenting adults is not intended to express my disapproval of the right of any such group, so constituted, to challenge and attempt to override the substantial findings of law and fact which the Commission has determined to be persuasive, in order to sustain their own deeply and widely held beliefs: a very considerable body of legislation in this country rests on just such a base of moral and social traditions.

It is a base, however, which is being undercut and eroded by the currents of the time and because this is so it may not now, upon fair and objective examination, be found to be of sufficient dimensions to sustain its burden.

11. The broadcasting or telecasting of explicit sexual material has not constituted a serious problem in the past. There is, however, a potential in this area for thrusting sexually explicit materials upon unwilling persons. Existing federal statutes imposing criminal and civil penalties upon any broadcast of "obscene" material do not adequately address this problem, because they do not describe with sufficient specificity what material would be prohibited, or under what conditions. Hence, the repeal of these statutes is recommended, upon the understanding that the Federal Communications Commission either already has, or can acquire through legislation, adequate power to promulgate and enforce specific rules in this area, should the need arise.

12. Commissioners Edward E. Elson and Winfrey C. Link.

13. Commissioners Otto N. Larsen and Marvin E. Wolfgang disagree for reasons stated in their separate statement. [*Report*, p. 375-77.] Commissioner Morton A. Hill, S.J. disagrees for reasons stated in his separate statement. [*Report*, p. 383-424.]

14. Commissioners Edward E. Elson and Freeman Lewis believe that segregating that material prohibited for sale to juveniles from that which is available to all would only enhance its appeal. Further, Commissioner Elson believes that juveniles would be protected from viewing sexually explicit

materials if the Model Public Display Statute were extended to apply to those places technically private but actually public, in the sense that they offer free and open access to all. Moreover, such an extension would significantly insulate the general public from such materials being thrust upon them without their consent.

15. Commissioner Morton A. Hill, S.J. See his separate statement for his reasons.

16. Commissioners Edward E. Elson, Thomas D. Gill, Joseph T. Klapper, Irving Lehrman, Winfrey C. Link, Thomas C. Lynch and Cathryn A. Spelts.

17. Commissioner Thomas D. Gill finds this conclusion acceptable at the present time, but if experience demonstrates that the effective enforcement of juvenile statutes which proscribe written as well as pictorial material is hampered by the problem of *scienter*, he believes the labelling statute promises to be an appropriate method of correction and should be tried. Commissioners Irving Lehrman and Cathryn A. Spelts join in this footnote.

18. Commissioners Edward E. Elson and Winfrey C. Link.

19. Commissioners Otto N. Larsen, Freeman Lewis and Marvin E. Wolfgang believe that a public display statute specifically aimed at erotic material is unnecessary. Very few jurisdictions have such a statute now. The execution of existing statutes and ordinances concerned with the projection of generally offensive objects, erotic or not, before the public provides all the spatial boundaries on public display of offensive erotica that is needed. Moreover, these three Commissioners believe that the offensiveness which may be caused by undesired exposure to sexual depictions is not so serious in scope or degree to warrant legislative response.

20. Commissioners Edward E. Elson and Winfrey C. Link believe that the model display statute should be so extended as to apply to those places technically private but actually public, in the sense that they offer free and open access to all. The statute would then cover, for example, retail stores, transportation terminals and building lobbies. It would then prevent potentially offensive sexually explicit materials from being thrust upon the public unexpectedly at any time.

21. Commissioners Edward E. Elson, Morton A. Hill, S.J., Winfrey C. Link, Thomas C. Lynch and Cathryn A. Spelts.

22. Commissioners Otto N. Larsen and Marvin E. Wolfgang. See their separate statement. Commissioner Freeman Lewis dissents for two reasons: (1) that legislation restricting only the mailing of sexually oriented materials, when so many other kinds of unsolicited mail also produce offense, is bad public policy because it is too particular and too arbitrary; and (2) that the frequency of offense caused by unsolicited sexually oriented mail is demonstrably so minute that it does not warrant either the costs of the requisite machinery for operation and enforcement or the exorbitant expenses which would be forced upon this particular small category of mailers in order to comply. In his opinion, the most effective resolution of this problem is to employ the same technique commonly used for any other kinds of unwanted, unsolicited mail: throw it in the garbage pail.

23. Potentially offensive sexual advertisement means:

"(A) Any advertisement containing a pictorial representation or a detailed verbal description of uncovered human genitals or pubic areas, human sexual intercourse, masturbation, sodomy (i.e., bestiality or oral or anal intercourse), direct physical stimulation of unclothed genitals or flagellation or torture in the context of a sexual relationship; or

(B) Any advertisement containing a pictorial representation or detailed verbal description of an artificial human penis or vagina or device primarily designed physically to stimulate genitals; provided that, material otherwise within the definition of this subsection shall not be deemed to be a potentially offensive sexual advertisement if it constitutes only a small and insignificant part of the whole of a single catalogue, book or other work, the remainder of which does not primarily treat sexual matters and, provided further, that the Postmaster General shall, from time to time, issue regulations of general applicability exempting certain types of material, or material addressed to certain categories of addresses, such as advertisements for works of fine art or solicitations of a medical, scientific or other similar nature addressed to a specialized audience, from the definition of potentially offensive sexual advertisement contained in this subsection, where the purpose of this section does not call for application of the requirements of this section."

24. Commissioners Morton A. Hill, S.J. and Winfrey C. Link.

25. Commissioners Morton A. Hill, S.J. and Winfrey C. Link.

26. Commissioner Cathryn A. Spelts.

5 Pornography—Raging Menace or Paper Tiger?

John H. Gagnon and
William Simon

Since the task of defining pornography has fallen more and more to the Supreme Court—and since not much research exists on what effect pornography has on the social actions of individuals—what standard is the court using?

The Supreme Court seems to be erecting a more complex standard for judging pornography to replace the old concern with individual morality. Some interesting insights into the confusion surrounding the topic can be drawn from three court decisions of March 21, 1966: *Ginzburg v. United States, Mishkin v. New York* and *Memoirs of a Woman of Pleasure v. Massachusetts*. Although this set of decisions was almost immediately accorded distinction as a landmark by the public, the Nine Old Men themselves did not seem quite so sure of the meaning of the affair. The justices produced among them 14 separate opinions in the three cases. Only three judges were in the majority in all cases. The decisions were divided, respectively, 5-4, 6-3 and 6-3.

Ginzburg is the key decision. The court reversed the suppression of *Memoirs*, better known as *Fanny Hill*, under the Roth test of 1957—that is, "whether to the average person, applying contem-

Reprinted from *trans*action (now **Society**) magazine, July/August 1967 Copyright © 1967 by Transaction, Inc., New Brunswick, New Jersey.

porary standards, the dominant theme of the material taken as a whole appeals to a prurient interest." The conviction of Edward Mishkin, owner of the Main Stem and Midget book stores in New York City, was upheld. In the words of the court, Mishkin "was not prosecuted for anything he said or believed, but for what he did." What he did was to commission, publish and sell such illustrated books as *Mistress of Leather*, *Cult of Spankers* and *Fearful Ordeal in Restraintland*, for an audience interested in sadomasochism, transvestitism, fetishism.

Ralph Ginzburg was being tried on postal charges of obscenity for three publications: *The Housewife's Handbook of Selective Promiscuity*; an issue of the bi-weekly newsletter, *Liaison*; and a volume of the hardbound magazine, *Eros*. In this case the court departed from earlier rulings by considering not the obscenity of the specific items, but rather the appeal to prurient interest made in the advertising campaigns. The court remarked, "Where the purveyor's sole emphasis is on the sexually provocative aspects of his publications, that fact may be decisive in the determination of 'obscenity.' "

To the court, one of the proofs of Ginzburg's motives was his request for second-class mailing privileges at Intercourse or Blue Ball, Pennsylvania, before obtaining them at Middlesex, New Jersey. One of the indicators of the social worth of *Fanny Hill*, conversely, was the translation of the book into braille by the Library of Congress.

Three of the justices voting for reversal filed written dissents, in which they argued that the court was creating a new crime—that of pandering exploitation, or titillation—which Ginzburg could not have known existed when he committed it. Furthermore, the dissenters said, if a statute creating such a crime had come before the court, it would be found unconstitutional.

It is the Ginzburg decision that gives us the primary thread to follow in seeking to understand "obscenity," as it is now seen by the Supreme Court and the sexual arousal caused by what is conventionally termed pornography. With this decision the court has moved—in a way that may be inimical to the conception of law as abstract principle—toward a more realistic determination of the factors relevant to triggering a sexual response. The court's sociological discovery—whether intentional or not—is that in sex the context of the representation is significant. That is, sex as a physical object or symbolic representation has no power outside a context in which the erotic elements are reinforced or made legitimate.

In doing this, the court did not change the rules under which any work will be considered outside its context. If a book is charged—as *Fanny Hill* was—with being obscene under the Roth decision, it will be treated in exactly the same way as it would have been in the past. When aspects of the context of advertising or sale—the acts of labelling—are included in the original charges, then the Ginzburg rules will be applied. This was demonstrated in the court's decision in May 1967 on a number of girlie magazines. Obscenity convictions against the magazines were overturned because, as the court stated, "In none was there evidence of the sort of pandering which the court found significant in *Ginzburg v. United States.*"

Whether the majority of the court was aware of the significance of the change it made in the definition of obscenity is not clear. From the tone of the opinions, it is obvious the court felt it was dealing with a problem of nuisance behavior—not only to the public, but to the court itself—quite analogous to keeping a goat in a residential area, or urinating in public. By making the promotion of the work a factor in determining its obscenity, the court was reinforcing the right of the person to keep his mailbox clean and private, not to mention the likelihood that it was cutting down the amount of misleading advertising.

TWO FACES OF PORNOGRAPHY

The court apparently considers pornography to have two major dimensions. The first can be defined as dealing with sexual representations that are offensive to public morality or taste, which concerned the court most importantly in the Ginzburg case. The second centers on the effect of pornography on specific individuals or classes, which is the focus of most public discussions and prior court decisions on pornography. This dimension was mentioned only twice in the array of decisions made in 1966, but much of the confusion in discussions of pornography reflects a difficulty in distinguishing between these dimensions, or a tendency to slip from one to the other without noting the change.

The first dimension—offenses to a public morality—not only appears more objective, but also has a cooler emotional tone. The problem becomes one of tolerating a public nuisance, or defining what constitutes a public nuisance. This issue becomes complex, because the heterogeneity of an urban society makes it difficult to arrive at a consensus on what the limits of public morality might be. We might also add the complicating factor of our society's somewhat uneven libertarian tradition, that affirms the theoretical existence of the right to subscribe to minority versions of morality. These obviously touch upon important issues of constitutional freedoms. As important as the implicit issues may be, however, the explicit issue is public nuisance, a misdemeanor, usually bringing only a fine or, at most, up to a year in the county jail. Talk of offense to public morality or public taste is relatively remote from the old fears of serious damage to the community or its members.

The second dimension—effects upon persons exposed to pornographic productions—generates more intense emotions. Claims are made that exposure to pornography results in infantile and regressive approaches to sexuality that can feed an individual's neuroses, or at the other extreme, that exposure tends to fundamentally and irreversibly corrupt and deprave. The latter argument asserts that exposure to pornography either awakens or creates sexual appetites that can only be satisfied through conduct that is dangerous to society. More simply stated: pornography is a trigger mechanism that has a high probability of initiating dangerous, antisocial behavior. There also exists what can be called a major counter-argument to these, but one that shares with them a belief in the effectiveness of pornography. This argument is that pornography serves as an alternative sexual outlet, one that releases tensions which might otherwise find expression in dangerous, antisocial behavior. For the proponents of this view, pornography is seen as a safety valve or a psychological lightning rod.

The very act of labelling some item as pornographic or obscene creates a social response very close to that brought on by pornography itself. The act of labelling often generates sexual anticipation centered on fantasies about the business of pornography and the erotic character of those who produce it. How else could such benign and hardly erotic productions as family planning pamphlets and pictures of human birth have come under the shadow of the pornography laws? As with other unconventional sexual expressions, in public consideration of pornography even the dreary details of production, distribution and sale of such material are matters for erotic speculations. This simplification—defining as totally sexual that which is only marginally connected with sexuality—is one of the major sources of the public concern over pornography.

Labelling can also be done by individuals, who can thus make pornographic the widest range of materials—*Studs Lonigan, Fanny Hill, Playboy,* the Sears Roebuck catalog. This ability leads to the assumption that sexual fantasy and its agent, pornography, have a magical capacity to commit men to overt sexual action. In this view the sexual impulse lies like the wild beast in every man, restrained only by the weak fetters of social repression. This assumption, founded on the Enlightenment's notion of a social contract, underlies most of our discussions of sex and its side show, pornography.

These serious views of pornography can lead directly to the formulation of an empirically testable question. Unfortunately, no one has provided an acceptable answer, based on reliable and systematic research procedures.

WHAT EFFECT—IF ANY

Of the data that are available on the effects of pornography, the best remain those provided by the investigations of the Institute for Sex Research. Kinsey and his associates indicate that the majority of males in our society are exposed, at one time or another, to "portrayals of sexual action." So are a smaller proportion of females. Further, 77 percent of males who had exposure to "portrayals of sexual action" reported being erotically aroused, while only 32 percent of women reported feelings of arousal. What is significant is that, arousal notwithstanding, no dramatic changes of behavior appeared to follow for those reporting both exposure and arousal. Perhaps even more significant is the fact that Paul H. Gebhard and his colleague in their book, *Sex Offenders,* report:

It would appear that the possession of pornography does not differentiate sex offenders from nonsex offenders. Even the combination of ownership plus strong sexual arousal from the material does not segregate the sex offender from other men of a comparable social level.[1]

Summing up their feeling that pornography is far from being a strong determinant of sexual behavior, and that the use of pornography tends to be a derivative of already existing sexual commitments, the authors observe: "Men make the collections, collections do not make the men."

However, given the intensity and frequency with which the argument of pornography's corrupting powers is raised, one might wonder whether thinking about pornography has not itself given rise to sexual fantasies, developing an image of men and women as being more essentially sexual than they may in fact be.

These two major dimensions—public offense versus public corruption—result in two different images of the pornographer. Projected through the rhetoric of public corruption, we see him as someone self-consciously evil, a representative of the antichrist, the Communist conspiracy, or at the very least, the Mafia. We also tend to see him in terms of the obscenity of ill-gotten wealth, since he deals in commodities that are assumed to generate high prices.

Thought of as a public nuisance, he appears in somewhat more realistic hues. Here we find not a sinister villain, but a grubby businessman producing a minor commodity for which there is a limited market and a marginal profit, and which requires that he live in a marginal world. Here our collective displeasure may be derived from his association with a still greater obscenity—economic failure. However, whether the pornographer is Mephistopheles or a Willie Loman, he is one of the few members of our society whose public role is overtly sexual, and that is perhaps reason enough to abandon any expectations of rationality in public discussions of the role.

THE FANTASY OF THE STAG FILM

We tend to ignore the social context within which pornography is used and from which a large part of its significance for the individual consumer derives. The stag film is an excellent case in point. Out of context, it is rarely more than a simple catalogue of the limited sexual resources of the human body. Stag films are rarely seen by females and are most commonly viewed by two kinds of male groups: those living in group housing in colleges or universities, and those belonging to upper-lower-class and lower-middle-class voluntary social groups. The stag film serves both similar and different functions for the two major categories of persons who see them.

For the college male they are a collective representation of mutual heterosexual concerns and—to a lesser degree—they instruct him in sexual techniques. For this group, the exposure is either concurrent with, or prior to, extensive sociosexual experience. Exposure comes later in life for the second group: after marriage or, at the very least, after the development of sociosexual patterns. For this audience, the group experience itself provides a validation of sexual appetites in social milieus where other forms of validation, such as extramarital activity, are severely restricted. The films primarily reinforce masculinity, and only indirectly reinforce heterosexuality. This reinforcement of heterosexuality is reflected in the way the films portray the obsessive myths of the masculine sexual fantasy. They emphasize, for example, that sexual encounters can happen at any moment, to anyone, around almost any corner—a belief that closely parallels the romantic love fantasy so characteristic of female arousal. In the case of the male, however, sex replaces love as the central element. These films also reaffirm the myth of a breed of women who are lusty and free in both sexual surrender and enjoyment. Last, given the kind of social context within which the films are shown, there is little reason to assume that their sexual arousal is not expressed through appropriate sexual or social actions.

Pictorial representations of sexual activity lend themselves to the same approach. Unlike films and more like written materials, their use is essentially private. Nonetheless, their patterns of use remain congruent with other patterns of social life and process; they do not represent the triggering mechanisms through which the social contract is nullified and raging, unsocial lust (whatever that might be) is unleashed. The major users of pictorial erotica are adolescent males. If these materials have any use, it is as an aid to masturbation. There is no evidence, however, that the availability of dirty pictures increases masturbatory rates among adolescents. This is a period in life when masturbatory rates are already extremely high, particularly for middle-class male adolescents. Indeed, in the absence of hard-core pornography, the boys create their own stimulation from mail order catalogues, magazine ads and so on. In middle-class circles, many young men and the majority of females may grow up without ever having seen hard-core pornography.

If exposure to this kind of pornography, while facilitating masturbation, does not substantially affect masturbatory rates, it is still possible that such materials may shape the content of the masturbatory fantasy in ways that create or reinforce commitments to sexual practices that are harmful to the individual or to others. In this area little is known. It may be observed that most pornographic materials share with the masturbatory fantasy a sense of omni-potence, but the acts represented are rarely homosexual, nor are they sadistic beyond the general levels of violence common in contem-porary kitsch. Once again, one suspects a reinforcing or facilitating function, rather than one of initiation or creation.

The pornographic book, in contrast to photographs and films, represents a very different social situation. Few books are read aloud in our society, and it is particularly unlikely that this would occur with a book of descriptions of overt sexual activity. In fact, prosecutors take advantage of this fact by reading allegedly obscene books aloud in court, with the aim of embarrassing the jury into a guilty verdict. The privately consumed erotic book merely provides fantasy content or reinforcement of fantasy that is already established. Few books lead to overt action of any kind, and the erotic book is unlikely to be an exception.

PORNOGRAPHIC FRINGELAND

The most difficult problem in considering pornography is the fringeland found on newsstands: the pulp books, national tabloids, men's magazines, and pinup collections which line the racks in drugstores, bus stations and rail and air terminals. The girlie magazines are often attacked for their use of nude pictures. The current magic line of censorship is pubic hair, although recently it was the bare breast or exposed nipple. Not so very long ago, navels were ruthlessly airbrushed away and Jane Russell's cleavage was an issue in gaining the censor's approval of the movie "Outlaw." The Gay Nineties were made gayer with pinups of strapping beauties clad in tights revealing only the bare flesh of face and hands.

In our era the pulp book freely describes most sexual activity with some degree of accuracy, although less explicitly and more metaphorically than hard-core pornographic books. Such books are clearly published for their capacity to elicit sexual arousal, and they are purchased by an audience that knows what it is buying.

To view these examples of fringe pornography exclusively in terms of a sexual function might well be misleading. Since we tend to overestimate the significance of sexual activity, we see the trends of representation in these works as indicators of sexual behavior in the community. An increase in works about homosexual love is taken as an indication of an incipient homosexual revolution, or even as the *cause* of a homosexual revolution. If we find more books about adultery, sadomasochism, or fast-living teenagers, we believe that there must be more adulterers, sadomasochists and fast-living teenagers in our midst. With a dubious logic reminiscent of primitive magic, many believe that if the number of such written representations increases, so will the frequency of such acts, and conversely that the way to cut down on this antisocial behavior is to suppress the pornographic representations.

In the fringeland, there is a greater attempt to place sexual activity in the context of a social script, with a greater concern for nonsexual social relations and social roles, and a more direct treatment of appropriate social norms. Some part of this, particularly its common trait of compulsive moralizing, is an attempt to establish a spurious—but defensible, under the Roth decision— "redeeming context." This may also represent the producer's awareness that more than simple lust is involved, that the reader may bring to the work a complex of motives, many of which are nonsexual.

For example, the psychiatrist Lionel Ovesey links some of the fantasies of his homosexual patients, not to their sexual commitments, but to their problems of managing other personal relations, particularly in their jobs. The management of dominance or aggression in nonsexual spheres of life, or the management of ideologies and moralities of social mobility, may be the organizing mechanisms of such fantasies—while sexuality provides an accessible and powerful imagery through which these other social tensions may be vicariously acted upon. It may be overly simplistic to view this marginal pornography as something exclusively sexual.

These items at the fringeland are of most concern in the formulation of community standards. The girlie magazine and the pulp book are visible and priced within the range of the mass market. The hard-cover book available at a high price in a bookstore may well cause no comment until it appears on the drugstore racks in paperback. Because such items are sold at breaks in transportation or in locations that tap neighborhood markets, they are the most visible portion of the problem and thus are the source of the discontent among those who are committed to censorship.

ELUSIVE STANDARDS

The dilemma, then, becomes the formulation of community standards, and this has been the dilemma of the courts themselves. One interesting attempt to strengthen enforcement of conservative standards is the interpretation of federal law to allow prosecution of a seller in the jurisdiction where obscene materials are received, rather than in the one from which they are mailed. Thus, in the rather liberal jurisdiction of New York, where the sale of obscene materials must be compared in the mind of the judge with all the other kinds of crimes that come before him, the seller may well be seen as a small-timer, his crime a misdemeanor. However, in a rural jurisdiction where religious standards are more conservative and a pornography offense is viewed more seriously—especially when compared with the strayed cows and traffic violations that make up the most of the court docket—the seller may appear to be a heinous criminal.

The Supreme Court may wish to establish a national standard, allowing some jurisdictions to be more liberal but none to be more conservative. Thus the Supreme Court may build a floor under the right of materials to be protected under the First Amendment, at the same time constraining, through the use of the Ginzburg decision, the importation of materials through wide mailing campaigns into conservative communities. In its more recent *Roth* decision, the court indicated—somewhat Delphically—that its concern in the future would be with three areas, none of them directly concerned with the content of any works charged as pornographic. These were sales of smut to minors, obtrusive presentation, and "pandering" à la Ginzburg. The court's decisions, however, may well be too conservative in a period when national society is being created through the penetration by the mass media into larger and larger elements of our society. Indeed, it is likely that most legal revolutions have been imposed from above and that communities will fall back to a narrow conservative position, if allowed to do so. To trust local innovation is to trust nothing.

Pornography is as elusive as mercury. That of the past seldom fills the bill today. The use and users of contemporary pornography vary. Indeed, it might be said that sex itself would not change if there were no more pornography. Pornography is only a minor symptom of sexuality, and of very little prominence in people's minds most of the time. Even among those who might think about it most, it only results in masturbation or in the "collector" instinct.

What is most important about pornography is not its particular relevance to sexuality, but rather the fact that it elicits very special treatment when confronting the law. In this confrontation the agencies of criminal justice, especially the courts, behave in a curious manner that endangers the freedom of ideas as they might be expressed in other zones of activity, such as politics, religion or the family. Our best protection in this regard has been the very contradictory character of the courts, which carefully excludes the consideration of sexual ideas from the general test of the expression of ideas: do they give rise to a clear and present danger? Our problem is not that pornography represents such a danger—it is far too minor a phenomenon for that—but that the kind of thinking prevalent in dealing with pornography will come to be prevalent in controlling the advocacy of other ideas as well.

NOTE

1. Paul Gebhard, John Gagnon, William Pomeroy and Charles Christenson, *Sex Offenders* (New York: Harper and Row, 1965).

6 Obscenity Laws—A Shift to Reality

Earl Warren, Jr.

In a world which is a massive crucible of questioning and change, where critical issues of poverty and war and disease and discrimination scream for solution, it is a peculiar phenomenon that the laws relating to obscenity have suddenly jumped into sharp focus in the eyes of both the public and the legal profession. Having lain relatively dormant and accepted for many years, they now strangely command attention of an unusually intense, and even violent, nature.

The emotional basis for this reaction may be obscure to those resilient few who adjust to change readily or who have early in life adopted a live-and-let-live philosophy. But to the great majority of others, who have been taught that proper conduct is largely governed by a certain number of "absolutes," the battle is very real. To such people, transgressions against what they believe to be the old norms are likely to seem to be a direct assault upon the entire structure of traditionally accepted forms of human behavior. Apparently, the public emphasis on sexual themes in recent years falls squarely into this category.

Reprinted with permission from *Santa Clara Lawyer*, vol. 11, no. 1, (Fall 1970): 1-19.

THE MERGER OF ECCLESIASTICAL AND CIVIL LAW

From a legal standpoint, the fundamental reason for this tension lies in the peculiar merging long ago of two distinct bodies of law—ecclesiastical law and the bodies of laws made by governments to regulate their everyday affairs. Therefore, any discussion of the legal aspects of obscenity must logically begin with an awareness of this fact.

In the days when religious bodies governed the citizens of a region just as much as did the civil authorities, the civil laws were mainly concerned with regulating conduct only as necessary to preserve reasonable order in the society—while matters relating strictly to morality were left to the workings of ecclesiastical law. However, as the civil governments became more powerful and the political control of the churches waned, the civil law gradually absorbed many of the ecclesiastical laws.[1] In doing so, these religion-based laws generally took on a revised nature so as to conform to the enforcement patterns for the civil laws. Hence, a religious law which perhaps called only for "atonement" or "confession" when broken in the ecclesiastical sphere, usually carried a penalty of jail, fine, forfeiture or worse when it became part of the civil law.[2]

Unfortunately, in the years since these mergers took place, the members of the legal profession, as well as governments and their citizens, have increasingly come to forget the derivation of the two bodies of laws and the distinctions between them which were once so important. Thus there has been a distinct trend to think of conduct as being legal or illegal instead of in terms of being moral or immoral.

Today, however, when nearly all traditional values and customs are being tested to see whether they are founded in logic and humanitarianism or only in special interest, the earlier distinctions are being consciously or unconsciously bared. And many citizens are insisting that civil laws return to the status of being those which secure an orderly, free and just society, leaving matters of an otherwise personal nature to the desires of the individual and the dictates of his God. Among these citizens are a great number of men of the cloth.

From a practical standpoint, this is difficult to accomplish completely, for there is an unavoidable amount of essential over-lapping of the two concepts. And from a human nature standpoint, history indicates that it is virtually impossible—because men and their governments will invariably attempt, to some extent at least, to impose their personal views on others by mandatory compliance with certain civil laws. It is thus an age-old battle; a battle between those who believe in influencing by intellectual persuasion and those who believe in achieving conformity by governmental fiat.

FREEDOM OF SPEECH
AND THE FIRST AMENDMENT

Those of us living in the United States have a rare means of challenging both our laws and public attitudes—a means which in some cases amounts to a mandate. This is the First Amendment's provisions for freedom of speech. As the cornerstone of any discussion involving the rights of an individual to express his ideas to others, and receive the thoughts of others, it provides that:

> Congress shall make no law respecting an establishment of religion, or prohibiting the free exercise thereof; or abridging the freedom of speech, or of the press; or the right of the people peaceably to assemble, and to petition the Government for a redress of grievances.[3]

Although the reference is only to "speech," this was early recognized to include non-verbal conduct which serves as a means of expression,[4] and there is no apparent vestige of challenge to that proposition today. Hence writings, photographs, movies, paintings, statuary, bodily gestures and other symbolic conduct are all recognized as being within the purview of its intended scope.[5]

However, it is equally clear that the courts have consistently held that obscenity is not, and never has been protected by the mantle of the First Amendment.[6] And it is here that the controversy really begins to swirl, for not only does the Civil Law vs. Ecclesiastical Law concept come sharply into play, the efficacy of the First Amendment itself is seriously challenged by how narrowly or broadly the term "obscene" is defined.

If some of the usual dictionary definitions of obscenity were applied (e.g. "disgusting to the senses," "grossly repugnant to the generally accepted notions of what is appropriate"), it is obvious that the hallowed free speech provisions of the Constitution would be of little moment, for, in that case, only "generally accepted" ideas would be protected. Particularly onerous is the fact that this would apply to expressions of a religious or political nature as well as to other types of expression. Fortunately, the First Amendment has always been interpreted as obviously carrying more potency than this.[7] Nevertheless, the laws relating to obscenity rocked along for many years without clear definition (often referring to accounts of such things as "bloodshed" and "crime")[8] until, in the landmark case of *Roth v. United States*,[9] the scope at last narrowed to matters of a sexual nature and an attempt was made to spell out how it should be determined if something was "obscene" in the eyes of the Constitution.[10]

Through this ruling, the Court hoped to provide a means of giving viability to reasonable laws relating to the problem, yet preclude them from unduly encroaching upon the sacred ground of the First Amendment. The Court was not unmindful of the public's "hang-ups" on such matters, and the general desire of the citizenry to keep unsolicited exposure to salacious themes at a minimum.[11] Yet it was also well aware of numerous past absurdities which are well illustrated by the notation in a later case[12] that the City of Chicago once censored a Walt Disney movie merely because it showed the birth of a buffalo calf!

THE ROTH FORMULA

Roth set forth a formula—a formula which was an earnest and thoughtful attempt to give guidelines in a highly confused and politically sensitive area. But it is equally apparent that the ruling was not to be a panacea—only the best that the Court could do at that time. Justices Black and Douglas dissented,[13] Justice Harlan concurred in the result in one issue and dissented in another,[14] and Chief Justice Warren concurred in the results but wanted them limited to the specific facts involved. Thus, although *Roth* became law, it did so with no great enthusiasm by the Court, for not only did it present a wide variety of differing views, subsequent cases[15] were to disclose that even those in the majority did not share exactly the same opinions of what the majority opinion appeared to say.

Nevertheless, *Roth* has been the foundation for all proceedings since its rendition, and therefore must be the starting point in analyzing where the law stands now. And its "formula" is still mandatory, although how it is to be practically applied, even in the simplest of cases, remains substantially in doubt these 13 years since its pronouncement.

Justice Brennan, the author of the majority opinion in *Roth*, clearly restated the formula in *Memoirs v. Massachusetts*.[16]

We defined obscenity in Roth in the following terms: '[W] hether to the average person, applying contemporary community standards, the dominant theme of the material taken as a whole appeals to a prurient interest.' Under this definition, as elaborated in subsequent cases, three elements must coalesce: it must be established that (a) the dominant theme of the material taken as a whole appeals to a prurient interest in sex; (b) the material is patently offensive because it affronts contemporary community standards relating to the description or representation of sexual matters; and (c) the material is utterly without redeeming social value.[17]

Prurient Interest

In the first element, which is that the dominant theme of the material must appeal to a prurient interest in sex, the first real obstacle of workability is encountered in the word, "prurient." The California Legislature has construed it as meaning "shameful" or "morbid"[18] and although this is probably a conceptually accurate approach, both constructions raise problems of interpretation and courtroom application which are typical of all of the definitions thus far put on the word.

"Shameful," for instance, has two distinct meanings, one of which is that the act is repugnant to the observer, while the other means that the act arouses a feeling of shame in the actor. "Morbid" has even more definite pathological foundations, inasmuch as its best known synonym is "unhealthy," and it is equated with "disease" in both medical and common parlance.

Hence at least two of these three meanings have medical overtones, and defense lawyers can legitimately seize upon this to insist that the prosecuting attorney must present expert medical testimony on the subject as a part of his prima facie case. Of course, this is a great burden on the prosecution, often an impossible one, and accordingly is usually rejected by the trial judge. But the defense can claim that surely the Court had something in mind other than merely whether or not the observer was shocked by what he saw.

Proceeding further into the area of practical application, we run into the word, "interest"—or more properly the phrase "a prurient interest." Who has such an interest? All of us? Or only certain deviant types? Does a homosexual act in front of a strictly heterosexual audience "appeal to a prurient interest"? Or is it non-appealing? Are we attempting to penalize actions which excite lustful inclinations, or are we attempting to penalize actions which instead create revulsion? Both? The answer is less clear now than it was prior to *Roth*.

We must also determine who that person is who must make the judgment as to whether there is such an appeal. We are told that it is the "average person."[19] Not just the young, or just the old, or just the sophisticated, or just the naive—but *all* of these and a lot more; sort of a composite person. Does such a human exist? Or are we merely falling back on one of those legal escape valves we sometimes manufacture in order to avoid reality? It is one thing to say that the "average man," by his nature, will take reasonable care for his safety, and that he will normally use good business practices and otherwise conduct himself in a certain manner in certain situations. But can we honestly expect a handful of people on a jury to know whether or not certain actions will appeal to a prurient interest of unspecified persons of unspecified ages, sexes and cultural and religious backgrounds?

And how, under this mandate, do we treat the wide variety of situations which obviously create completely differing results? For instance, a nude in a nudist colony has a different impact on his observers than does a nude walking along the main street of a town, yet the formula seems to say that we must nevertheless think of the

effect on the same average man in each instance without consideration as to where the conduct occurs.

At this point, it might be wise to pause and consider whether all
this is merely nit-picking. These things are not, of course, merely
pulled out of the sky to carp at, for they are issues trial attorneys
and trial court judges must wrestle with on a very real, day-to-day
basis.

"But, after all," we might say (as so many do) "if something is
bad, it's bad, and we shouldn't have to worry about such niceties."
Or should we? If we were the board of censorship which was
squeamish about the Disney movie, the Supreme Court would not
think much of us for simply following our gut reaction. And it
would be naive to assume that such learned justices agonizing over
such a difficult problem would not try to say what they mean.

Naturally, the Court intended that we use our common sense in
applying the formula. But "common sense" alone has not solved its
inherent dilemmas. Justice Stewart delighted everyone when he said
he could not define hard-core pornography, but he knew it when he
saw it.[20] However, at the enforcement level we are not permitted
the luxury of this approach, for the Court obviously would not
evaluate the Disney movie in the same way as the Chicago censors
did, and the records are replete with cases where the substitution of
personal leanings for constitutional requirements at the trial level has
resulted in convictions and reversals with all their traumatic consequences.[21]

Hence it is patently apparent that those who deal in the enforcement of obscenity laws must diligently attempt to ascertain
not only the true ingredients in a formula such as that of *Roth*, but
also their respective dosages.

Community Standards

Assuming, then, that we somehow get by the first element in the
formula, we must next determine if "the material is patently
offensive because it affronts contemporary community standards
relating to the description or representation of sexual matters."[22]
This has generally been interpreted to mean that the act or material
must go "substantially beyond" existing community standards of
"candor" for that type of representation.[23]

Immediately we are faced with the problem of what is meant by the "community," and here we run into a fiction which is almost as perplexing as that of the mythical "average man." For it is not the immediate community which most people think of—namely, their town and its environs—but probably at least the entire state,[24] and it may even be much larger than that.[25]

Little quarrel can be made with the proposition that it would be wrong to allow a certain community to unreasonably label as criminal certain conduct which is proper elsewhere. But neither is it reasonable to expect sheltered communities to readily adapt to the more bizarre conduct of the "wide-open" communities.

And when a huge state like California is involved—where there are the most rural of communities and the most cosmopolitan, and every conceivable degree of sophistication in between—the task of determining a statewide standard is one of incredible magnitude and highly doubtful potential success. The same, of course, would also be true of a national standard.

Beyond that, we have a problem as to whether we are talking about a standard which relates to what takes place within the physical borders of the community, or whether we are really talking about an environmental community—namely, what the people within the community are exposed to.

In many places, a very straight-laced city in State A lies adjacent to a very libertarian city in State B, and the citizens in each city are just as much exposed to the goings on in the other city as they are to those of their own. Therefore, it is legitimate to ask if it serves the constitutional mandates, in this age of great mobility, to rely on the tenuous environmental importance of historical lines of political demarcation.

Going deeper into the thicket, we run into the phrase "standards of candor," and must ask if we are talking about what "exists," or only what is "accepted"? Certainly it is not in keeping with our American way of life to suppress a form of otherwise legitimate expression, merely because it is looked upon unfavorably by the majority. Yet simply because something undesirable has negligently been allowed to exist is not reason to give it sanction. So again we are faced with a requirement which, no matter how it is interpreted, does not accurately take into account the various cultures, conditions and attitudes which are present in any specified inhabited area.

As a last ingredient of this second part of the formula, we note that the complained of conduct must go "substantially beyond" the existing standards.[26] While this is an understandable attempt to give further protection to the constitutional freedom of thought and expression, it does suggest that the boundaries of obscenity can be nibbled away by going "a little beyond" but not "substantially beyond." It suggests that the standards will gradually become more and more relaxed, regardless of the fact that there may come a point at which the welfare of the entire system will be seriously jeopardized by further inroads.

Redeeming Social Value

Finally (assuming that we successfully traverse the mazes of the first two elements), we come to the no-man's land of the requirement that the conduct or material must be "utterly without redeeming social value."[27]

The first curious thing we note about this point is that it violates the general rule that the prosecution must prove every element of the offense in order to present a prima facie case.[28] For, of course, it would be patently absurd to require the prosecuting attorney to speculate in this regard by even beginning to attempt to prove that the matter or conduct is totally devoid of any value.

While this procedural quirk is perhaps really not too bothersome, we do face a problem of fantastic latitude in interpretation and application, for the term "social value" is terribly imprecise and carries different meanings to different people. The usual response tends, in human nature, to be an emotional one—namely that if a person is sufficiently offended by what he has observed, he is not likely to be willing to see any value in it even if considerable value truly exists. And yet, we are told that, no matter how overwhelming the damning evidence is on the first two elements, such evidence cannot overrule the effect of existing social value. If value exists, the matter is automatically not obscene.[29]

Although court decisions following *Roth*[30] have virtually erased any viability from the word "redeeming," it strangely remains in the formula and in the instructions the judge must give the jury. And the issue is also very unclear as to how far the trial judge must go in making an independent determination of the existence of social value.[31]

The concept additionally snags upon the question of "social value to who?" This is frequently raised when psychiatrists testify that exposure to pornography is helpful in the treatment of certain patients, thereby implying that obscenity has some intrinsic social value. Is this enough to give protection to materials which have no such value to the rest of the population? If not, how large must the benefitted group be before the material or conduct becomes constitutionally acceptable?

THE UNWORKABILITY OF THE PRESENT APPROACH

All these questions about the formula remain essentially unanswered. Naturally, individual defense attorneys, prosecutors, policemen and judges have personal opinions as to what some of the answers should be, but there is nothing approaching unanimity on any point, and a well-handled case is likely to bring most of them into serious dispute.

The legal result is that cases of alleged obscenity are extremely difficult to prosecute, to defend and to preside over, and the cost to the taxpayers is huge. With this goes a disproportionate amount of publicity, a rising of public frustration and, not infrequently, attempts by legislative bodies to meet the problem by enacting repressive and constitutionally defective laws.[32] In short, it is historically apparent that the formula falls far short of providing a workable solution to the problem of handling what we now term obscenity.

These failings are not pointed out by way of criticizing the thoughtful efforts of the courts to define what is obscene, for the formula is probably as good a one as could be devised for this purpose. But they are noted by way of illustrating the unworkability of this overall approach to the problem, and by way of suggesting that another approach is both desirable and necessary.

A DIFFERENT APPROACH

The correct tack is simply to abandon the concept of labeling any particular act or material as inherently obscene, and instead determine whether it is actionable within the context of how it is employed. It is not a new concept—just one we seem too timid to adopt fully.

It would far better protect the constitutional principles we operate upon, and yet at the same time give more effective protection against those unwarranted activities which so disturb the citizenry. And it would additionally help alleviate the dilemma created by the question as to what extent a government may go in attempting to legislate the morals of its subjects.

Happily, the concept also squares with the natural inclinations of human nature, and is consistent with what governments and their citizens *actually* do in the everyday conduct of their affairs. For example, nudity on a public street is taboo, yet we tolerate it in nudist camps. Naked models and racy plays are old hat in college classes, yet we don't allow them in grammar schools. The "dirty joke" may be commonplace in meetings of men's clubs, but distinctly out of line in mixed meetings. A book like the *Kinsey Report* would certainly never be labeled as pornographic today, yet if pandered to young children, it would raise the ire of most everyone.

The list could go on and on, hypocrisy after hypocrisy. Not hypocrisy within the context of human nature, but hypocrisy within present legal concepts. For, in the logical application of putting labels on matter as such, if that naked model in the college art class does not offend the fictional "average man" in that fictional "community," then he or she does nothing "obscene" by sitting in the grammar school art class. And, conversely, if the off-color joke is offensive to the mixed group, then it is legally wrong for mature males to tell it to each other.

No approach to the problem will be totally effective or as efficient as we would wish—and, in fact, some of the concepts and problems of *Roth* must necessarily be included. But it should be remembered that there are existing laws governing human conduct which we have lived gracefully with for many, many years and which, if amplified a bit and applied to this problem, could far better accomplish what we need to achieve in the regulation of obscenity than do the laws we are now using for this purpose.

Nuisance

We have, for instance, the laws of "nuisance," which, though

often cumbersome in application, have considerable potential for
meeting many of the problem areas in a realistic manner.[33] Such
laws give maximum leeway in the area of personal conduct, but at
the same time provide the means of abating that conduct if it goes
beyond what is legally permissible.

The opponents of this approach can rightly claim that it is very
difficult to enjoin threatened offensive activity, and that by the time
the conduct is stopped, the "damage" is often done. Also there
usually isn't a workable "penalty" which attaches so as to prevent
further such activity.

But it must be conceded that it is a unique area of the law, from
the standpoint of procedural fairness and from the standpoint of the
fact that the issues are usually tried in very close proximity in time
to the inception of the complained of conduct. Also, it cannot be
denied that, more than any other established procedure, the laws of
nuisance faithfully adhere to the constitutional abhorrence of "prior
restraints" of freedom of expression.

Disturbing the Peace

There is also a very intriguing possibility in those quaint old laws
which are generally classified in the category of "disturbing the
peace." Although rather imprecise, somewhat vague and usually
archaic in language, they have flourished in every community since
the inception of the nation because of a need for them, and because
they peculiarly recognize the vagaries of human nature.

In legal analysis, there is often little to recommend them, yet
they have constantly proven their worth and therefore probably
represent an important phase of "natural law." Since it is this very
element which is now lacking in our approach to obscenity, and
since somehow these half-forgotten laws once did a pretty fair job of
regulating lewd conduct, they ought to be looked at again from a
conceptual standpoint.

California provides that:

Every person who maliciously and wilfully disturbs the peace or
quiet of any neighborhood or person, by loud or . . . tumultuous
or offensive conduct . . . or uses any vulgar, profane or indecent
language within the presence or hearing of women or children . . .
is guilty of a misdemeanor. . . .[34]

Like all such laws, it is imperfect, leaving ambiguities in definition and scope. But it nevertheless very firmly puts the spotlight on conduct and willfulness, and upon the effect the conduct actually achieves or is likely to achieve. And when compared with more modern legislative attempts to meet the problem, it looks very good indeed.

For example, nudity in California is now largely penalized by a re-enacted "disorderly conduct" law[35] and by a revised "indecent exposure" law.[36] Conviction under either statute requires subsequent registration as a sex offender.[37]

Hence, it is disorderly conduct to engage in "lewd or dissolute conduct in any public place or in any place open to the public or exposed to public view."[38] There is no consideration as to whether there are observers, or likely to be observers, of the conduct involved—just the question (1) whether the conduct is "lustful," "lascivious," "immoral" or "wanton"[39] and (2) whether it takes place in a "public place."

What if the conduct occurred in the center of a deserted national forest? What about the young couple that parks at the end of a deserted country road and engages in sex play?

The same concern is even more applicable to the first part of the indecent exposure statute, which condemns anyone who "[e]xposes his person, or the private parts thereof, in any public place. . . . "[40] With not even a requirement of lewdness, how do we view a troop of Boy Scouts innocently skinny-dipping in a lake in the center of that remote forest?

The exposure statute goes on to add another catchall provision: "or exposes his person in any place where there are present other persons to be offended or annoyed thereby. . . . "[41] What if someone (as many do) goes to a theater expecting to be "offended"? And isn't there a great distinction between a person being "annoyed" or even "offended" and involuntarily having his "peace" disturbed?

Assault and Battery

Another possibility is to expand the concepts of assault and battery. California defines a criminal assault as "an unlawful attempt, coupled with a present ability, to commit a violent injury on the person of another"[42] and a battery as "any willful and unlawful use of force or violence upon the person of another."[43] These definitions do not substantially vary from the patterns which exist in a rather universal form throughout the world.

Again, these are well-tested laws of exceptionally long-standing application[44] which have successfully dealt with man's unfortunate tendency to frequently use unjustified physical violence on his neighbors. If extended so as to adequately encompass assaults of a visual and audible nature, as has been done in the case of civil assaults and batteries,[45] these laws could well help fill one of the greatest gaps now existing in the obscenity field—namely, the need to protect people from being unconscionably preyed upon by those who deal in sex themes.

Thus it could be actionable, as a battery, if a patron of a theater or tavern was not warned of the heavy sex theme of the entertainment inside before he entered. And it could be actionable to sell the *Kinsey Report* to young children, or otherwise assault a nonconsenting person with a sex theme going beyond what is normally tolerated and expected in such situations.[46]

Adoption of these concepts would basically allow mature, consenting adults to expose themselves, if they so desired, to matters now considered obscene, but would far better protect them from sex themes they would not want to be exposed to. It would give a freedom of choice which is not now present because of the constant uninvited deluge of such themes in the mails, periodicals, theaters, stores and nearly every facility and media utilized by the public.

Those who desired to disseminate a sexual theme would do so at their peril—not at a risk of having the theme declared inherently bad, but at a risk of assaulting someone or, as in the case of children, creating a degree of risk of harm which is too high to be tolerated.

Hence, legitimate expression could be better protected, the citizen's right of privacy could be enhanced, and a definite lessening of the present tensions should occur. Additionally (and this is a point quite important to priests, ministers, rabbis and others who educate and counsel in matters of religion), there hopefully would be a substantial return from the present unnatural reliance on the concept of "legal-or-illegal" to concepts of "right-and-wrong."

THE FUTURE

Is there hope that the law may eventually shift over to this new course? The answer must be guarded, for it is a most difficult transition to make. But there are signs which give a basis for cautious optimism.

Roth was the product of widely diverse opinions and, therefore, did not close the door to later modification. Nor did any of its authors abandon an open mind on the subject—as is amply illustrated by their decisions in subsequent cases. So, although *Roth* has survived, there has been a distinct branching off which now appears to be leading in the direction of judging the use of the matter instead of the matter itself and which, if continued, could form the main channel of legal thought in the area.

The first big breakthrough came in *Ginzburg v. United States*,[47] where the Court introduced a new element. It said that matter which is not obscene, as such, can be rendered obscene if pandered in a commercial manner.[48]

Although the prosecution conceded that the publications themselves were probably not obscene, the defendant was convicted under a federal statute which made it a crime to knowingly use the mails for the mailing or delivery of any "obscene, lewd, lascivious, or filthy book, pamphlet . . . or other publication of an indecent character. . . ."[49]

Upon reaching the Supreme Court, Ginzburg, the editor of several publications including a magazine called *Eros*, found himself tripped up by such things as the fact that the magazine bore the provocative postmarks of two little Pennsylvania hamlets called "Intercourse" and "Blue Ball." Because of such evidence, the Court simply held that it was apparent that the intent of the defendant was solely to minister to the baser passions of the reader.

Justices Black, Douglas, Harlan and Stewart dissented vigorously,[50] but the majority decision was written by Justice Brennan, the author of *Roth*, and therefore must be considered as an amplification of that earlier decision, not an abandonment of it.

In short, then, the Court said that a course of conduct can be actionable, even though the basic subject matter involved is not obscene, and even though no individual element of the conduct is itself obscene.[51] But, while the ruling was a shock to many who viewed it as an erosion of the First Amendment, it actually had the effect of raising the converse question as to whether it might be possible to utilize "obscene" matter in a nonactionable way.

Then along came *Stanley v. Georgia*,[52] which held that a person may possess obscene matter and not be liable therefore until he does something else with it. Justice Marshall, in delivering the majority opinion, flatly stated that neither *Roth* nor the Court's decisions subsequent to it, ever involved prosecution for mere possession of obscene materials, but instead dealt with the power of government to "prohibit or regulate *certain public actions* taken or intended to be taken with respect to obscene matter."[53]

Having thus cast a different light upon *Roth* than was apparent before, the majority held that the Constitution gives a right to receive information and ideas, regardless of their social worth, and that this right is "fundamental to our free society."[54] Further, the opinion contained the pervasive statement that, "[w]hatever the power of the state to control public dissemination of ideas inimical to the public morality, it cannot constitutionally premise legislation on the desirability of controlling a person's private thoughts."[55]

Stanley has also been widely claimed to stand for the proposition that a state may never prohibit mere possession of obscene matter on the ground it may lead to antisocial conduct, but this blanket interpretation may be a bit premature. First, the Court conceded that there is always the danger that obscene material might fall into the hands of children, or that it might intrude upon the sensibilities or privacy of the general public. But it found that, "[n]o such dangers are present in this case."[56]

Secondly, the Court's precise ruling was that, although the states have power to regulate obscenity, "that power simply does not extend to mere possession by the individual in the privacy of his own home."[57]

And lastly, it must be noted that, although Justices Brennan and White concurred in the result, they did so on the basis of unlawful search and seizure, not on the grounds stated in the majority opinion. As architects of many of the earlier decisions in the field, their absence in the majority in this case may carry considerable significance in projecting the probable results of the many cases which will seek to amplify the ruling.

The argument is now being made that if there is a constitutional right to "receive," then there must also be a right to disseminate; and it is here that the battle will be most intense. One federal trial court has already ruled that if there is a right to possess obscene material, there is a right to buy it and receive it, and this means that the federal government cannot constitutionally prosecute a seller for sending such materials to a consenting adult through the mails.[58]

It is a likely extension of *Stanley* that at least private dissemination will be held to be protected in most cases, but the line between public and private dissemination will be most difficult to draw—and the results of even private transfers, as between some individuals (e.g. from adult to child), could be noxious.

In any event, *Stanley* takes a giant step toward saying that all the circumstances of the individual case must be considered, and that mere classification of matter as obscene or not obscene is only one factor to be considered in determining whether the course of conduct is actionable or not.

The opinion also puts heavy stress upon the right of privacy—at least from the standpoint of "unwanted governmental intrusions into one's privacy"—but does not quite reach the important question as to how far government may go in protecting the individual from intrusions into his privacy by commercial and other private interests. However, in spite of language which frowns heavily on any governmental action which seems to be aimed at controlling what ideas its citizens might receive, *Stanley* does not appear to preclude governmental action which is reasonably designed to give citizens a freedom of choice as to what ideas they may elect to receive or reject.

Therefore, out of all the turmoil and trial and error which we have had to endure in this difficult area, a pattern of workability appears to be forming as great legal scholars and practical men courageously wrestle with the immense problems inherent in the subject matter. And it is to the great credit of most of them that they have remained receptive to new ideas and change, and have carefully avoided being absolutist in their initial theories.

Because of these attributes, the law on the subject has not vacillated in recent years, but has built upon itself and gradually metamorphosed, instead of making disruptively abrupt changes. The landmark case of *Roth*, for example, is still valuable and, in fact, has gained viability with each succeeding interpretation, even though it now bears little resemblance to what we originally thought it to be.

As the law progresses in this field, it is apparent that it more and more squares, not only with the Constitution and with the natural laws of man, but also with the historical concepts of jurisdiction between ecclesiastical and civil law. The judiciary thus finally appears to be working on a true course, and it is hoped that legislators and members of the executive branch of government will follow suit and not encumber or deter this trend by advocating and enacting unconstitutional or unworkable laws which run counter to it.

NOTES

1. Louis Henkin, "Morals and the Constitution," *Columbia Law Review* vol. 63 (March 1963): 391-414; G. Mueller, *Crime, Law and the Scholars* (Seattle: University of Washington Press, 1969) p. 1-30.

2. J. Wharton, *Criminal Law*, 11th ed. (London, 1912) p. 2234-39; L. Stephen, *A History of the Criminal Law of England* (London, 1883); W. Blackstone, *Commentaries* (New York: Adorno, reprinted in 1972, original, 1769).

3. U.S. Constitution Amendment I.

4. Thornhill v. Alabama, 310 U.S. 88 (1940).

5. Joseph Burstyn, Inc. v. Wilson, 343 U.S. 495, 500-05 (1952); Chaplinsky v. New Hampshire, 315 U.S. 568 (1942).

6. *Ex parte* Jackson, 96 U.S. 727, 736-37 (1877); Roth v. United States, 354 U.S. 476, 481, 485 (1957).

7. Grosjean v. American Press Co., 297 U.S. 233 (1936); Bridges v. California, 314 U.S. 252 (1941); *cf.* Dennis v. United States, 341 U.S. 494 (1951).

8. Winters v. New York, 333 U.S. 507 (1948).

9. 354 U.S. 476 (1957).

10. "The early leading standard of obscenity allowed material to be judged merely by the effect of an isolated exerpt upon particularly susceptible persons. *Regina v. Hicklin*, (1868) L.R. 3 Q.B. 360. Some American courts adopted this standard but later decisions have rejected it and substituted this test: whether to the average person, applying contemporary community standards, the dominant theme of the material taken as a whole appeals to prurient interests." Roth v. United States, Ibid., 488-89.

11. "But implicit in the history of the First Amendment is the rejection of obscenity as utterly without redeeming social importance. This rejection for that reason is mirrored in the universal judgment that obscenity should be restrained, reflected in the international agreement of over 50 nations, in the

obscenity laws of all of the 48 states, and in the 20 obscenity laws enacted by the Congress from 1842 to 1956." (*See also* the concurring opinion of the Chief Justice at 495, and the separate opinion of Justice Harlan at 501-02.) Roth v. United States, Ibid., 484-85.

12. Times Film Corp. v. Chicago, 365 U.S. 43, 69 (1961).

13. Justices Black and Douglas felt that "[w]hen we sustain these convictions, we make the legality of a publication turn on the purity of thought which a book or tract instills in the mind of the reader. I do not think we can approve that standard and be faithful to the command of the First Amendment. . . . By these standards, punishment is inflicted for thoughts provoked, not for overt acts nor anti-social conduct." Roth v. United States, 508-9.

14. Justice Harlan stated, "[m]y basic difficulties with the Court's opinion are threefold. First, the opinion paints with such a broad brush that I fear it may result in a loosening of the tight reins which state and federal courts should hold upon the enforcement of obscenity statutes. Second, the Court fails to discriminate between the different factors which, in my opinion, are involved in the constitutional adjudication of state and federal obscenity cases. Third, relevant distinctions between the two obscenity statutes here involved, and the Court's own definition of 'obscenity' are ignored." Ibid., 496.

15. Note Justice Clark's concurrence in the Chief Justice's dissent in Jacobellis v. Ohio, 378 U.S. 184, 199 (1964). Compare the majority opinion in Roth with the majority opinion in Ginzburg v. United States, 383 U.S. 463 (1966).

16. 383 U.S. 413 (1966).

17. Ibid., at 418.

18. Californian Penal Code Sect. 311(a) (West 1970).

19. Roth v. United States, 354 U.S. 476, 489-90 (1956); Memoirs v. Massachusetts, 383 U.S. 413, 418 (1966).

20. Jacobellis v. Ohio, 378 U.S. 184, 197 (1964).

21. Winters v. New York, 333 U.S. 507 (1948); Joseph Burstyn, Inc. v. Wilson, 343 U.S. 495 (1952); Gelling v. Texas, 343 U.S. 960 (1952).

22. Roth v. United States, 354 U.S. 476, 489 (1956).

23. *In re* Giannini, 69 California 2d 563, 572, 72 California Reporter 655, 661-62 (1968).

24. Ibid., 577, 72 California Reporter 665.

25. *See* the diverse opinions in Jacobellis v. Ohio, 378 U.S. 184, 192-94, 200 (1964).

26. *In re* Giannini, op. cit., 572, 72 California Reporter at 662.

27. Roth v. United States, 354 U.S. 476, 484 (1957).

28. 1 WITKIN, CALIFORNIA CRIMES Sects. 88, 90 (1963).

29. Zeitlin v. Arnebergh, 59 California 2d 901, 31 California Reporter 800 (1963).

30. Ibid., 920, 31 California Reporter at 812-13.

31. *See* Annot., 5 A.L.R.3d 1158, at 1190-91 (1966).

32. Times Film Corp. v. Chicago, 365 U.S. 43, 69 (1961) (dissenting opinion by Warren, C.J., joined in by Black, Douglas, and Brennan, J.J.).

33. For an excellent treatment, see Comment, *"Obscenity: The Pig in the Parlor*," SANTA CLARA LAW. vol. 10, 1968, p. 238.

34. CALIFORNIA PENAL CODE Sect. 415 (West 1970).

35. Ibid., 647.

36. Ibid., 314.

37. Ibid., 290.

38. Ibid., 647(a).

39. People v. Babb, 103 California Appellate 2d 326, 229 P.2d 843 (1951).

40. CALIFORNIA PENAL CODE Sect. 431 (1) (West 1970).

41. Ibid.

42. Ibid., 240.

43. Ibid., 242.

44. BLACKSTONE, COMMENTARIES, p. 120; BLACKSTONE, COMMENTARIES, Ibid., p. 216; BURDICK, LAW OF CRIME (New York: Bender, 1946) p. 338.

45. R. PERKINS, CRIMINAL LAW (Mineola, N.Y.: Foundation Press, 1969) p. 107; W. PROSSER, LAW OF TORTS (St. Paul: West, 1964) p. 32-52; 1 RESTATEMENT (SECOND) OF TORTS Sect. 46 (1965); Southeastern Greyhound Corp. v. Graham, 69 Georgia Appellate 621, 26 S.E.2d 371 (1943); Ft. Worth & R.G. Ry. v. Bryant, 210 S.W. 556 (Texas Civil Appellate 1918); Birmingham Ry., Light and Power Co. v. Glenn, 179 Alabama 263, 60 So. 111 (1912).

46. In Williams v. District of Columbia, 419 F.2d 638 (D.C. Cir. 1969), there was an interesting joinder of the three concepts (nuisance, breach of peace, and assault). The defendant had been convicted under a statute which made it unlawful to use "profane language" or "indecent and obscene words" in a public place. The question before the appellate court was whether the statue was constitutional, and to this the Court replied:

That portion of [22 D.C. Code Sect. 1107 (1967)] which makes it illegal for any person "to curse, swear, or make use of any profane language or indecent or obscene words" is on its face extraordinarily broad, so broad in fact that it would allow punishment of the hapless stonemason who, after crushing his toe, innocently utters a few relieving expletives within earshot of a public place. . . .

Both the facts of Chaplinsky [v. New Hampshire, 315 U.S. 568 (1942)] itself and the cases which followed it, indicate that the circumstances under which words are spoken are of critical importance in deciding whether the Constitution permits punishment to be imposed. Apart from punishing profane or obscene words which are spoken in circumstances which create a threat of violence, the state may also have a legitimate interest in stopping one person from "inflict[ing] injury" on others by verbally assaulting them with language which is grossly offensive because of its profane or obscene character. The fact that a person may constitutionally indulge his taste for obscenities in private does not mean that he is free to intrude them upon the attentions of others. . . . We therefore conclude that Section 1107 would not be invalid if the statutory prohibition against profane or obscene language in public were interpreted to require an additional element that the language be spoken in circumstances which threaten a breach of the peace. And for these purposes a breach of the peace is threatened either because the language creates a substantial risk of provoking violence, or because it is, under "contemporary community standards" so grossly offensive to members of the public who actually overhear it as to amount to a nuisance. Ibid., 644-46.

47. 383 U.S. 463 (1966).

48. Ibid., 467-71, 474-76.

49. 18 U.S.C. Sect. 1461 (1964).

50. Justices Black and Douglas adhered to their previously expressed beliefs that government lacks the constitutional power to "put any type of burden on speech and expressions of ideas of any kind [as distinguished from conduct].... " Ginzburg, at 476. Justice Black further felt that the case's new guidelines were " ... so vague and meaningless that they practically leave the fate of a person charged with violating censorship statutes to the unbridled discretion, whim and caprice of the judge or jury which tries him." Ibid., 478.

Justice Douglas added, " ... a book should stand on its own, irrespective of the reasons why it was written or the wiles used in selling it." Ibid., 482. Further, "I find it difficult to say that a publication has no 'social importance' because it caters to the taste of the most unorthodox amongst us. We members of this Court should be among the last to say what should be orthodox in literature.... However plebian my tastes may be, who am I to say that others' tastes ... have no 'social importance'?" Ibid., 491.

Justice Harlan stated that "[n]ow evidence not only as to conduct, but also as to attitude and motive, is admissible on the primary question of whether the material mailed is obscene. I have difficulty seeing how these inquiries are logically related to the question whether a particular work is obscene." Ibid. at 497.

Justice Stewart felt it was unfair to convict the defendant of "Pandering" when he was not charged that way, and concluded, " ... there is even another aspect of the Court's opinion in this case that is even more regrettable. Today the Court assumes the power to deny Ralph Ginzburg the protection of the First Amendment because it disapproves of his 'sordid business'. That is a power the Court does not possess." Ibid., 501.

51. Ginzburg v. United States, 383 U.S. 463, at 465-66, 474-76 (1966).

52. 394 U.S. 557 (1969).

53. Ibid., 561 (emphasis added).

54. Ibid., 564.

55. Ibid., 566.

56. Ibid., 567.

57. Ibid., 568.

58. United States v. Letha, CRS-884, Memorandum and Order filed April 29, 1970, United States District Court for the Eastern District of California. *See also* Karalexis v. Byrne, 360 F. Supp. 1363 (D.C. Mass. 1969). *But see* Marvin Miller, Covina Publishing, Inc. v. United States, Court of Appeals, Ninth Circuit, decision filed September 16, 1970, (No. 23935) which shows reluctance to extend Stanley.

PORNOGRAPHY
AND
DILEMMAS OF MORALITY

Pornographic Theaters
Off Times Square

Joseph P. Slade

I was pleased when the President's Commission on Obscenity and Pornography decided that serious collectors of pornography, while at first attracted by the possibility of erotic stimulation, gradually began collecting for other reasons—the same reasons which motivate philatelists and numismatists. Such an imprimatur would seem to make me a respectable dirty old man, though I have never pretended to be interested in pornography only for its artistic significance or its redeeming social importance. I cheerfully admit to enjoying the sexual stimulation, which to me is a perfectly legitimate reason for reading a book or watching a movie. Ultimately the test of appeal hinges on personal predilection, or, in the argot of the young, "whatever turns you on." Perhaps because of simple satiation, however, my interest in pornography has become more or less academic. In short, it isn't as much fun anymore; pornography is too available. Back in the fifties, part of the thrill lay in its forbidden nature; one had to ferret it out, acquire it by stealth, and pay enormous prices (measured, at least, by the proceeds from my paper route). On the other hand, living in New York provides me with the

Reprinted from *trans*action (now **Society**), magazine November/December 1971. Copyright ©1971 by Transaction, Inc., New Brunswick, New Jersey.

opportunity to observe the porno phenomenon at more leisure and, at present, on a still manageable scale.

In case there are any doubts about the matter, New York is an up-and-coming distribution center of pornography in the United States. (I use the word pornography in its generally accepted etymological sense—as material intended to arouse. I would not even try to define obscenity.) There is little cause for hysteria. Compared to Copenhagen, New York is still in a kind of pornographic infancy. It also lags behind San Francisco, Los Angeles or even Hollywood, where the spread of pornography has reached explosive proportions. I doubt that New York will overtake the California cities, for lifestyles are too different. New York is cool, sophisticated and imperturbable in the face of minor cultural revolutions, much more obsessed with real upheavals (which pornography is not), in contrast to frenetic and faddish San Francisco. Nevertheless, to judge from the flourishing business in Times Square, pornography is clearly turning on a sizeable segment of the native population.

Incidentally, most but not all of the pornography in the bookstores along 42nd Street comes from California. The competition in America between the major producers of porno is rather like the traditional rivalry over wines between California and New York state. In terms of sheer bulk and, perhaps as a consequence, quality as well, California supplies the lion's share of pornographic books, magazines and films, but the New York stores stock the homegrown variety also, along with lesser vintages from Miami, Dallas and Atlanta. Unlike our native wines, American pornography is successful in the international market place. Most European countries do not permit the open sale of Danish hard-core, but American salesmanship has flooded the Continent with soft-core picture books and tawdry paperbacks. Fifteen or 20 years ago, Americans ransacked Paris and Amsterdam for French postcards and dirty books. Now a sailor on the prowl in Amsterdam finds glossy "art" printed in Los Angeles or New York, and the American tourist looks in vain for titillation he would not find in his corner drugstore back home. What about the "exhibitions" in Paris—you remember? Closed for lack of customers, but check your *local* paper for live sex shows here. Unless one goes to Copenhagen, the acknowledged pornography capital of the world, a trip abroad will not garner much foreign erotica. Amsterdam holds an occasional erotic film festival, it is true, yet the last one was won by an American entry.

Sexual explicitness in movies, in spite of a lingering cachet attributed to foreign films, is becoming more and more an American prerogative—the Danes always excepted. Again the Californians are the leaders in the field, and here in New York, Times Square provides the showcase. Arcades along Sixth, Seventh and Eighth Avenues are lined with projection machines requiring a steady stream of quarters to view an endless supply of 8mm reels. Usually these are of the soft-core variety. Models of all four sexes engage in hilarious positions to be as graphic as possible without crossing the borderline (accepted by police and exhibitors) of actual sexual contact which would make the films hard-core. Vulnerable to official harassment, the arcade owners tend to be cautious. It is in the theaters of the area that one is startled by the new freedom. Not every theater in Times Square goes in for hard-core; those which do advertise in code words like "heavy" and "strong." Nor are such theaters limited to Times Square. In Manhattan they range north and south from 14th Street to 57th, as far east as Third Avenue; even Brooklyn has two or three. Still, the heaviest concentration is in the grind circuit of West midtown between 42nd and 50th. The number is presently around two dozen, with a new one opening at the rate of about one a month. Some deal exclusively in homosexual fare; the majority stick to heterosexuality, which should reassure New Yorkers who worry about the city's going gay.

Inside one sees explicit, hard-core pornography, or what used to be called stag films—not the old skin flicks or nudies, which have been swamped by a rising tide of lovingly pictured semen—thanks to a combination of general public tolerance, recent court decisions and a reluctance on the part of district attorneys to prosecute. Periodic police raids, once a source of intimidation, have all but ceased. The recently publicized July drive to clean up Times Square hit primarily prostitutes and *live* sex shows, intimated only the most timid of porno entrepreneurs, and affected the blue movie operators hardly at all. The new frankness has not gone unnoticed. The *Village Voice* has already begun *auteur* discussions of the leading porno directors, and Andrew Sarris has predicted that Lincoln Center will hold an erotic film festival within a few years. Every now and then the *New York Times* or the *Post* dispatch a reporter to sit through an afternoon of sleazy movies. They do not send a Roger Greenspun, who confesses to liking exploitation films and who chose *The*

History of the Blue Movie as one of the Ten Best of 1970. They send
a journalist of standard sociological bent. Because as a liberal he
cannot condone the idea of censorship or inveigh against immorality,
he simply delivers a condescending verdict: the stuff is boring.
Naturally (one is tempted to reply) anything to surfeit is boring. But
the reporter misses the very real interest.

SEX FILM REGULARS

On a weekday morning, say between 9:30 and 10:00, Times
Square looks innocuous. Rush-hour workers have filed into office
buildings, and Broadway and Seventh Avenue retain a virginal
quality. Burglar-guards still cover the plate glass which glittered the
night before. The shopkeepers are out sweeping refuse into gutters.
Cowed by the freshness, the shlock vendors have their merchandise
under wraps. Pedestrian traffic is thin compared to the usual bustle,
but energetic. Among the passersby are the sex film regulars, men
heading for the first show of the day. Some merely look for one
they haven't seen, alerted by ads in the *Daily News* or for true
aficionados, by capsule commentaries in *Screw*. Others know the
schedules of all the theaters by heart and whether the features
change on Mondays or Thursdays. The titles of the films help very
little anyway; a great many have none, and those which do are
hopelessly garbled on marquees or in newspaper ads, partly from the
necessity of avoiding public display of taboo words (no prurient
advertising, orders the Supreme Court), partly from surrealistic
impulses of the theater owners.

Determined to search out the dens of iniquity, the veterans
trudge up stairs to second-story halls or descend into damp
basements on side streets just east of Broadway. On Broadway and
Seventh Avenue the choices are more elegant. Scattered among
conventional movie houses are little pocket cinemas, like the lushly
carpeted, brand-new Circus Cinema or the Cine Lido, constructed
from the faded rococo of the old Latin Quarter. Farther west, along
Eighth, customers pick from clusters of tawdry crackerboxes ranging
from the Cameo at 44th to the Tivoli at 50th. Much farther west, in
the wilds of 42nd Street around the West Side Airline Terminal, the

storefront theaters of the New Era chain (formerly the Seymore Domore—get it?) draw crowds.

Some of these establishments sandwich films between performances by strippers of "live" (a misnomer) sex shows. At the 47th Street Playhouse, for instance, a packed house peers around basement pillars at a minuscule stage. The mistress of ceremonies pulls a frayed curtain over a 12-foot screen and then pulls off her clothes. An aging and poorly costumed, decidedly overplump Puerto Rican, she grins her way through a ponderous dance to canned music. She is followed by a succession of black and Latin girls, who strip completely and quickly, then redress and dash off individually to the 49th Street Playhouse to do the same act. The last one says she hopes everyone will tell his friends of the show and asks that they all please come again next week. She tugs the curtain back, exposing the movie screen, as she leaves. At the Club Zsa-Zsa, on West 42nd, a man and a woman squirm on a mattress in a dingy store front. Their heavy breathing and transparently fraudulent squeals of ecstasy are almost lost in the foot-shuffling of the sweating audience. When they finish, the movies start.

Most theaters, however, show only films. They are either 16 or 35 mm. The Mike Todds of the circuit, the Tivoli owners, offer their programs in wide-screen Panascope. The New Era chain uses the cheaper rear-projection screens; even shoddier are the homemade videotapes in the same neighborhood. Among the various houses considerable commercial incest takes place. The Tivoli passes on its Panascope to the Metropolitan on 14th Street; the Mini-Cinema delivers to the Harem; a first-run program at the 50th Street Cinema will play successive one-week stints at the Mermaid, the Masque and the 42nd Street Cinema, so there is no danger a patron will miss one he specially wants to see. The same holds true for the Avon chain.

A fair proportion of viewers drift into the emporiums of this chain, which has grown impressively from a single house (now demolished) on Sixth Avenue. The original Avon was the first in New Yo k to screen "beaver" films—i.e., those showing pubic hair—five or six years ago. With business booming, the management moved into the old Hudson Theater on 45th between Sixth and Broadway, a huge, still thinly gilded barn with a double balcony, and steadily acquired or built four others, including the shocking-pink upholstered Orleans on the opposite side of Broadway. Though challenged briefly by latecomers to the field, like the Mini-Cinema, the first in the city consistently to deal in hard-core, the Avon chain has never lost its eminence.

Each theater has its own odor, degree of comfort and general ambience. Some even sell popcorn. The Avon Hudson is typical of the type, and the most interesting, for it is easily the largest. Seven days a week, 16 hours a day, it serves a generous helping of garden-variety heterosexual pornography. On the program will be two or three 16 or 35 mm features of 45 minutes or an hour, plus several shorts and 20 minutes or so of coming attraction previews. For every competently lighted and photographed sequence, three are grainy, out-of-focus, underexposed or so badly edited as to be incomprehensible. They have little in common with the quasi-respectable mammalian comedies of Russ Meyer or the baroque sex *opera* of Radley Metzger, other than a fondness for flesh. These are perhaps unfair standards. After all, Meyer has been feted at Yale, and Metzger at the Museum of Modern Art. Still one likes to remember that cameramen like Lazslo Kovacs (*Easy Rider*) once received their training in nudies. To be fair in this regard, I should point out that the Orleans, the pearl of the Avon chain, regularly shows the more tutored craftsmanship of directors like Bill Osco and Alex de Renzy; neither is likely to win an Oscar for technical skill, however. The Hudson's films are produced by the most mediocre of amateurs. All are in color. One of the features may have sound, out of synch; the tape-recorded music froths romantically for the rest. According to my computations, the Hudson projectionist plays "Hey Jude" and the theme from *Dr. Zhivago* 73 times a day.

Screening begins promptly at 10:00. By 10:30 dim shapes (the theater is always dark; there is never an intermission) occupy each quadrant of the house. If it is Wednesday, the day the program changes, there will be more than on other days. These first patrons are of indeterminate background, moderately well-dressed, vaguely middle-class, footloose at this early working hour. Ages vary. The majority fall between 35 and 60, or even older. Men who can barely walk totter down the aisles and grope painfully into the damaged seats, where they often snore peacefully. The Hudson cashier scrutinizes IDs to keep out the very young. Yet not all the patrons are over 30, as the Woodstockers would have us believe; a sprinkling of beards attests to the presence of the liberated generation side by side with veterans of the unemancipated fifties. Blacks are by no means rare. Perhaps they are here to indulge Eldridge Cleaver fantasies about the white ultra-feminines, for few black men or women appear on screen, though theoretically they should be plentiful, since sexual relations between the races is one of our most cherished and titillating taboos. Surprisingly, Puerto Ricans seem to be boycotting. Machismo, as we shall see, does not thrive at the Hudson.

From 12:00 to 1:00, the lunch crowd swells the audience. Nattily tailored executives unwrap sandwiches from sleek attaché cases. In the late afternoons, tourists wander in; the theater belongs to them in the evenings. They betray themselves by arriving in groups of conventioneers. They giggle defensively, like at the American Legion smokers back home, or twist their heads in mild panic until, realizing that no one is paying them attention, they allow their embarrassment to settle into raptness. They have stumbled into a temple of sex. Eroticism is a palpable force in the air, inhaled by a reverent congregation.

Except for the cloying music or the clumsy dialogue, the silence is profound. Once, however, when an especially lovely young lady appeared on screen, I heard a "she's beautiful" gurgle involuntarily from an elderly man three seats to my left. Yes, the seating order is odd, as the newspaper reporters have noticed. At least one seat separates each member of the audience. This territorial imperative is enforced to permit masturbation—the Hudson deserves the sobriquet "Masturbation Emporium" as much as the burlesque houses of Henry Miller's novels—and to allow space for private musings and individual fantasies. The atmosphere is superficially passive, charged with underlying tension.

Now that McSorley's has been breached, one might expect that the sex films would remain a last exclusive preserve of the New York male. Sitting in the Hudson, I have often hoped to hear Lucy Komisar leading in the troops. Actually the theaters have never discouraged female attendance. Women trickle in, rarely alone, never in groups, escorted by bold husbands or boyfriends, usually to one of the more artsy cinemas. Students frequently took dates to *The History of the Blue Movie* when it played the Orleans. The women's reactions range from amusement to terror, and a few argue their companions into leaving. Those who stay are ignored by the men in the audience. The indifference is not hostility; it results, again, from the function of the theater as a place of private fantasy. The real woman within touching distance has not the attraction of the images. A few years ago, when the theaters were still showing nudies, prostitutes occasionally infiltrated the back rows. Once the films went all the way, the prostitutes returned to the streets, presumably because business fell off. The real thing, as always, just doesn't compete with the silver screen.

One sympathizes with the discomfort of the unsuspecting women visitors. The films are slanted toward men (though women do respond, as the Presidential Commission discovered). Were Miss Komisar's myrmidons to arrive, they would surely attack the treatment foisted on women in pornography: women are exploited, treated as objects, and degraded by sexual contempt—with an ultimate effect of fostering an unreal view of sex and impersonal and therefore dehumanizing attitudes. These are serious contentions, far more important than the common bluestocking objections to pornography. While there is truth to them, to one who has sat through literally hundreds of stag films they seem reflex, unexamined reactions. Moreover, these arguments indict the men in the audience as sexual criminals, as it were, an accusation I think unfair.

In the first place, it is difficult to think of the women as exploited, save in an abstract sense. After all, they are paid, and no one forces them to do it. A facile argument? Did not Stepin Fetchit degrade himself and his race by accepting exploitation from Hollywood? Perhaps, although scorn is easy in retrospect from an era of black militancy, but he took such roles because blacks then could act no others. Women are not so limited today. Are prostitutes (and that is what the sex film roles come down to) necessarily exploited if they receive their asking price? Are the female models any more exploited than the males?

In regard to the question of sexual objects, I must admit to some prejudices. We are all objects to one another, as Sartre would say, if only because we can never really know another human being. Like Harriet Van Horne, I see nothing wrong in regarding others as sexual objects. Logically, to do otherwise in our casual dealings with the majority f the opposite sex would be impossible; better to regard others as sex objects than not to regard them at all. If a male glances at a pretty young lady on the street, in order not to regard her as an object (a merely esthetically attractive, sexually stimulating member of the opposite sex), he would have to accost her, strike up a conversation, discover her traits, interests and intelligence, a process which could take days or weeks, and slowly learn to appreciate her as a human being who can be understood as such. The same holds true for females. Sexual roles on so casual a level are simply social short cuts and time savers, like knowing whether a man you meet but never expect to see again is a butcher or a lawyer, and governing your response accordingly. To attempt to learn to know every person you meet, to upgrade him from his status as object to yourself, would be like trying to support every good cause or giving a dime to every beggar in the Village. Deliberately to treat (as opposed to regard casually) as an object someone who has a claim on you to be treated otherwise, to refuse to acknowledge him as an individual human being is another question, and to the extent that pornography encourages such behavior, it should be condemned. I am not sure that the pornography theaters do encourage men to treat women impersonally, because of the way audiences respond to the films. Just as American males have traditionally divided, women into "good" and "bad" girls, so they make distinctions between the girls in the films and the women they know or meet. They have come to the theater to cinder their imaginations, and they know that their fantasies *are* fantasies. They are there to see what they do not get at home, and they are hardly likely to rush home and order their wives to perform fellatio just because they saw a stud do so in the movies.

All of this would be academic to the Hudson's clientele. Most of them have never read Kate Millett's simple-minded thesis on sexual power, or Norman Mailer's loony rejoinders. If they think of exploitation as they sit in the dark, they complain of the high price of admission. Tickets at the Hudson are four dollars, at the Mini-Cinema and others, five; the West Side storefronts offer a bargain two dollars. And they do not like to think of the women as objects. Fantasies do not thrive on impersonal, reified sex. Film producers, and indeed, most purveyors of pornography know this. Consider a pertinent example, *Playboy* magazine (not that *Playboy* is particularly pornographic). The editors write (create?) carefully detailed biographies of the Playmates and print them alongside the pictures, to reduce the possibility of the girls' becoming mere objects to the reader. How successfully the editors achieve this end is debatable, but without the text the Playmate is simply a steatopygic Barbie Doll. The biographies furnish the models with some degree of personality, a sort of psychological clothing which intrigues; the more a reader knows about the nude girl, the less an object she is to him. (Written pornography, as opposed to pictorial, requires somewhat different treatment. Written pornography cannot be too sharply defined, so as to leave space for the reader's imagination.) A skilled movie pornographer has similar intentions, but he is limited by the medium itself and by the necessity of including actual sex.

Current hard-core films in New York break down into two categories: the documentary of allegedly serious purpose or redeeming social importance, and the stag, presented without any justification, spurious or otherwise. Examples of the former are *He and She, Censorship in Denmark* and *The History of the Blue Movie*, which proved so lucrative that they have since moved into neighborhood houses. Such films adopt a pseudosociological voyeurism; a narrative on how-to-do-it or look-who's-doing-it splices together footage of people doing it. The rationale is that the film itself is educational, or that it is not pornography but about pornography. As a legal argument, this rationale works; *Censorship in Denmark* was recently cleared for exhibit by the courts. Aside from the legal advantages, the documentary has other virtues. It seems to be about real people, photographed as they are being photographed. After showing a film clip of a sex act, a narrator interviews the participants. The questions are predictable—"What's a nice girl like you doing in a film like this?"—as are the answers, which range from personal capitalism—"They pay well"—to high moral purpose—"Well, uh, you know, maybe people watching us will get over their sex hangups." This last answer, to make the world safe for sexual honesty, is the most common. The audience doesn't believe it for a second, but it's a popular technique.

So popular that it carries over into the other genre, the stag, which can take the form of a movie about making movies. A couple gets hold of a camera, telephones another couple, and they take turns aiming the dummy lens as the others whoop it up, all the while glancing coyly at the real camera off-screen. The extra camera attests to the "reality" of the situation. The stag is in a process of evolution. As demand increases, quality should improve—in theory. Right now, the crudest examples still litter the market. Fifteen-minute shorts present two naked robots hopping into bed for awkward, rapid intercourse. The decor of the setting is standard Motel Modern, or, if the director has a penchant for the gothic, Early Vincent Price. On a somewhat higher level, a film may employ an elementary plot. A hackneyed device is to set the action in a doctor's office, because it makes credible the removing of the female's clothes, which is followed by the doctor's seduction of his patient (or more likely, her seduction of him). The lady has come for advice on a sexual problem. The doctor's advice progresses to demonstration, with student swiftly outpacing mentor. The better stags, and there are infinite gradations of quality, utilize elaborate story lines and rudimentary characterizations, as in *Mona* by Bill Osco of California. Intent on preserving her virginity until her marriage, Mona initiates oral sex with several available males and one female (Osco likes to cover all bases), until her fiancé discovers her activities and demands the same. Mona's proclivities stem from a father who forced his daughter to perform fellatio—shown in flashback—and from a hypocritical mother, who seduces the fiancé behind her daughter's back. Mona thus becomes a product of her upbringing: a nymphomaniac trying to be good by conforming to a traditional American double standard which permits heavy petting (in this case, very heavy) so long as it does not lead to intercourse.

Such attempts to characterize rarely rise above the level of stereotypes, although I have never understood why sexual stereotypes deserve more scorn than accepted dramatic stereotypes, or for that matter, living stereotypes. In her sterling essay on "The Pornographic Imagination," Susan Sontag suggests that stereotypes are inevitable in pornography, that characters must be two-dimensional in order to permit the imagination to fill in the gaps with fantasy or personal identification with the protagonists. Sontag is referring to written pornography. Filmed pornography involves a larger problem, for here one has the element of visual physicality to contend with. It is a formidable and disconcerting element. Unlike written pornography, nothing is left to the imagination. The man in the audience does not control the pacing of the action or the explicitness of the images, as he does when he reads; he may see more than he wants to see. When a girl on screen spreads her legs so wide that her ovaries are visible, her sheer presence forestalls consideration of her other attributes.

Salvador Dali has warned against using full frontal nudity in painting, because, he says, the vector of pubic hair draws the eye immediately and destroys the effect of the whole composition. Nudity alone may not reduce artistic possibilities in film, but graphic sex does. Sex, being an activity both intensely personal and publicly taboo, jolts the mind. It intrudes on our consciousness and wipes away everything else; its force, enhanced by the inhibitions we have toward it, makes the sex, and the sex alone, the "reality" of the situation. While the actor and actress (to use euphemisms) may have been playing roles, the characterizations slip away, leaving only the immediacy of two people making love. Again unlike the author of written pornography, the cameraman cannot get inside the performers' minds, so the audience does not know what they are thinking. And how does an actor express emotion in the throes of orgasm? Heavy breathing, squealing or screaming do not seem sufficient. Conceivably a filmmaker might employ expressionism— i.e., try to indicate thought and feeling by things external to the performers. For example, we apprehend King Lear's state of mind from the clashing elements in the storm scene. But what would a stag film cameraman use? A phallic bedpost, a rushing, piston-driven locomotive? Why, when we can see in detail the act these metaphors would merely represent? In *He and She*, as She reaches climax, a collage of images—a romp in a wheat field, a baby, a kiss, etc.— creates a mood of tenderness, but does not tell us anything. Gothicism, that traditional American refuge of sex in its flight from the Puritan ethic, might be another answer, since it could perhaps heighten emotion or tension.

The situation recalls Bertolt Brecht's *Verfremdung*, the alienation of the audience from the performers, the prevention of identification with the people on screen. A kind of distance is created: the audience cannot forget that these are men and women caught in the immediacy of the sex act, playing roles, just as the audience in Brecht's theater is continually reminded by the actors themselves that what is going on is illusion, fantasy. The reality on screen is simply physical presence wrapped in artifice, and the audience, fighting the threatening impersonality, turns in desperation to the little individuality that physicality can reveal. Thrown back on apprehension of one dimension, the patrons plumb it for a source of fantasy. Physical idiosyncrasies are savored: moles, caesarean and appendectomy scars, a tattooed "Property of Hell's Angels" on a buttock, even hairstyles, dangling earrings, a crucifix bumping between breasts. Fantasy requires fairly specific stimulus, and wherever fantasy is thwarted, the mind searches for some individuality to offset the impersonality.

For this reason, a good stag film will concentrate on the faces of the participants, especially the females, for faces indicate dimly what the actors think and feel. The face may not be the mirror of the soul, but it certainly furnishes some index of the personality and of the person's sexuality, as Freud understood very well in his discourse on the Medusa's head. Benjamin Franklin, perhaps the first American to notice the phenomenon, put the idea differently in his *Advice to a Young Man* (1745): if you put a basket over their heads, all women look alike. When a novice cameraman focusses on what he thinks should be the center of interest in a sex film, holding closeups of churning genitals, the audience goes to sleep. When an ingenue accidentally glances straight into the camera and smiles shyly before averting her face, the ripple of attention from the silent rows is perceptible. She has become vulnerable—and more real.

No one would dispute the charge that women are often humiliated and degraded by the sexual treatment they receive in the films. In many instances, however, they suffer less than the males. Virtually all the female recruits are pretty, some are beautiful, a few are exquisite. The audience is drawn esthetically, even romantically, toward them. One of several conversations I have held with stag patrons—they are generally an uncommunicative lot—began when a fortyish business type confided that he had seen the feature at the Capri, *Voluptuous Vera*, four times because the star was his "dream girl." She was lovely enough to stand the competition in a Roger Vadim opus, and in addition seemed thoroughly to enjoy her role. My friend's enthusiasm was understandable. He hunted for her pictures, he said, a quest made difficult by not knowing her name, which was never given in ads or credits. His chances were good nevertheless; I have seen Voluptuous Vera in no less than seven films since. One sees the same girls again and again. Some always perform with the same partner, some take on all comers. The real beauties are popular and acquire followings of fans. To my friend and his fellow regulars, their idols are not objects; the males are. The men are interchangeable, ciphers of no consequence, while the women reacquire their virginity from one picture to the next. If this seems to run counter to common conceptions of pornography, it is merely that the nature of the stag film conspires to produce a peculiar romantic elevation, even exaltation, of women.

The women, not the men, are the stars. They stand on pedestals by virtue of their necessity as the focus of a male-oriented film. One can argue that this worship of her as a sexual being is simply the obverse of the "degradation" visited upon the female, that the males elevate her only to gloat over her abuse. Still, in the films, male revenge does not come easily, and one wonders just who is being exploited.

Sexual myths nurtured by generations of literary pornography collapse visibly on screen. The rampant satyr of the dirty novel proves visually incapable of sustaining an erection. In the movies, frailty's name is man; he tires quickly and falls far short of the multiple orgasms of his literary counterpart. (On screen, an orgasm must be proved, in accord with the traditional code of the stag film. The male invariably ejaculates—if he can—in view of the camera.) Generally (there are exceptions), the females are the aggressors and initiators of sexual contact and experimentation. They are beautiful, haughty, vaguely menacing—definitely knowledgeable. They seize penises, demand erections, stuff organs into mouths and vaginas.

A typical example might be the appropriately titled *Dirty Old Men Need Love Too*, which recently finished a run at the Hudson and the Love Cinema. The protagonist is a middle-aged Milquetoast married to a wife who refuses to sleep with him more than once a week. Frustrated, he writes "horn-books" in which he fantasizes freely. When one day his wife turns a cold shoulder to his pleas, he stalks to a massage parlor, run, as it happens, by the girl who played Voluptuous Vera. The plot thickens when the wife, suspecting infidelity, follows her husband to the masseuse's. Having delivered herself of a homily on the sexual ignorance of married couples (redeeming social importance), V.V. dispatches a male staff member to educate the wife, whose presence in the place is unknown to the husband, while she attends to her client. After halting reluctance, the wife sexually exhausts the masseur, having learned instantly from his ministrations. Cut to V.V. and the husband. He protests; he loves his wife and does not want to commit adultery. V.V. whips open her robe, forces a breast into his mouth, literally manhandles him onto the table, fellates him and climbs aboard in the position the marriage manuals delicately call "female superior." At film's end, a reunited husband and wife join hands and gallop off to their own bed—or rather, the wife drags the husband off, eager to put her lessons to use. The inference is clear: within the woman reposes sexual knowledge and skill.

One of the functions of pornography is to reassure males threatened by the virile roles expected of them. Literary pornography commonly assuages anxiety by portraying indefatigable males dominating females. Filmed pornography tends to be less reassuring even as it caters to an equally old male fantasy: that the sexual appetite of the female is as great or greater than the male's, a conception that probably reaches back to the Cuna Earth Mother, and that therefore part of the responsibility for successful sex belongs to her. Because of the ambivalence which persists in this conception, one suspects that behind the silence of the sex film audience lies fear. Patently powerful women "drain" men as they demand satisfaction. The inadequacy of the males is painful. In literary pornography, because it is not seen, only imagined, the male can dominate and humiliate. Dominance is much more difficult to render pictorially. (Things might be different if producers learned to splice and edit, but most stags are shot continuously from a single can of film.) For instance, consider (heterosexual) fellatio. The incidence of fellatio has risen from something less than 50 percent in stags of the thirties, forties and fifties to nearly a 100 percent in those of the seventies.

In part, obviously, this rise has resulted from relaxed sexual taboos; oral sex is now a practice endorsed by nearly everyone but the PTA. Then, too, in mass-produced pornography, what else is there for the models to do? Probably also the increase reflects modern male fears of assertive, confident women. On the one hand, fellatio can be considered degrading to the female, forced to kneel and submit to her partner, which gratifies the male ego. On the other hand, fellatio is symbolically dangerous because of the implied possibility of castration. She could bite. I have watched patrons wince at an overzealous actress. There might also be latent homo-sexual suggestion here, since fellatio is often associated with homoeroticism, which opens up a real can of worms, if you will pardon the phallicism. In this regard, incidentally, the isolation of the men in the theaters from one another prevents the comforting camaraderie of the fraternity or American Legion smoker with its undertones of homosexuality. The laughter and shouting at these events are defensive, rather like the old street-corner gatherings where boys stood around giggling and swapping lies of sexual prowess. Without this kind of relief in the theaters, fears are aggravated, and the "subjugation" of women does not convince.

The films can hardly be satisfying in another respect. They lack the ingredient of sin, the weight of guilt which has in the past given pornography its piquancy. Nudity and intercourse in themselves are not necessarily arousing. What is required to make them so is what Sontag calls "moral resonance." Earlier stag producers achieved a certain sly furtiveness by dressing the males in black socks and masks. Now randy burglars are out. Nobody winks or leers. There is very little of the clandestine in the modern stag film, no conscious-ness of treading on public taboo or personal sensibility. The whole business has become so matter-of-fact, so bereft of humor or even corrupted glamour, that at times one might as well be observing carcasses on a meat rack. At least the old skin flicks spiced things by a "Tsk! Tsk! Look what these naughty people are doing!" attitude of pretended shame at the silly knee bends and push-ups of naked amazons.

That obscenity is in the mind of the beholder has long been an article of liberal faith, but no one really believed it. Perhaps the lack of moral resonance is healthy, a logical extension of the "to the pure all things are pure" argument. Yet it must be bewildering—and dull—to middle-aged viewers raised in the school of inhibitions. It is hard to rid one's self of awe at sex, or the expectation that others will be awed too. Almost gone are the days when an audience could bask in the delicious sense of transgression emanating from the screen or tremble in anticipation of a policeman's bellowing, "This is a raid!"

It is no accident that the stag performers are almost exclusively hippie types, for the sexual rhetoric and ethics of the young have carried the day. The popularity of casual sex and the growing acceptance of sex without guilt by other segments of society have been boons for the stag producer. He has only to hire talent from a large pool of willing young people and make his product available—he need not any longer bother attempting to appeal to prurient interests while disguising his intent. Poor Ralph Ginzburg is at last going to prison for doing just that. Adolescent though he may have been at times, at least Ginzburg had imagination. Today's pornographers have none.

This impoverished imagination manifests itself in a moral blandness which may or may not reflect the tastes of the viewers. So far, sexual practices in films are not particularly vile or guilt-inspiring, by liberal standards. Two people or a dozen make love pretty much like any other couple or group. The positions and combinations, unless the participants are gymnasts or adept in the *Kama Sutra*, are not infinite. Their intercourse is of a depressing conventionality. The imagination of most stag producers rests heavily on a solid Western preference for the missionary position. Parenthetically, by the way, Americans historically have demonstrated little pornographic imagination. The United States has had no "Other Victorian" period such as that English era chronicled by Steven Marcus, let alone an erotic genius like de Sade. Among the classics of our literature one finds only a few essays on flatulence and the equally scatological *1601* by Mark Twain; Frank Harris might qualify, were he not a transplanted Briton; Henry Miller's work is purgative rather than pornographic. There may be some hope in Terry Southern's comedies and in the cartoons of R. Crumb; the work of these two resembles pornography current in socialist countries, in which bureaucrats get buggered, or the older type prevalent in church-oppressed countries, in which nuns are sexually defiled or priests pictured as satyrs. Sex is a great leveler.

In Times Square films, oral sex is universal and group sex has become more than a novelty, but overt sadism, masochism and bestiality are rare, dildos and other props are only now making widespread appearance, male homosexuality is confined to theaters specializing in it, and weird fetishism and pedophilia are virtually nonexistent. This picture could change, of course, contingent primarily on the ingenuity of the Californians.* Barring new developments, for that added fillip patrons must bring their own

* A year after this essay was written, West Coast producers have indeed moved into anal intercourse, urolagnia, caprophagia and bestiality, while still resisting out-and-out sadism. Such films have been introduced tentatively and in limited quantity to Times Square. New York audiences viewing them react restively.

guilt. They do. While hardly anyone turns up his coat collar any more, men do not dawdle as they enter, and many case the street first in case they might be spotted sampling the mysteries.

Except that "mystery" does not quite apply here. Critics deplore the lack of mystery, of anything's being hidden in the clinical renderings of a human activity they think should be shrouded. They point out that graphic frankness deprives the sex of eroticism. A more stimulating film sequence, for instance, is Bibi Andersson's monologue in Bergman's *Persona*, during which she recalls a group sex encounter. The account of this persona leaves audiences gasping. The technique here is that of literary pornography; there is no visual representation of the acts she remembers so vividly, and none is needed. The camera focusses on her face, and because Miss Andersson is an excellent actress, the scene is charged with eroticism and emotion as she tells her story; actual sex would only detract from the moment. But while the stag patrons may miss the more complete dimensionality of such scenes, they seem also to require specific stimulus into which, conversely, emotion could only intrude and prevent their own fantasy. This is probably why prostitution, strip shows and pornography continue to flourish in spite of the new sexual freedom. When the level of general sexual stimulation in a society is high, as no one familiar with modern advertising, television or fashions would deny, then stimulation needs to be made specific, if only on occasion. Fantasies cannot always be manufactured out of whole cloth.

If the stag films are so depressing, why are they well attended? For first-timers, the answer is easy enough. The stuff is stimulating (to liberals, at least, says the President's Commission) in short doses, because it caters to the voyeurism inherent in most of us. In New York, in particular, voyeurism is almost a way of life—witness the binoculars beside apartment windows. Perhaps the isolation of citizens in the city encourages them to violate the privacy of others. After they have indulged a natural curiosity, however, why do the regulars risk boredom by returning again and again?

I think that the sex in the films fills a vacuum. The sex for some is immediate, hence the masturbation in the theater. For others it generates fantasies which can then be grafted on to real sexual experiences or take their place. Does this mean that the porno parlors in Times Square prefigure the feelies of Huxley's *Brave New World*? Well, yes, except that Huxley's patrons enjoy the inestimable advantage of being tuned in sensually to the action on screen by electrodes, which New Yorkers do not, and Huxley's feelies successfully create an aura of romanticism, which New York's do not. Does this also mean that such films reflect, as Huxley meant to imply, a divorce of sex from human warmth and personal contact? Perhaps, though it would be erroneous and unfair to single out pornography as cause rather than symptom of growing dehumanization in our society. It is well to remember that pornography has flourished in eras we call humanistic without observable deleterious effects.

And, lest we champion the supremacy of real sex over fantasy too quickly, we should remember as well that whatever else sex may involve, and that is considerable, it includes fantasy. This should be so obvious as not to need stating. Sex is in part mental, in spite of D.H. Lawrence's reactionary hopes to the contrary, and not just gonadal. The gonads provide a necessary force, but emotional and intellectual energy carry it forward. When one makes love to someone else (and the else says it all—the other, the object), one really makes love to a matrix of complex experiences, a continuum, as it were, of past sexual feelings and associations, present sensations and momentary anticipations, perhaps centered around the partner, perhaps not. The obvious analogy is that we have a kind of sexual movie reel inside our consciousness—an idea derided without explanation by so astute a sexual theorist and practitioner as Gore Vidal in his otherwise admirable hatchet-job on *Everything You Always Wanted to Know About Sex But Were Afraid to Ask* in the *New York Review of Books*. This personal projector may play back impressions of someone seen on the street—like the pretty object I mentioned earlier. The person being made love to is not thereby necessarily excluded. Or the projector can draw on fantasy from whatever source it can, and that includes pornography. The sex in the films may be impersonal, for all the miserable plots, the beauty of the women and the romantic music, but it does not stay that way for the patron. The viewer's mind uses the scenes as grist for his own imagination. To fantasize sexually is not to be crippled psychologically. On the contrary, accumulated fantasies contribute to a richer sex life. One could go further. Fantasy is the rock on which a stable marriage stands, since it permits mental adultery while preserving monogamy.

Fantasized sex, a critic would say, is autoerotic and masturbatory, and consequently bad. This viewpoint overlooks an important fact: sex, even that between two people, is masturbatory in one of its aspects. In his outburst against pornography in the *New York Times Magazine*, Irving Kristol calls masturbation "adolescent." This is an improvement on saying that it causes madness or pimples, but is still an insult to us all. Ask an ardent feminist how she achieves that clitoral orgasm. As has often been remarked, love and sex are frequently narcissistic. One perceives a reflection of one's self in the partner or makes love to a projected image. The nature of sex is ambiguous: it is both creative and destructive. Love is the flip side of hate, as the adage has it. If sex be ideally defined as an attempt to merge with another, in one sense it requires a willingness to lower the barriers to one's self, and in a similar sense, to break through the barriers of the other's self. This penetration or violation of the other's self is fully as destructive as the willingness to let one's own self be shattered is creative. For a fanciful example, think of Spock's orgasmic mind-probes on the reruns of "Star Trek."

The total fusion of two selves is probably only rarely if ever achieved. The legacy of the greatest and most misunderstood pornographer, the melancholy Marquis de Sade, is a reminder that whatever you do to another, love or hate him, torture or kill him, you can never break through his self—or your own. In any case, the attempt calls for enormous emotional and intellectual energy. For this reason, autoerotic, masturbatory intercourse may at times be an acceptable alternative to ideal sex. It is less debilitating. When the ideal does happen, love or deep personal involvement with the other person cuts through fantasy and renders it superfluous. To expect the earth to move every time, like a Hemingway heroine, is unrealistic. (In choosing sympathetic literary heroines, I side with Lady Chatterley when she says sex is faintly ridiculous.) That would be like constantly trying to reach the simultaneous orgasm the marriage counselors used to prattle about; it's a lovely idea, but when was the last time you made it? Or to put it another way, intercourse is like our modern narcissistic dance: it's nice if you groove with your partner while you frug, but it's still fun even if you don't.

While fantasy can take the place of real sex, it can never wholly supplant it, except, I suppose in psychotics. But the men in the pornography theaters are our next-door neighbors and not certifiably insane. "No, it isn't real," admitted a visitor to the Eros I on Eighth Avenue. Then why had he come? "I wish it was." The impulse seems to be simple wish fulfillment, a desire to experience a pure, physically raw sex unfettered by responsibility. Romantic and adolescent perhaps; dangerous, no. The patrons know what they are watching is artifice and illusion, that real sex involves responsibilities, respect for others, and emotional and intellectual involvement. They have fled those bonds in coming to the theaters, and they know they will return to them.

Distinctions must be made, of course. The stags are not necessarily representative of all pornography, and they may be condemned individually on grounds of morality, taste or art. But the pornographic film at this juncture is probably no more sinister than the related sexual phenomena of our time, like communal marriage, gay liberation or unisex fashions. Besides, the films can boast of one advantage. As one patron put it after watching two hours of predominantly long-haired performers at the Tivoli: "You sure can tell the boys from the girls."

8 The Pleasures of Commodity, or How to Make the World Safe for Pornography

Peter Michelson

After being "five times fairly lost in supreme rapture" with the fair Louisa, James Boswell in his *London Journal* admits to being "somewhat proud of my performance." Louisa, having greater moral sensibility than temperance, "said it was what there was no just reason to be proud of . . . . She said it was what we had in common with the beasts. I said no. For we had it highly improved by the pleasures of sentiment." Even in the sack, Bozy and Louisa are deep in the usual sex bag: they deny what both *need, want* and *do*. This mechanism of denial is itself worth pursuing because it connects us with the psychic process of displacement whereby sexual energy is transformed or sublimated. Advertising has for a good while recognized this, and when it drapes juicy ladies or chiseled he-men about a Dodge Polara, Aerosal shaving cream or Maidenform bras, it woos our eager displacement apparatus to gratify sexual pressures by transforming them to less "dangerous" analogues. So, rather than loosing our lust on the world, we acquire a new car—another kind of potency. But as this advertising technique has developed (largely since World War II and the popularizing of depth psychology), its

Reprinted from *The Antioch Review*, vol. 24, no. 1, by permission of the editors and the author. This essay also appears in *The Aesthetics of Pornography* published by Herder and Herder, 1971.

profound materialism has been not only obvious but also disturbing. For a Judeo-Christian society, no matter how materialistic its practices, cannot *morally* justify them. The options are clear enough, therefore: change the morality or change the practice. Which means, realistically, that there are no options and we are confronted with time-honored sophistic problem of moral revisionism.

If, as Boswell's anecdote suggests, we will not change our habits; and if, as poor Louisa's lamentation suggests, we feel morally obliged to refute our bestiality, then we must understand how our intractable beastly behavior gets sublimated to civilized virtue, and we make peace with our nastiness. History, here in the guise of Boswell, shows us—our naturalistic selves have been, over the past 300 years or so, "highly improved by the pleasures of sentiment." Since Boswell's time, sentiment figures so centrally in our cultural tradition that it may be said to be the primary phenomenon in what Leslie Fiedler calls "the Break-through" to modernity.

In its largest generic sense, sentiment refers to emotion, and the capacity for emotion, as Boswell says, signifies those higher functions of mind by which we distinguish ourselves from beasts. It was used as an analogue of *affection, feeling, belief* and *sensation* by such eighteenth-century philosophers as Hume, who were exploring the philosophy of consciousness and interior reality. But the scientific exploration of such psychic machinery required a more sophisticated clinical context, and the more popular and culturally significant use of the term was Laurence Sterne's moral elevation of humane *feelings* over the pompous absurdities of *reason*. Toby Shandy, the moral hero of *Tristram Shandy*, transformed the western heroic concept irrevocably when he, rather than killing, liberated a fly out the window saying, "This world is surely wide enough to hold both thee and me."

This fictional incident is very likely the source of that epithet which signifies for us the highest refinement of human sensibility— and Toby Shandy is thereby the sentimental model for Albert Schweitzer; neither of them would hurt a fly. Before Toby, this richly foibled and often fuddled image of human sensibility, Sterne routs the pretensions of reason and dialectic, represented in such characters as Walter Shandy, who regulates his connubial "obliga-tions" by machine—the first Sunday of each month, after he winds the clock. In articulating this dialectical opposition, *Tristram Shandy* may be the most profound and optimistic statement of humanism possible. It celebrates imagistically what theologians, philosophers and psychologists have sought mechanistically. It celebrates mind, that elusive touchstone, the thing that makes men men. Thus the ubiquitous human urge for univocal morality was provided with the univocal image of moral virtue—the man of feeling. Moral needs were better served by an idealistic synthesis than by the disconcerting diffusion of scientific analysis. Sentiment, therefore, came to signify the apex of human virtue.

In the hands of an existentialist like Sterne, such a theory was good, but it did not everywhere have such integrity. Samuel Richardson, for example, extracted sentiment from its existential roots and made it the rhetorical servant of a middle-class ethos. For Sterne, sentiment—the capacity for feeling—was its own standard of human being. It assumed the status of a moral paradigm. But, while Sterne's sentimentality argued the philosophical case for moral idealism and its resultant ethical charity, Richardson's was made a tactical weapon of liberation for the culturally emerging business class. Thus sentiment was accommodated to commerce. What, after all, beside a nicely turned haunch, has Pamela to "sell" Squire B.—other than those hundreds of pages of high sentiment which punctuate the narrative of her heroic preservation of virginity? And a well-turned virgin haunch, as Fanny Hill's or Moll Flander's narratives tell us, was easily obtainable for any squire of the realm. So, though fine feeling has sexy packaging, it is nevertheless sentiment that is for sale. And Richardson makes the Squire buy his dearly. It cost him, and all his kind, a way of life. The battle between Pamela and Squire B. signifies a historic moment of natural selection in the cultural evolution of the West. The business ethos, in England for example, having shut down the theaters and having harnessed kings, had finally worked its way into art. It was not, of course, a revolutionary moment. The business ethos had no particular interest in a better world and certainly had no strategy to achieve one. It didn't want an end to aristocracy; it wanted to *be* the aristocracy. The profit principle (not to be confused with the greed principle, which is an unequivocal vice even in the business ethos), therefore, needed elevation in the cosmic moral scheme. When Pamela marries "up" into aristocracy, she carries the middle class and all its baggage (servants, peasants, etc.) with her. It was the best deal Business ever made: exchanging what all men had a lot of—sentiment—for what up to that time most men had very little of—value. With Richardson, sentiment is transformed into commodity, and commodity, by his association, is transformed into moral virtue. Ultimately, in our time, it becomes *the* moral virtue. What's good for business is good for man.

KNOW YOUR NOSE, PICK YOUR FRIENDS

The way, therefore, to make the world safe for pornography is to show it that sex is good for business. It sounds simpler, however, than it is. It won't do, for example, to say that sex *is* good business, because one becomes, then, a greedy sex-monger. Greed and profit, remember, are not the same. Profit is good; greed is bad. How much profit is equivalent to greed? "If you don't like it here go back to Russia where you came from." Besides, we're enlightened now and we know that sex is bad only when it's *dirty*. How does sex get dirty? "It gets dirty when there's too much of it." How much is . . . ? "Well, you don't have to have your nose rubbed in it to know about it." Couldn't those with sensitive noses decline the gambit? "It would be nice to think that people knew their own noses, but it's not realistic." What we must do, in short, is to clean up sex and show that, though it's perfectly businesslike, it isn't tainted by filthy lucre. For however much we may think that money is its own reward, we'll not risk its spoilation. Help us, ye gods, to keep money clean.

Playboy magazine, perhaps more than any other single pop culture phenomenon, has managed to change sex from a dirty joke into "entertainment served up with humor, sophistication and spice," to purloin a phrase from its original apology. *Playboy* has been a paradigmatic force in making the world safe for pornography, because it has always been careful to use sex for "higher" ends—essentially for the establishment of its fundamental image, the well-heeled Playboy who can and should afford his monthly Playmate. From its beginnings, *Playboy* projected the image of a latter-day (executive *ne* business) man of mode; again from the credo of its first issue, "We like our apartment. We enjoy mixing up cocktails and an hors d'oeuvre or two, putting a little mood music on the phonograph, and inviting a female acquaintance for a quiet discussion on Picasso, Nietzsche, jazz, sex." The audience was intended to be, as it has proved to be, "young men-on-the-move" (another *Playboy* PR phrase). It was intended to be and has become a magazine for the young executive and, more inclusively, for the hopeful fantasies of aspiring pre-executives. But, more than anything else, it is a monumental pop celebration of commodity.

Playboy has grown, in 15 years, from the twice-hocked furniture of its founder Hugh Hefner's apartment to a $54 million "empire," as we are told in the 1968 financial report from *Playboy*; and we are reminded by Hefner—president of the enterprise—that, being a private corporation, *Playboy* is not required to make a public financial statement. He does it, presumably therefore, because he *wants* to. And if there is any question about *Playboy's* most important product, one need only check its own public relations brochures. The introductory paragraph of one, the cover of which shows the new Playboy Building backed up by Chicago's Gold Coast, goes thus:

> Topped with the world's largest aviation beacon, the Playboy Building at 919 North Michigan Avenue in Chicago is today the headquarters of one of the brightest lights in the world of entertainment for men—*Playboy*. A landmark since its construction, the building, formerly called the Palmolive Building, is a fitting symbol for a magazine and subsidiary enterprises which have witnessed lightning success during the past decade.

One might note here that, after *Playboy* moved out of its old Ohio Street buildings, it took the United States Post Office and the Museum of Contemporary Art to fill its "shoes." Another blurb, entitled "The Playboy Empire," begins thus:

> The $12,000,000 Playboy Club-Hotel at Lake Geneva, Wis., represents one of the most ambitious projects in the history of the Playboy empire. It is the 19th Club in the international chain which includes locations in Atlanta, Baltimore, Boston, Chicago, Cincinnati, Denver, Detroit, Kansas City, Los Angeles, Miami, New Orleans, New York, Phoenix, St. Louis and San Francisco, plus Montreal and London. It is the second Club-Hotel to be

operated by Playboy Clubs International, Inc.—the first one debuted in Ocho Rios, Jamaica, in January 1965. Today the Playboy Clubs have some 650,000 keyholders and additional Clubs and Club-Hotels are now being planned for areas including New Jersey, Southern Spain, San Juan and Acapulco.

So Alpha, and so Omega:

> As *Playboy* grew, so did its related enterprises. A Playboy Jazz Festival featuring practically every name jazz artist was held in Chicago in 1959. It was the largest in history, with 68,000 people attending. Hefner conceived and produced Playboy's Penthouse, a syndicated latenight television show. A second TV show, Playboy After Dark, is now being shown. Playboy Press, the book division, and VIP, the magazine for keyholders, were organized. The Playboy Theater, specializing in outstanding U.S. and foreign films, opened in Chicago; Playboy Models was set up; and Playboy Products, marketing apparel and gifts, was initiated.
>
> With the continuous growth of the Playboy empire, plans are now under way for a major expansion into the motion picture and television industries.

Commodity is the beginning and the end.

But profit is really the simplest and even most predictable of *Playboy's* achievements. More complex and more culturally significant is the cause of that awful success—*Playboy's* adroit use of sex. So adroit has it been, in fact, that one has the uncomfortable feeling that Pamela, our old flame, has not done with us yet. One feels, in the image of the Playboy, that Pamela's Squire has been mightily domesticated (and calling domesticity "urbanity" or "sophistication" doesn't relieve the anxiety). Yet again from the original credo: "Most of today's 'magazines for men' spend all their time out-of-doors—thrashing through thorny thickets or splashing about in fast flowing streams. We'll be out there too, occasionally, but we don't mind telling you in advance—we plan on spending most of our time inside. We like our apartment." Etc. The rest we've already seen. And not the Playboy's broadest, knowingest wink, not even a desperate psychedelic discussion of Picasso, Nietzsche, jazz *and* sex all at the same time can dissuade us that Pamela hasn't stuffed that velvet smoking jacket and silk scarf with the carcass of her long-tamed Squire, put a highball in his hand, a cigarette holder in his teeth, an impressionistic nude on his paneled den wall and called him PLAYBOY. At last Pamela and the Squire are on equal terms (a fact which *Cosmopolitan* magazine has recently recognized, much to its own advantage), and Pamela, our vital parts firmly in her grip, demands, "and now, Monsieur, your wallet." Hemingway warned us, but we wouldn't listen.

The first thing, then, that *Playboy* has done by equating sex with profit is to sublimate it from its fearful psychic depths to the heights of that "fitting symbol formerly called the Palmolive Building." And, by being made into capital, sex has been psychologically neutralized. It has become a contemporary (and historical) community standard: it has proved profitable and therefore socially redeeming. Concomitant, of course, with *Playboy's* showing cause for sex has been its cleaning up of the image of sex. Attributing the observation to a Kinsey Institute authority, Nat Lehrman, a senior editor of the magazine, says that *Playboy* has raised sex to respectability, made it fit matter for coffee conversation (along, remember, with Picasso, Nietzsche and jazz). This is probably true, but in the beginning *Playboy* had some difficulty getting launched into the antiseptic sex imagery which is its present-day hallmark.

SEX IN THE STONE AGE

The early foldouts, called "Playboy's Eyeful" then, were standard lowgrade skin pictures. Nor did they have the now-familiar personality sketch accompanying them. It took three years for the Playmate to find the girl-next-door quality that is now current. *Playboy* legend has it that one Janet Pilgrim, a circulation secretary whose name is still on the masthead, went to Hefner requesting a new typewriter. He told her she'd have to pose nude for it, à la Lady Godiva. She did, and the Playmate image was born—bright eyed, bushy-(I beg your pardon) tailed and clean, clean, clean. Until this time (about 1955), as one editor acknowledges, the magazine had been obliged to use either "hookers" or professional models for its foldouts and the image, except, perhaps, for the celebrated Marilyn Monroe calendar nudes featured in the first issue, was more sleazy than piquant. And, though Jack Kessie, *Playboy's* managing editor, claims that the sublimated *Playboy* image we can now perceive was planned from the magazine's inception, sleaziness pretty much describes its character for at least the first four or five issues. Such photographic features, for example, as "Strip Quiz," a Paris bistro strip routine, or Beaux-Arts Ball, a portfolio of prurient snapshots, or illustrations of criminal assault, indicate something of the imagistic tone of the first three issues. The fourth issue, though, presented two marvelously prophetic features. One is called "Sex Sells a Shirt," and simply shows a girl taking off her clothes— including, of course, her shirt. The text, in its banal way, discusses sex and merchandising for a few column inches. It intends to say nothing, and it does. Nevertheless, this was the first public presentation of the profit formula on which *Playboy* was to ride to fiscal glory. The other feature is billed as "A Pictorial History of Surgery," and it is essentially a vehicle for showing naked ladies, pictured in the context of medical history. Sex, thus, is both a delight and an instruction, satisfying not only classical poetics, but, also more importantly, providing the proper scholarly elevation for an essentially base subject. This kind of augmentation was also to become an editorial staple of the magazine's success formula.

Today's Playmate, through which the *Playboy* Image is projected, is the scrupulously antiseptic incarnation of almost virginal contemporary community standards, an occasional lapse into prostitution notwithstanding. She even has sufficient social redemption potential to be rented out to colleges over football weekends. At which, to show her healthy respect for the Working Man (or Labor, The People, or the Dollar—as you prefer), she will charge overtime for conversation above and beyond an eight-hour day. Playmates, lest their title be misleading, do not indulge in idle pleasure for its own sake; the meter on these puritanic taxi-dancers is always running. And well it might, for, Nathanael West to the contrary, a clean young girl is always worth more than a clean old man—especially on a college football weekend at an all-male college.

Especially, too, when one notes that *Playboy's* notion of its editorial "responsibility" is to serve, according to managing editor Jack Kessie, as a guidebook to the good life for the young, university-educated man. The vocabulary *Playboy* editors use to describe their magazine and its goals reads like Dr. Johnson's own lexicon of esthetic terms: Balance, Proportion, Taste, Elegance, Imagination, Wit, etc. And it is easily acknowledged that *Playboy* is the most balanced, tasteful, elegant, imaginative and witty skin book in the business. (By "skin book" I don't, of course, mean *skin* itself, but rather, skin sublimated to *capital*. In this sense, one understands that *Playboy* is the more honestly pornographic analogue of *Fortune* magazine—though it is less honest, and therefore more obscene, than the *Evergreen Review*. So much for the periodical scheme of things.) Of all the terms in the *Playboy* vocabulary, "taste" is perhaps the most significant. "We present sex," says Kessie, "in proportion to its overall degree of importance in man's life." This is true, but it's not the whole truth. In modesty, Kessie ignores the fact that, in making sex a respectable thing and in demonstrating its commodity quotient, *Playboy* expanded the popular horizons for sex's overall degree of importance in man's life. What he means by *Playboy's* tastefulness is that, *visually*, there is no more sex showing than there should be.

This is elaborated in Kessie's notion of *Playboy's* editorial contribution to the culture. *Playboy* was, he says, the first to assert not only nudity and sex, but also something else—a well-rounded view of the good life. He points out, for instance, that if *Playboy* "advocates materialism, so do we advocate other things—civil rights, for example." And what, after all, is the end of Taste (not to mention Balance, Proportion, Imagination and Wit), if not to give a well-rounded view of the good life? The *Playboy* editors are tastefully aware that "too much" of anything—such as civil rights activism, or an eyeful of genitals—is bad for standards, of both business and taste. Thus the Playmate has breasts with glamorized nipples, a groin without pubic hair, vagina, or urinary tract, and a backside without anus. She has feminine shape without female, or for that matter even human, function. She is not made for coitus or procreation or motherhood. She has body without consequence. So when it comes to nakedness (absolute nudity), as distinguished from "tasteful" nudity—guess whose taste: yes, Pamela's—the "cleanliness" of sex is threatened, and so, therefore, is business: "Our standard has been taste," Kessie says, "and of course there is the risk of legal action. We like to think of ourselves as trend setters, but here we have, for business and other reasons, to wait for society to know its own mind." So, despite the PR assurance that "it was

Hefner's unorthodox belief (a belief he still holds today) that editing a magazine should be a personal matter, that the primary criteria for choosing content should be the editor's own taste and judgment rather than the preferences of a preconceived audience," there is in fact a preconceived audience—the young, university-educated man— and the taste of the *Playboy* editors has long since been determined by the sublime cultural marriage of commodity and morality. And *Playboy*, one of the massive offsprings of that union, has as much as any other cultural product reaffirmed the fact that its parents are indeed of one flesh.

The effect of sentimentalizing materialism—i.e. of giving it the moral value of an ideal—is to transform the natural world into a pop art toy which exists for the Playboy's *well-earned* amusement. After all, he brings home the fatback. (Nor can we, in honesty, be condescending to the *Playboy* Image, for it symbolizes all of us, the whole consumer culture on which our egos, economics and politics depend.) Therefore, all things are seen in the context of *Playboy's* peculiar ethos of amusement. Women, particularly, are *objets d'art*, created for the Playboy fantasy by the photographer's air brush and in the Image of *Playboy* by the sketch writer's Playmate-as-home-town-girl fictions. The mere idea of his Playmate menstruating, is enough to make the Playboy impotent. The Playmate is the Playboy's Beatrice. She does not function, she *is*. Like Shakespeare's Cleopatra, age cannot wither nor custom stale her infinite variety; Like Keats's still unravished bride of quietness, she is forever warm and still to be enjoyed, forever panting and young, far above the stinking breath of human passion, and with *her* we avoid after-sex hangover, that "heart high-sorrowful and cloy'd/ burning forehead, and a parching tongue." The Playmate is not an object of sex. She is an object of art, low art to be sure, but art nonetheless. And who put her on that pedestal and on the mantelpiece of our den? Pamela, we smell a rat.

MAKING IT, SPENDING IT, LYING IN IT

Playboy's pornography consists in its transformation of female human beings into Playmates and bunnies, erotic art objects designed to titillate the sexual sense and then sublimate it into spending money (in the Playboy Clubs, hopefully), or into fantasizing about spending money (in *Playboy* magazine). The greenback dollar, in the *Playboy* ethos (and the *Playboy* ethos is fundamentally the capitalistic ethos) is the sublimated analogue of sperm. Money and the making of it is the masculine symbol in this cultural climate. Spending money, therefore, is the masculine privilege. It is no accident that the verb *spend* is a common pornographic metaphor for the male orgasm. And since, in a capitalistic democracy, money can buy everything, women are, as they have really always been, a commodity; and all commodity is available to him who has the power to take it. Thus the power to buy becomes, in the capitalistic ethos, the sign of sexual power. So the world is sexualized, sex is commercialized, and we have a pornographic image of the world—an idealized, socially lionized metaphor of prostitution as a way of life. And that, traditionally, is what pornography is—the literature of whores and whoring.

But then this process is rather subtle, and one is seldom conscious of himself as the Playboy. Nor does one think of his woman as a whore. So long as he has Playmates, Bunnies and their analogues, the movie sex stars (who of late have been knocking one another's knockers for the chance to appear nude on *Playboy's* pages), he needn't think of her—if he thinks of her at all, his mind being filled with more enticing fantasies—as such, or as property. She may continue in her time-honored rhetorical role of the sometimes dull, sometimes bright but always slightly irrelevant companion. So it is a curiously lonely bed that Pamela after all has made and in which she must lie. But she is not through yet. Having established her ethos, she labors now to imprint her personality. She has before her, therefore, the task of creating a feminine pornography.

Feminine pornography requires a fastasy structure in which women are invited, as women, to be sexually excited. For the socially redemptive pornography we have been considering, this means an alteration of the sex-profit nexus. Theoretically, it needs a shift from money and expenditure as an exclusively masculine symbology. Imagistically, it involves a transition from the *Playboy* cultural mode to that of the Career Girl. The basic model, of course, is still that of *Playboy*. The emphasis is merely reversed—from male cultural potency to female cultural potency. The woman's magazine most perspicacious in recognizing the *Playboy* mode and in exploiting it for its own audience and purposes is the new *Cosmopolitan*. *Cosmopolitan* has only recently tapped into the pornographic tradition we have been considering. And, coming from its own imperial stock—the Hearst syndicate—*Cosmo* is not a pornographic empire builder, but is merely capitalizing on the female potential of the ethos *Playboy* had long since stabilized. Thus, although *Cosmopolitan* has its own cultural significance as a feminist pornographic voice, it isn't as historically significant as *Playboy*.

Cosmopolitan emerged from the maze of what William Iverson, in a marvelously witty series of *Playboy* articles—"The Pious Pornographers" (1957 and 1964)—called "the bizarre bulletins on glands, guilt, grief, gynecology and intercourse which are the peculiar specialty of some of America's most widely read sex books—the women's magazines." His general thesis is that women's magazines offer sentimentalized sexual voyeurism which takes the form of a "sick, sad sex approach to the problem of getting a [man to drop his pants or a woman to lift her skirts], so that a million-odd women [can] get a few vicarious kicks from 'playing doctor.' " Here is part of what Iverson calls a "sampler" of prurient ladies' home preoccupations:

> "That inverted nipple seems better than it was," the doctor told Evelyn Ayres after he had concluded his usual examination. "Have you been pulling it out gently several times, morning and night, the way Mary Ann showed you?"
>
> "Yes, Doctor. . . . "
>
> "I believe I told you that there is a difference of medical opinion as to the best method of toughening the nipples. . . . "
>
> "Your uterus is small and firm. . . . Your breasts show no signs of pregnancy engorgement. . . ."
>
> "This was an atavistic dream of a man and woman alone in a Garden of Eden, perfumed, flecked with butterflies. A red petal fell from the African tulip tree. . . . "
>
> "Oh, Bill," she whispered, half-choking. . . . Then he kissed her. Her lips were like orchids—crumpled, soft, cool, moist. They clung to his. Her arms were around his neck. . . .
>
> The range of frequency in intercourse for couples of 25 to 35 is great. A few have intercourse as often as 20 to 30 times a

month; others only twice a month. For the majority, the average is 2 or 3 times a week. . . .

"If he has his way, it would be every night. It isn't that I'm a frigid wife, for I am not. Once a week (which is my preference) I respond readily. . . . "

Q. What about the forceful technique of making love? Do you think that women prefer it?

A. Sometimes. Many couples think that variation in sex simply means a different position. Variation can also mean a different psychological attitude. If a man surprises his wife, spontaneously, on a Sunday afternoon, or in a different room of the house, aggressively taking her, this type of approach can make their relationship enormously more erotic. . . .

"He said I was cold, and I said he was oversexed. Once he even wanted to make love at lunchtime!"

"Of course it's awfully hard not to. You both want to so much. Sure, Jim used to get fresh with me now and then, but I'd always handle it by saying 'Look at the television' or something. But once I thought, Oh, why not? . . . "

"The hymen is a thin little membrane, Phyllis, stretched across the lower end of the vagina. . . . "

"Am I afraid to use mine?" I said.

"No," George said, "like I say, you're naturally lascivious. You use your pelvis. . . . "

I did a little bump.

"But I wouldn't go too far," George said. I could feel from his neck that he was beginning to color.

"Why do men want sex to be like a burlesque show? Why can't they realize that it is a solemn thing?"

"And . . . well, one night I drank a can of beer in the car with him, and it happened again. . . . I just couldn't help it. After all, girls want it just as much as boys do, don't they?"

In summing up, Iverson recalls:

the curious saga of Evelyn Ayres, troubled heroine of another stirring episode of "Tell Me, Doctor," the *Ladies' Home Journal's* long-playing feature on clinical sex and gynecological horrors. Years of familiarity with its format of fear, disaster and medical

salvation had led me to think of this ever expanding anthology of
female malfunctions as a kind of cryptoprurient *Memoirs of a
Woman of Misery*, in which Evelyn Ayres now starred as the
anxiety-fraught Fanny Hill of Breast Feeding.

This is a latter-day version of that same morbid sentimentalizing of
the faithful servant woman (not Moll Flanders, but Pamela), as she
resists the forces of aristocratic evil and guile that Richardson
exploited for his social class in the eighteenth century. The heroine
is essentially the same, but, with her social and even economic
success in molding the Squire into the Playboy, the nature of the
villain has transformed itself into neurosis, obstetrics and gynecology, things unheard of in Richardson's day. That, if you are not
too particular, is progress. But, being an extension of the
long-familiar soap opera, it is pretty much predictable. And so one
suspects that Iverson's anxiety (*Playboy's* anxiety) is crowding his
condescending wit.

For his real complaint, *Playboy's* complaint, is not that the
women's magazines are *pornographic* (he and *Playboy* know all
about that, although such language makes them nervous, being bad
for business), rather it is that they are *obscene*. Nor is his objection
to their piety (sentimentality); he and *Playboy* know all about that
too, as we have seen. The problem is that these magazines undermine
the Playmate image. Think of the Playmate. Imagine her with
inverted nipples! Or menstruating! Or, worse still, imagine her being
sexually unsatisfied *after* a bout with the prodigiously phallic
Playboy!; smearing her neuroses, obstetrics and gynecology all over
the hard-earned sanctuary of his den. Not only that, as if it weren't
enough, they also undermine the *Playboy* image. Iverson's citation
of the following rebuke of vertigial "Nineteenth-century Puritanism"
is revealing in this regard:

All shapes and varieties of marital anguish were laid squarely at
the door of the clumsy husband. It was the man, the marriage
manuals unanimously declared, who was responsible for success in
sex, and equally responsible for its failure. For the enlightened
readers of the manuals, making love became a kind of
challenge. . . .

Frequently couples spent so much time worrying about

whether their technique was right, whether their climaxes occurred simultaneously, as the book said they should, whether the wife really had an orgasm, that they lost all the meaning of marital intercourse, not to mention the pleasure. . . .

"Pleasure" was a word that the ladies' books had seldom mentioned in connection with sex, and T.F. James' reference to it came as a welcome surprise.

Iverson argues, though with more clever outrage than analytical energy, for a "recognition of the need for greater sexual responsibility in women . . . [to] reduce the impossible number of restrictions . . . imposed upon the sexual deportment of the American male." The *Playboy* spokesman is annoyed that women, too, want some fun but aren't getting it and are imposing their frustrations on his fantasies. Women, alas, want to *feel* something down there and, alack and alas, they want to feel it more often than men want to make them feel it. *Playboy* may or may not acknowledge the problem. That isn't clear, either from Iverson's articles or from *Playboy* generally. What is clear, however, is that *if* there is a problem, it is a problem for *women*, so *Playboy* lays it discreetly at their door and strides manfully off to a rendevous with mood music on the hi-fi and a quiet discussion of Picasso, Nietzsche, jazz and (still undaunted) sex.

STONED IN THE SEX AGE

Perhaps *Cosmopolitan* got the message, for five months after Iverson's articles had been concluded it appointed Helen Gurley Brown (author of the best-selling *Sex and the Single Girl*) as its editor. *Time*, in March of 1965 (the same month Miss Brown was appointed *Cosmopolitan's* editor), noted the magazine's transition from a "rather bland" publication into a female counterpart of *Playboy*. And in July of 1966, *Newsweek* observed that Helen Gurley Brown had sexed *Cosmopolitan* up, especially in terms of its advertising and the identification of its audience. So *Cosmopolitan's* press noted the terms of its new formula very quickly. *Cosmopolitan*, or more likely the Hearst hierarchy, had recognized how

Playboy was making the world safe for pornography, and it very neatly cut itself in on the sex-profit nexus. It took women out of the home, away from children, housework and suchlike dowdiness, and put them into careers. It imagistically paired up the Playboy with the Cosmopolitan Girl. This advertisement copy defines her, accompanied by the usual photograph of a sleek and sexy career girl: "A girl can do almost anything she wants to, don't you agree. She can tan instead of burn, look sexy but also look like a lady, have a job that PAYS because she's smart and still stay fascinating to men. I've done all these things and thank goodness there's one magazine that seems to understand me—the girl who wants everything out of life. I guess you could say I'm that Cosmopolitan Girl." It also counterpointed its editorial image with that of *Playboy*. If Hugh Hefner, complete with smoking jacket, pipe, hi-fi mood music, girls, quiet conversation, etc., is the *Playboy* incarnate, so is Helen Gurley Brown the complete woman and therefore the Cosmopolitan Girl's ideal tutor. Her New Year greeting for 1969 repudiated the "sick, sad sex approach" with a vengeance:

Happy New Year! I can't even hope 1969 is going to be any good for me personally because 1968 was so great! Are you as superstitious—or fatalistic or something—as I am? I feel no matter where you start from—rich, poor, smart, dumb, beautiful, plain, or whatever—people have their good years and bad years. Mine have been running so good lately . . . marrying David, writing *Sex and the Single Girl*, getting to edit *Cosmopolitan* . . . I'm afraid it may be time for a change! I do think if you put a lot in every day . . . like you're too tired to pick up your dumbbells to do your chest exercises at night because you gave already that day . . . life gets better! Oh, the scruffy years a young girl goes through! In my teens I was at the doctor's three times a week with the worst case of acne you ever saw. Then into the twenties with different doctors . . . to cure all the psychosomatic illnesses brought on by terrible love affairs! Things only began to get better in my thirties and now (forties) I think is the best time of all. Honest! I can't help but try to impose my philosophies on you, of course, through the pages of *Cosmopolitan*, to tell you that if you hang in there and give everything you've got—yes, that

means self-discipline and having ambition—every day the rewards
can be scintillating, notwithstanding a 'bad year' that creeps in
now and then.

During the tenth scintillating month of 1968, I flew to Paris
for the weekend to go to a party (Darryl Zanuck's gala for
Maxim's seventy-fifth birthday and the world premiere of *A Flea
in Her Ear* plus a fascinating short film, *The World of Fashion*). I
love the sound of Paris for the weekend, don't you?—although I
must admit I spent most of my non-party time flaked out at the
George V trying to grapple with the time change! They help you
in European hotels. The maids close the draperies so you can't tell
whether it's day or night; consequently, you don't have to get up.
The next week . . . off to Shawnee, Oklahoma, to see my mother.
Mother actually lives in Osage, Arkansas (population: 98), but,
since they don't have a landing strip in Osage yet—they only got a
paved street 12 years ago—it was easier to meet at my sister's in
Shawnee. It's good for a girl to go home to her family; no matter
who you think you are in your own world, they see you as the
not-altogether-bright creature you were 30 years ago and manage
not to let you get too uppity. I went shopping at Sears,
Roebuck . . . still the best values anywhere on earth . . . and
visited an AA meeting (no, I'm not a member!). Gad, but they're
fabulous. I can't even give up chocolate-chip cookies for five days
(much less, cocktails), but some of the members I chatted with
had not been off the wagon for 10, 12, 15 years.

What's in *Cosmo* this month? Oh, you know . . . making it . . .
making good . . . making love . . . loving men . . . loving yourself . . . a great mystery novel, short stories . . . the usual birthday
package. I hope you like all of it.

The *Cosmopolitan* "moral" is just the other side of the *Playboy*
coin—every girl/woman can be rich, alluring, sexually satisfying and
satisfied and, if she wishes, happily married.

Cosmopolitan is not through with neurosis, obstetrics and
gynecology, but it says they are no longer occasions for morbidity.
It fosters the fantasy that every woman can be taught what she
doesn't know or be artificially augmented with what nature hasn't
awarded her. A sampler of titles alone gives a fair idea of
Cosmopolitan's vast pornographic curriculum: Why I Wear my False

Eyelashes to Bed; How to Make Your Figure More Perfect; What
Keeps Some Girls from Getting Married and What to Do About It;
How to Turn a Man On; Spectacular Beauties Reveal Their Special
Tricks; Get Him to Marry You with this Revolutionary New Method;
How to Make $100,000 Before You're 35 (Without a Man), and so
on into infinity. There is also, of course, a good deal of voyeuristic
entertainment (and mayhap instruction) in such features as: The
Men Surrounding Jacqueline Kennedy—and the One Who's Winning
Her (they pick wrong); One Young Wife's Shocking Marriage, or
When a Young, Pretty Girl Discovers She's Married a Homosexual
(which subject, incidentally, *Playboy* won't touch); Jim Brown is
Coming on *Strong* and *Big* (and with that pun twister, we may
desist). *Time*, in February of 1968, accused *Cosmopolitan* of
exploiting every sexual anxiety and every sexual fantasy of "the 18
to 34-year-old single women who are not knock-outs, who are
unsure of themselves, who are searching for a man." This is probably
true, though there is no reason to put a lid on at the age of 34.
Voyeurism is for all seasons, and sexes too, for that matter.

But, if one can provide instruction while celebrating commodity,
as both *Playboy* and *Cosmopolitan* do, then one has not only an
acceptable, but even a socially redemptive license for pornographic
fun. The trick, quite simply, is to make it slick. The Cosmopolitan
Girl may not be so slick or affluent as the Playboy, but then she is
15 or so years younger, and it really does seem more difficult to
sublimate gynecological messiness into profitable status than it does
to do so with crudely simple phallic power. Bathyspheres will never
capture our imagination so well as space rockets, and the idea of a
concave skyscraper with a miner's beam at its bottom just won't do.
Nor is the Cosmopolitan Girl so intellectually pretentious as her
Playboy friend. Miss Brown disclaims intellectual ambitions for her
magazine. "We don't want very many cosmic pieces—about space,
the war on poverty, civil rights, etc., but will leave those to more
serious general magazines." But *Playboy*, too, made similar
disclaimers at the beginning: "Affairs of state will be out of our
province. We don't expect to solve any world problems or prove any
great moral truths." So if the Cosmopolitan Girl has not yet devised,
let alone published, a philosophy, she does at least read the poetry
of Dorothy Parker, which the Playboy has never done. And the
future lies, after all, securely ahead. Standing on the troubled shores

of our land, looking neither too far out nor in too deep, haunch by hip, these twin colossi, guarding the divine grace of capital, are beacons telling the world that, with "taste" and a little Yankee ingenuity, all is safe for pornography.

Moral Principles Towards a Definition of the Obscene

Harold J. Gardiner, S.J.

It is all very well to say that an effort should be made to evolve a set of standards about what is or is not obscene. Such standards would safeguard the community and, at the same time, preserve individual freedom and the due process of the law, upon which, to a large measure, the protection of civil society depends. But such safeguards and procedures will only be ephemeral if they do not rest on some permanent basis of moral principle. So, too, must individual freedom, if it is not to be protected today and endangered tomorrow, find its stability in the moral basis of the dignity of man.

The core problem, then, is how to formulate moral principles by which the obscene can be determined. Catholic moral theology with which I, as a theologian, am most familiar, has little to offer in the matter of defining the obscene. This may come as a surprise, especially to those who may have thought that the Catholic church has succeeded in reducing life and thought to a precise set of neat axioms or has an exact formula to be applied in all contingencies.

It is quite true that Canon Law refers to obscenity with obvious severity. This occurs, of course, in the legislation of the Code of

Reprinted with permission from a symposium on Obscenity and the Arts, appearing in *Law and Contemporary Problems*, vol. 20, no. 4 (Autumn, 1955), published by the Duke University School of Law, Durham, North Carolina. Copyright 1955 by Duke University.

Canon Law that deals with the censorship of books (Canons 1385-1399).[2] These passages do not take us very far, however. Canon 1399, numbers eight and nine, for instance, lists among general classes of literature that are forbidden to the reading of Catholics, books which "professedly (*ex professo*) discuss, describe or teach impure or obscene matters." But there is no definition, either here or in any other place in Canon Law, of what the obscene is. Legislation simply says that *if* a book is obscene, it is forbidden; it does not say what constitutes obscenity.

When the codifiers produced the corpus of legislation now known as the Code, they were, as lawyers must be, at pains to clarify anything that seemed open to misunderstanding or obscurity, and their successors in the various Roman commissions are constantly receiving *postulata* (requests) from all parts of the world for clarification of such words and passages. We may presume, then, that since the word *obscenum* has rarely come up for any extended elucidation, it remains uncomplicated and clear in Catholic legal and moral thought; that it is, in fact, thought of as being rather self-evident. The interpretations that have actually been given by canonists and moralists have been by no means exhaustive; they have generally been little more than somewhat sketchy paraphrases.

ARRIVING AT A DEFINITION

There is, of course, agreement among all canonists and moralists that the word *obscenum* is to be interpreted, as far as possible, in a restricted sense (*strictiori modo*). This is a corollary to the whole tenor of the interpretation of Canon Law, which declares that restrictive legislation (Canons that curtail freedom) is to be interpreted at its minimum extent; that is, human liberty is to be curtailed as little as possible in the achievement of the ends of particular legislation.

Guided by this fundamental principle, canonists and moralists have been cautious not to widen the meaning of *obscenum* so as to include anything and everything that may be offensive to good taste or even to morals. So, for example, Noldin states:

For a book to be prohibited [by reason of its obscenity], it is necessary that from its whole tenor the author's intention is evident of teaching the reader about sins of impurity and arousing him to libidinousness (ut prohibitus sit liber, requiritur ut ex tota ejus indole appareat scribentis intentionem lectorem de peccatis turpibus instruendi et ad libidinem excitandi). [3]

Interpretations of this cautiously restricted nature have been re-echoed time and again by commentators on the Code. To quote one recent commentary, Bouscaren-Ellis state that the *ex professo* phrase of the Code's prohibition "indicates the principal purpose of the author or the principal scope of the work";[4] moreover, in determining what that intention and scope are, Abbo-Hannan explain that "useful books imparting scientific information do not deal *designedly* with obscene matter as such and do not fall within this category" of obscene books.[5]

Canon Law and moral theologicans, strict as they are in the matter of obscenity, especially in books, are not, shall we say, overly anxious to scatter shots against books that may, at first sight, seem to be obscene, but which more mature reflection will prove not to fall within the carefully restricted legislation.

The best beginning to a satisfactory definition of obscenity that has come to my attention is contained in a phrase used by the famous Father Arthur Vermeersch, S.J., who wrote most extensively and lucidly on the matter of sex morality. Speaking of nudity in art, this wisely moderate moralist says:

Not every nude can be called obscene; in common estimation an obscene nude is a nude that allures, and obscenity may be defined as 'a degrading manifestation or solicitation of the soul in the nudity.' (non omne nudum dici potest obscenum; sed vulgo dicitur obscenum nudum allectans et dici potest; turpis in nuditate manifestatio animi vel solicitatio).[6]

This suggestion seems to have been in the mind of the Rev. Gerald Kelly, S.J., when he wrote:

The term *obscenity* is frequently used with a rather wide and vague meaning, but with the moral expert it is very technical. Let us illustrate from things to which the term is especially applicable, namely "obscene" literature and theatrical productions. For such things to be obscene, two elements are required: a) their theme, or content, is of an impure or sexually-exciting nature; and b) their manner of presentation is such as to throw an attractive emphasis on that impure or sexually-exciting element. For instance, adultery is a sin of impurity; so when a book or play not only centers about adultery, but portrays it in an attractive manner, such a book or play is obscene. Again, excessive nudity, and especially disrobing of a woman in the presence of a man, are commonly recognized as strongly stimulating to the sexual passions. Hence, when such things are alluringly emphasized and advertised . . . they must be called obscene.[7]

There may be a slight ambiguity here, especially, in our efforts to determine what constitutes obscenity in literature. The "attractiveness" with which a theme, say of adultery, is treated may be taken in two senses. First, if the characters who commit adultery are to be portrayed convincingly, the adultery *must* be portrayed as attractive to them, else they would never have ventured on the downhill path. This follows from the general moral principle that no one ever sins save *sub speci boni*—when he thinks and feels that he is getting some good out of it. If I may quote myself:

But [sin] cannot be made so attractive that the reader, in his turn, is so swayed by the attractiveness as to have his judgment warped and his conduct misguided. Despite what will be said later [in the book] about the sympathy that good literature ought to foster between reader and character portrayed, the reader can never legitimately identify himself fully with the character. Those who think they are Napoleon are, after all, put away safely.

This is a psychological problem. . . . Authors have resorted to the phrase 'esthetic distance,' or 'psychical distance,' to describe the necessary detachment which enters into the contemplation of any artifact. If it is true that the viewer of a still-life, let us say, of a table spread with succulent viands should not experience the reaction of having his mouth water, it is equally true that one who reads of sin that proved fatally attractive to a character ought not feel himself drawn by the same attraction. But it is possible for a

reader, too, to violate the 'esthetic distance' by unintelligent
reading of a book that keeps the distance very well indeed.[8]

THE CONTEXTUAL ISSUE

The emphasis in Canon Law and in its continuing interpretation is
always on the *tendency* of the book, of the work of art, to exude
some sort of allure that panders to the passions of sex. This
tendency is not to be judged by some sort of mystical reading of the
mind of the producer. It is to be judged from objective elements in
the thing produced; the author's "intentions" externalize themselves
in his work. This is as much to say that the subjective element is a
two-way street between the author and the reader or viewer. It is not
to say that the judgment of whether or not a certain artifact is
actually obscene is a purely subjective decision. There are, moral
teaching firmly declares, objective norms by which obscenity can be
discovered. The main point of interest to the legal mind, however, is
the remarkable similarity of advertence to the *tendency* of the work,
both in the discussions of the moralists and in legal decisions that
were for a long time the basis for most of the legislation in England
and the United States.

The famous (and recently rewritten) judgment handed down by
England's Lord Chief Justice Cockburn in 1868 stated that the test
of obscenity was:

> whether the tendency of the matter charged as obscene is to
> deprave and corrupt those whose minds are open to such immoral
> influence, and into whose hands a publication of this sort may
> fall.[9]

And, appositely echoing the views of the moralists that the whole
tenor of the work must be taken into consideration (ex tota ejus
indole), Judge Woolsey, in handing down the famous *Ulysses*
decision in 1933, stated:

> the same immunity should apply to literature as to science, where
> the presentation, viewed objectively, is sincere, and the erotic

matter is not introduced to promote lust and does not furnish the dominant note of the publication. The question in each case is whether the publication taken as a whole has libidinous effect.[10]

THE MORAL AND THE OBSCENE

Moral teaching on the whole process of sex holds, as a basic and cardinal fact, that complete sexual activity and pleasure is licit and moral only in a naturally completed act in valid marriage. All acts which, of their psychological and physical nature, are designed to be preparatory to the complete act, take their licitness and their morality from the complete act. If, therefore, they are entirely divorced from the complete act, they are distorted, warped, meaningless and hence immoral. It follows, therefore, that any deliberate indulgence in thoughts, words or acts which, of their intrinsic nature, are slanted toward, destined for or preparation for the complete act, and yet performed in circumstances in which the complete act is impossible, have ceased to be a means toward an end and have become ends in themselves. All sin, whether sexual or otherwise, always entails such a confusion, in one way or another, of means and ends.

There is a vast literature on this matter of the relation of means and ends, with special reference to the role of sex in life. One of the best popular expositions will be found in *Christian Design for Sex*,[11] in which the author asks, "why may not man use sexual intercourse and *seek the pleasure attached to it*, contrary to its natural pattern?"[12] He answers: "Because man is not the master of this function. Human life is God's domain . . . and so, likewise, is the process that leads to human life. A process belongs reductively to the same category as the object to which it leads."[13]

It is for this reason that true sex morality has always held that any sins against purity are serious sins. Commenting, for example, on the statement of Father E. Mersch, S.J., the "the importance of the degree of the [sex] activity that has been aroused does not enter into the reckoning [of the gravity of the sin],"[14] the translator of the book, one A.S., who also adds illustrative notes, goes on to say:

Because, whether this voluntary activity of the sex instinct is more or less, the same essential consequences are involved, namely, the emotional consequences, which the author calls 'the psychological link' between the will and the bodily state, and the acceptance of this motion by the will, in virtue of its acceptance of the bodily sensation and activity which caused the emotion.[15]

He then goes on to illustrate this idea, which would be accepted, I feel, by psychologists and even by the general public of this day when we hear so much of psychosomatic medicine.

> Thus, pressing the button of a small electric switch can start the most powerful machinery. The least voluntary degree of sex activity is like a switch which brings into action beyond our power of control "primordial forces that move in the depths of our nature." If it is always gravely sinful to bring these into action, except in conformity to moral law, it must be equally sinful to do what is to them the same as the pressing of the starting-switch is to all the machinery connected with it. It does not matter whether this activity be physical or mental ("bad thoughts"), for both kinds have the same effect on the deeper forces connected with them; that is, of course, provided they are voluntary.[16]

The libidinous effect of the work, therefore—of which both the moralists and the law speak—can always be determined by an investigation of the tendency of the work to stimulate sexual passion. The reactions of the individuals may, of course, differ considerably—one may be more suggestible, the other more sluggish in his responses—but if the subject matter—the statue, the painting, the book—because of its very nature, stimulates in the person of average sex instincts those preliminary commotions which are of their very nature preparatory for the complete sex act, then the subject matter has the character of stirring to libidinousness and is, consequently, obscene.

In order, however, to define this whole matter more closely, and to emphasize Father Kelly's important statement that, for the moralist, "obscenity" has a very precise meaning, it will be necessary to delimit what the moralists mean by "sexual passion." For sexual passion, pleasure that is called "venereal" is always concomitant. But there are three types of sense-pleasure that are not venereal.

The first non-venereal sense-pleasure has been named *delectatio mere sensibilis*: merely sensible pleasure. This has been described as "the pleasure proper to the harmonious functioning of the external senses."[17] In other words, the senses—taste, smell, the sense of touch, and so on—reacting to a stimulation proper to themselves, experience a pleasure that perfects their operation; a pleasure that is not, per se, physically or psychologically geared to even a remote connection with the sexual act. So, a man feeling the delicate texture of a rose petal may indeed be sexually aroused, but, if he is, it is not something in the rose petal that had any connection with sexual activity. All the senses return a pleasure that is properly and uniquely theirs. If the pleasure fulfills the function of "perfecting operation," then the object which stimulates such pleasure cannot, of itself, be called an "obscene" object. A perverted person may misuse the object and read into it a lubricious character, but the object does not actually possess such a character.

The second non-venereal pleasure is called *delectatio spiritualis-sensibilis*: a psychosensible pleasure. This has been described as:

> the satisfaction that a noble love takes in the external acts which are proper to the *delectatio mere sensibilis* [as outlined above]. It is essentially an act of the spiritual appetite which, nevertheless, has a redundance [an overflowing] on the sensitive appetite.[18]

This "redundance" is often manifested physically in such ways as a rapid heartbeat, a mounting color and so on. Examples, such as the physical reactions of a mother greeting a long-unseen son, have been adduced to show this intimate connection between psychic and physical reactions. But, again, the point to be made is that there is no intrinsic connection between the pleasure experienced and the sex act.

Finally—and here we are on slightly more difficult ground—the third non venereal pleasure is *delectatio carnalis-sensibilis*: a pleasure carnally sensible. It is:

> the satisfaction taken in the same physical acts [as mentioned in the *delectatio mere sensibilis*] by a love which, though not strictly

impure, is nevertheless carnal and strongly centered on physical characteristics.[19]

Its psychic contours are quite different from the reactions mentioned earlier in either of the other two non-venereal pleasures, and it is often the prelude to venereal pleasure. An example might be the physical pleasure experienced in the fondling of a child.

This breakdown by the moralists is a wonderful example of the care with which "obscenity" is not charged against every sensible human pleasure. The peculiar characteristic by which these types of pleasure are distinct from venereal pleasure is that they have no intrinsic, no per se connection with genital commotion. It is this last element, the actual arousing of genital commotion, or the intrinsic tendency of an object so to arouse, which must be present if a book, a work of art, etc., can objectively be called obscene.

Such an approach to the question of defining obscenity, though it may strike one as being a mere process of rationalization, is actually an objective method. The distinction between venereal and non-venereal pleasure is one based on an objective study of how men actually do react, and it is a distinction that must be made if, as I mentioned above, the label of obscene is not to be slapped indiscriminately on works of art or literary productions which, by their nature, minister legitimately to a proper sense-pleasure.

This method of objective study, of determining moral norms from a consideration of men in action, is, of course, not of recent vintage, though the present-day emphasis on a sociological approach to morals often gives the impression that only nowadays are moralists interested in leaving their ivory towers to consider man in his true human condition. Actually, however, the construction of moral science by the method of observation goes back to Aristotle. I refer my reader to the admirable *The Conflict between Ethics and Sociology*,[20] especially chapter seven, "Toward the Solution," wherein the author expounds at length on how St. Thomas Aquinas, following Aristotle, states, for example:

In moral questions we must start with certain effects produced by human acts . . . because in moral questions the first principle is the existence of the moral act; and we attain knowledge of this existence by experience.[21]

Again, St. Thomas states:

> It is necessary for anyone who wishes to be an apt student of moral science that he acquire practical experience in the customs of human life and in all . . . civil matters, such as are laws and the precepts of political life.[22]

If these principles by which we are attempting to define the obscene are based on the objective study of man in society, do they not, nevertheless, rest on a chimera? Do they not presuppose something that cannot be experimentally determined—namely, the existence of a uniform and normal human nature? It seems that they do. The moralists quoted have referred constantly to those "of normal sex instincts," and a phrase they are fond of is *homo quadratus*, which we would translate, oddly enough, "the well-rounded man." Speaking of such a man—if he exists—Father Kelly says:

> And this habitual disposition or latent appetite, should naturally pertain in some way to the parts that minister to the pleasure in question. Hence the natural constitution of man contributes the latent appetite, and the perception of the apt object is the stimulation that arouses the power from latency to activity. Thus . . . man's perception of a venereally apt object by means of one of the external senses writes on his subjective apprehension: "Genital pleasure—something good for me, but absent": and nature's response is the actuation of the appetite in the form of venereal pleasure, an attempt to make the object present.[23]

Does not such an approach presuppose that there *is* a uniformity of response to the appeal of the alluring object; a uniformity in human nature that is a figment of the moralists' imagination, rather than a fact that can be experimentally shown? In other words, does the nature of individual men so differ that it is impossible to set down some norms by which a certain thing can be called obscene? Is what is obscene for one capable of being not obscene for another?

As one might expect, St. Thomas has a great deal to say on this matter—not, it is true, with respect to obscenity, but in terms of the general problem of the immutability or variability of the moral law. Let it be said forthwith that St. Thomas, precisely because he worked from the data of experience, never affirmed that moral laws oblige "with the same force every reasonable free human being without distinction of time or place."[24] Instead, as Deploige states:

> Anyone would have to be ill-informed to believe that St. Thomas ignored the external world and was absorbed in drawing up a plan for the ideal state or a code of the perfect life, without any advertence to the possibility of the plan or the code being practicable. Before occupying himself with what ought to be St. Thomas inquires into what is. And he observes precisely, as a fact of capital importance, the diversity of rules of conduct, of laws, and of institutions.[25]

To give but a few instances of St. Thomas' grasp of reality in this matter:

> Concerning virtuous works, men have no certain knowledge, but their judgments about them differ greatly. For there are works which are reputed just and upright by some, and, according to differences of time and place and persons, as unjust and dishonorable by others. Something is considered vicious at one time or place, which in another time or locality is not thought to be vicious.[26]

On account of the uncertainty of the human judgment, especially on contingent and particular matters, different people form different judgments on human acts; whence, also, different and contrary laws result.[27] From this difference of opinion it happens that some believe that nothing is naturally just or honorable except by reason of positive laws.[28]

This "uncertainty of the human judgement" is caused by many things: by ignorance, by passion, and so on. Moreover, when, to return to our matter of the obscene, we are striving to lay down rules of conduct, we must remember that we are here in the realm of what St. Thomas calls the "practical reason," as distinguished from the "speculative," and

> The practical reason is busied with contingent matters, about which human actions are concerned: and consequently, though there is necessity in the general principle, the more we descend into matters of detail, the more frequently we encounter defects.[29]

This allowance for the variations in practice, however, does not mean that there is no immutability in principle, and it is the speculative reason that discovers the principles. St. Thomas will say, for example, over and over again:

> There are certain actions naturally becoming to man, and in themselves right by nature, and not merely because they are prescribed by law.[30]
>
> Now the right ends of human life are fixed; wherefore there can be a natural inclination with respect to those ends.[31]

Here we pass, it seems to me, from the general principle which we have laid down from experimental data to the application of that principle to particular cases. We are, in other words, now dealing with the minor premise of a syllogism that runs:

> Any object which per se tends to rouse the sexual passions is obscene. But this particular object tends per se to rouse the sexual passions. Therefore this particular object is obscene.

How may we take the step from theory to practice and determine that this particular object *does* have such a tendency? In the matter under discussion, the general principles which concern the ends of human life are the principles we have examined on the morality of venereal acts outside of marriage, even those preparatory acts whose whole bent is toward the complete act. On those principles, Catholic moralists all agree.

When we come to the use of the practical reason, however; when we come to the question "does this piece of literature, this work of art, actually arouse the average person to genital commotion, to sexual passion," then we are in the domain of probability, to some extent.

> All discussions about things to be done must proceed on the ground of probability, not of certainty, for everything is contingent and variable in moral transactions.[32]
>
> There is much uncertainty in things that have to be done; because actions are concerned with contingent singulars, which, by reason of their vicissitudes, are uncertain.[33]

These remarks of St. Thomas may perhaps be restated thus, with regard to our matter: it is certain that if this object rouses to genital commotion, it is obscene; and it is obscene only if it so arouses; but it is not a matter of absolute certainty that this particular object will so arouse even the normal man. This, however, is not an impasse. Since, in these matters of the practical reason, what is looked for is action, we may lay down the further principle that, even if it is not certain that such and such an object will arouse to sexual passion, nevertheless, if the probability swings in that direction, then the object is, for practical purposes, obscene. Here are some of the observations of St. Thomas on this matter:

> It is because the infinite numbers of singulars cannot be comprehended by the human reason, that our counsels are uncertain. Nevertheless, experience reduces the infinity of singulars to a certain finite number which occur as a general rule, and the knowledge of these suffices for human prudence.[34]
>
> We must not seek the same degree of certainty in all things. Consequently, in contingent matters, such as natural and human things, it is enough for a thing to be certain, as being true in the greater number of instances, though at times and less frequently it fails.[35]

It would seem to follow, then, that though we cannot say with absolute certainty that such-and-such an object will infallibly rouse the viewer to sexual passions, yet if the object is of such a nature that it generally does so arouse, then for practical purposes we have a "law" for determining the obscene.

THE MORAL AND THE OBSCENE: A FINAL NOTE

In all the discussions about defining the obscene—in the courts, by advisory counsel to publishers, and so on—perhaps not enough account is taken of what the ordinary man means and understands by obscenity. It is all very well to call upon "experts" to testify that such-and-such a work is not obscene, but in the effort to refine the definition to a razor-fine edge, perhaps the force of the common estimation is being watered down. Precision of definition is good, but not if it will blunt custom which knows pretty well what obscenity is. Here is one statement of St. Thomas' doctrine on law and custom:

> change in human law is justified only to the extent that it benefits the general welfare. Now the very fact of change in the law is, in a certain sense, detrimental to the public welfare. This is because, in the observance of the law, custom is of great importance; so much so that any action which is opposed to general custom, even if itself of little importance, always seems more serious. . . . Thus human law should never be changed unless the benefits which result to the public interest are such as to compensate for the harm done.[36]

This brings the consideration of moral principles for determining the obscene to a close. There is little need to recapitulate, I feel, but perhaps two summary observations are in order.

First, moral theologians are not vague or too far-ranging in their concept and statements of what constitutes obscenity or makes an object obscene. The word has a very precise meaning; it does not include such neighbors as "vulgar, distasteful, unpleasant, brutal," and so on. This, of course, is not to say that any moralist would therefore recommend reading books that are "vulgar." But it does mean that obscene has a restricted meaning, which the whole tone and practice of moral theology and Canon Law refrain from extending to works which, however much to be discouraged on other grounds, cannot be called objectively obscene.

Second, the determination whether this given work falls within that carefully staked-out definition is a matter of prudential judgment, in which there is no absolute certainty. In the dearth of such certainty, the probability that the work falls within the definition is enough to have the force of law.

In conclusion, let me say that, though I have not examined many of the legal decisions that have been handed down in this matter, I have been struck by the great amount of similarity existing between the approaches of the lawyers and the courts and the Catholic moralists in the matter of arriving at a workable definition.[37] This is, surely, a good sign, for it shows that, though differences may and do exist, those interested in the civil and the moral law are linked in a common work of trying, in this difficult and delicate field, to work together for the common good.

NOTES

1. Catholic Theological Society of America, *Proceedings of the Ninth Annual Convention* (New York, 1954), pp. 127-39.

2. Codex Juris Canonici 403 *et seq.* (1917). These Canons and their interpretations can be most conveniently found in Redmond Burke, *What is the Index?* (St. Paul: Bruce, 1952).

3. H. Noldin, *De Preceptis Dei et Ecclesiae* (1926), p. 658.

4. T.L. Bouscaren and Adam Ellis, *Canon Law Digest* (St. Paul: Bruce, 1946), p. 716.

5. John Abbo and Jerome Hannan, *The Sacred Canons*, vol. 2 (New York: Herder, 1952), p. 638. (Italics supplied.)

6. Arthur Vermeersch, *Theologiae Moralis*, vol. 4 (1926), p. 94.

7. Gerald Kelly, *Modern Youth and Chastity* (St. Louis: Queens Work Press, 1941), p. 73.

8. Harold Gardiner, *Norms for the Novel* (Beirut: America Press, 1953), pp. 53-54.

9. Regina v. Hicklin, L.R. 3 Q.B. 360 (1868). The recent case of Regina v. Martin Secker and Warburg, Ld. [1954] I Weekly L.R. 1138, however, has been seen by many as resulting in a modification of the *Hicklin* rule. Mr. Justice Stable's summing up to the jury in this latter case can be found in the *London Bookseller* for July 17, 1954. The preceding and subsequent issues of that trade magazine contain some very interesting comments on the whole matter of English concern for and treatment of obscenity in literature.

10. United States v. One Book Called "Ulysses," 5 F. Supp. 182 (S.D.N.Y. 1933), aff'd, 72 F.2d 705 (2d Cir. 1934). The decision may be conveniently consulted in the Modern Library edition of James Joyce, *Ulysses* (1942), where it is printed in full with an introduction by Morris L. Ernst.

11. Joseph Buckley, *Christian Design for Sex* (Paris: Fides, 1952).

12. Ibid., p. 35.

13. Ibid., p. 37.

14. E. Mersch, *Love, Marriage and Chastity* (New York: Scheed, 1939), p. 19.

15. Ibid.

16. Ibid.

17. Gerald Kelly, *The Theologian's Concept of Venereal Pleasure* 270 *et seq*. A doctoral dissertation presented to the Theological Faculty of Pontifical Gregorian University, 1937.

18. Ibid.

19. Ibid. Father Kelly's treatise contains a full study of the approaches of earlier theologians to the matter.

20. Simon Deploige, *The Conflict between Ethics and Sociology*, translated by C. Miltner (New York: Herder, 1938).

21. Ibid., p. 278.

22. Ibid., p. 274, n. 42.

23. Kelly, *The Theologian's Concept*, pp. 37-38.

24. This is the charge made by Levy-Bruhl in "La Morale et la Science des Moeurs" (1903), p. 278; S. Deploige, *Conflict between Ethics and Sociology*, p. 309.

25. Ibid., p. 310.

26. Ibid., p. 311, n. 161. The texts of St. Thomas to which this note and notes 27 to 35 *infra* refer are quoted from the Burns and Oates edition, London.

27. Ibid.

28. Ibid., p. 311, n. 162.

29. Ibid., p. 313, n. 170.

30. Ibid., p. 312, n. 165.

31. Ibid., p. 316, n. 179.

32. Ibid., p. 314, n. 170.

33. Ibid., p. 313, n. 169.

34. Ibid., p. 276, n. 45.

35. Ibid., n. 46.

36. J. Langmead Casserley, *Morals and Man in the Social Sciences* (New York: Scribner, 1951), p. 57.

37. This similarity can be traced to the accounts carried, for example, in Thomas I. Emerson and David Haber, *Political and Civil Rights in the United States* (Boston: Little Brown, 1952), pp. 602-24, where, under "Freedom of Speech: Untruthful and Harmful Communications," section A is concerned with "Obscenity and Related Matters."

The Modern Machiavellians: The Pornography of Sexual Game-Playing

John MacGregor

While much of this volume has been concerned with the controversy over hard-core pornography, a great many other kinds of obscene phenomena are going on in American society today. Some of this obscenity is reflected in what might be called "soft-core" literature—guides to pornographic relationships among individuals in contemporary American society. To the extent that a society and its literature reflect one another, social relationships reflective of pornographic literary themes may be said to be obscenity writ large.[1]

Richard Means has argued that social scientists can and should develop objective yardsticks for making judgments about ethical and moral systems. According to Means, the further extension of amoral relativism is likely to be unproductive or deleterious to social science and to the larger society.[2] Objective standards against which we can measure the social utility of an ethical or moral system include survival of the species or fulfillment of individual human potential (self-actualization). The latter is the implicit standard by which the literature discussed in this chapter will be evaluated.

The author wishes to thank Ray Rist for his most helpful criticism of an earlier draft.

175

SOFT-CORE, PROSTITUTION, AND OBSCENITY

The particular body of literature to which we refer might be called "guides to seduction and swinging." Representative examples are periodicals such as *Playboy, Cosmopolitan* and *Penthouse*; and books like *The Art of Erotic Seduction*[3] and *Sex and the Single Girl.*[4]

We call these publications "soft-core" because they are not so blatantly obscene as hard-core pornography, especially in the language they employ to describe sexual activity, and because they have, or pretend to have, "redeeming social value" in the form of plot or theme, usually concerning the etiquette of living a "liberated" sexual life. Despite the fact that soft-core pornography is obviously important to any analysis of the moral aspects of pornography, hard-core pornography has received far more moral (and legal) attention. Yet much hard-core pornography is so removed from the reader's actual experience that it can hardly be taken as anything but fantasy—at most, an aid to masturbation.[5] Further, it is repetitious to the point of boredom, and obviously has little point *but* repetition.[6]

Not so with soft-core pornography. The *Playboy* philosophy and Cosmo Girl "Guides to Etiquette" are believable. They provide explicit instruction to real people about how to live the swinging life. One can easily identify with them. Further, unlike hard-core pornography, which even today is usually kept "under the table," soft-core pornography has the advantage of being acceptable. It can sit respectably on the coffee table along with *Reader's Digest* and *Newsweek*—which makes it quite insidious.

While our clarification of "soft-core" may have cleared up some questions for the reader, he may have some questions about our use of the term "pornography." Literally, pornography means "writing about whores or prostitutes." While this sometimes applies to the contents of soft-core, it often does not, in a literal sense. But the more general definition of prostitution, "to put to any base or unworthy use," is, it seems to us, precisely what soft-core does to its readers and what it would have its readers do to themselves and others. The bulk of this chapter is devoted to vivid examples of such prostitution; for the moment simply contemplate this advice to the teeny-bopper set from Ellen Peck's *How to Get a Teenage Boy and What to do With Him When You Get Him* (while you're at it, comtemplate that title too):

> Party behavior is an exaggeration of real behavior. People let themselves go. Flirts become more flirtatious. And, because they get scared by all the action, mice become mousier.
>
> Don't be a mouse. Be flirtatious. If you *do* have to get sunglasses tomorrow, you can say so. But make the sunglasses comment more FUN by exaggerating a bit. Like, 'I've got to buy some sunglasses; I want a pair with a matching foreign spy to go with them.'
>
> And *now* you and Neil can start talking about foreign-spy films on TV and maybe mimicking the cloak-and-dagger bit. Or, later in the evening, after you've wandered around talking to some other people (that is, *boys*), you can bring Neil a drink, wearing dark glasses and delivering a mock warning that the drink is poison.[7]

The prostitution here has nothing to do with the fact that sexual flirtation is involved; it has to do with the phoniness and duplicity of flirting behavior, which makes a mockery of genuine, intimate, honest human relationships. "Peck's bad girls" are plastic harlots, despite the fact that they never bed down with their young swains (at least, not according to the book).

Elsewhere in this volume, George Steiner expresses his own concerns about sexually explicit material, particularly hard-core pornography and the "high pornography" of erotica. He sees it as an "onslaught on human privacy which does our imagining for us and which may lead to the withering of our power to feel, to experience, and to realize the precarious uniqueness of each other's being."[8] In our view, Steiner is saying that *such material strips us of our own humanity and the humane qualities of our relationships with other human beings*. If this is true of hard-core and high pornography, then it is even more true of soft-core. We are all the poorer because we are all prostituted by it.

Such an expanded view of pornography and prostitution leads us, of course, to an expanded definition of obscenity. Acts are obscene precisely when they diminish the essential humanity of the human being, when they prostitute the individual. Thus, hard-core pornography is obscene because it reduces the person to nothing more than a set of genitals,[9] but soft-core pornography is obscene because it reduces the person to nothing more than a phony game player—a plastic mannequin, a shill or a con-man. The obscenity of soft-core pornography is the obscenity of *machiavellianism*.

THE MACHIAVELLIAN AS SEXUAL GAME PLAYER

While few would single out the fifteenth century as especially significant in the development of pornographic literature, Machiavelli's *The Prince* can be regarded as the original sourcebook for soft-core pornography.[10] Machiavelli provided one of the most influential rationales in modern European times for a morality based on something other than religious principle. The particular principle emphasized by Machiavelli was *pragmatic political expediency*, summarized in the ubiquitous, "the end justifies the means." A Prince did what he must to gain, maintain or regain power—guile, deceit, opportunism, all could be justified as in the best interests of the people they were used upon. The Prince was a phony, but like most phonies, he probably believed his own rationalizations.

Because of its break with churchly morality, *The Prince* is a watershed statement of the early Renaissance period. By itself, though, it could hardly be said to have spawned the likes of *Playboy* and *Playgirl*. Pragmatic expediency is only one of many Western values which are both sources and consequences of literature like *Playboy*. Another is materialism, as is so wittily argued by Michelson:

> Thus the power to buy becomes, in the capitalistic ethos, the sign of sexual power. So the world is sexualized, and sex is commercialized, and we have a pornographic image of the world—an idealized, socially lionized, metaphor of prostitution as a way of life, and that traditionally, is what pornography is—the literature of and about whores and whoring.[11]

But Michelson's focus, like Machiavelli's, gives us only part of the picture. This is not the place to go into an extended analysis of other values which are peculiar to Western pornographic themes, but

certainly objective "scientific" detachment, success, egoistic freedom, social darwinism and active mastery are all also important.[12]
Such value orientations are synthesized—in both pornography and in
actual flesh-and-blood relationships—into a pattern between the
sexes which has been aptly called the "rating-dating-mating
game."[13] Prostitution is the essence of the pattern. But Michelson is
concerned with a broader kind of prostitution, in which the medium
of exchange is by no means limited to money, and the commodity is
often the very humanity of the individual. This is what machiavellianism has become in rational-bureaucratic, secularized, industrial-
ized, commercialized, urbanized, technologized America; we are
virtually all princes and princesses, and we have the resources and
techniques to play games that Machiavelli never envisioned.

A considerable body of research has developed around the
concept of machiavellianism. Christie and Geis,[14] taking their cues
from the master himself, list the following attributes of machiavellians: use of guile, deceit and opportunism in interpersonal relations;
possessing an unflattering view of the nature of man as being weak,
cowardly and easily subject to pressure from others; and lack of a
well-defined abstract moral system. Guterman presents a parallel
definition: an amoral, manipulative attitude toward others, combined with a cynical view of men's motives and character, emotional
detachment and a lack of commitment to conventional moral
norms.[15]

While Christie and Geis list numerous correlates of machiavellianism, only a few are important behavioral and attitudinal characteristics for our analysis. Machiavellians are interpersonal game players,
remain detached from ego-involving elements in bargaining and
concentrate on winning, are less "transparent" or predictable in
personal relationships, are "cool," tend to stereotype others as weak
and subject to pressure, have a singular disregard for others, engage
in duplicity and show an ability to lie more plausibly than others
(and use more eye contact when doing so).[16]

These characteristics sound like an operational definition of the
seductive swinger, whether he or she be a "teen-angel" of the 1950s
or one of the (supposedly) liberated "playboys" or "playmates" of
the contemporary era. Whatever sexual liberation has meant, it has
not meant a reduction in the general level of alienated, game-playing,
object-related sexuality in our society. The stimulation of the mass

media, particularly the type of books and magazines explored in this analysis, can be viewed as a major factor in helping to preserve and extend a tradition of alienated sexuality in American society.

The essence of machiavellian sexuality (pornographic relationships) is the *using* of another person as an object to gratify one's own needs. In Martin Buber's terms, it involves an "I-it" relationship rather than an "I-thou" relationship.[17] The *context* of personal relationship is missing, just as it is in pornographic literature (as opposed to erotic literature). The work of Erving Goffman[18] is particularly illuminating in this respect, and it provides a general background for the analysis which follows. Goffman emphasizes the conscious, deliberate, calculating behaviors of participants in interaction, vis-a-vis presenting and maintaining a desired "front" or "face." A particularly relevant concept is that of "frontstage" vs. "back-stage" behavior,[19] which distinguishes between those situations when the actor must be "on guard" because he is in the presence of an audience of others (who might see through his facade), and those times when he can relax and/or prepare his mask and costume for the next encounter. Goffman's "dramaturgical model" is not intended so much to depict people as crass, calculating con-men, as it is to emphasize the ways in which our behavior is consciously linked to the affirmation and enhancement of our self-concepts. Nowhere though, is Goffman's approach more applicable than in the analysis of the crass, calculating machiavellian, who enhances his own self-concept at the expense of someone else. It doesn't take a very sophisticated background in social psychology to understand that in such a relationship the user, as well as the used, is himself degraded and impoverished. The alienator becomes the alienated.[20] Thus, the authors and purveyors of the "how to" primers on machiavellian sexuality collectively epitomize the alienated individual. Let us sample their wares.

THE BOOKS AND THE GAMES THEY DESCRIBE

The specific books chosen for analysis in this chapter were selected virtually at random from our rather large shelf of "soft-core pornography." They happen to include two books written for women, *The Cosmo Girl's Guide to the New Etiquette*[21] and *How To Get A Teenage Boy And What To Do With Him When You Get*

Him[22]; and one written for men, *The Art of Erotic Seduction.*[23] This selection is appropriate, we feel, for two reasons: first, given the sexual "double standard" in this culture, women are programmed for sexual game-playing to an even greater degree than men. This is the essential reality to which the women's liberation movement is responding. Second, the great classic of male "how-to-pornography," *Playboy* magazine, is widely read by both sexes and is generally well enough known to need no explication here. Any who feel that the male sex has been slighted in this analysis are free to add their own favorite examples from *Playboy* (particularly from the "Playboy Philosophy" articles).[24]

Finally, these books are examples of a type of communication that is widespread in our culture and that is beamed sometimes at men, sometimes at women, and sometimes indiscriminately at either sex in commercial advertising, in soap operas and a variety of mass circulation magazines.[25] Thus they are intended to be illustrative, not definitive.

Con games of the sort we are concerned with can be divided into four major types plus a variety of more complex combinations of the basic types. The labels used describe the effect of the game upon the "victim" or "patsy." The basic games are the "put-on" or phony game (the patsy is *fooled* into thinking the player is something other than what he actually is); the "put-off" or evasion game (the patsy is *eluded* by the player); the "set-up" or seduction game (the patsy is *used* by the player); and the "put-down" or humiliation game (the patsy is *degraded* by the player). Typical combination types are the set-up/put-off or flirtation game (the patsy is used and then eluded by the player), and the "set-up/put-down" or sadism game, (the patsy is used and then degraded by the player).[26] It's worth noting that all games involve phoniness by definition; thus a put-off, for example, involves phoniness *plus* evasion. The most basic game, then, is "playing the phonies," and it's not surprising that most "pornographic manuals" start with some rich instruction on how to manipulate the image one presents to others.

GETTING THE GAMES STARTED: PLAYING THE PHONIES

The publisher's blurb on the frontispiece of *How To Get A*

Teenage Boy and What To Do With Him When You Get Him boasts: "at last—a teen-age guide book that doesn't cop out! ... pick-ups and put-ons ... first date tricks ... super-effective props ... and the list goes on .... " Advising girls that they've got to "have a crowd" for contacts with boys, Peck launches into a list of steps for getting into a crowd. Detailed instructions are provided for making the first front-stage overtures to crowd members:

> Your first Candystriper meeting will give you your first contact with a crowd member. But for the time being, *forget* that she is a crowd member. She's not with her crowd now; she's just herself. You can start a conversation with her. In fact, since you're from her school, it would look funny if you didn't. Simply walk up. Friendly and casual. (Like, imagine seeing *her* here!) Here's what you say, if you know her fairly well:
> "Hi Barb. Guess what I finally talked myself into." Or, if you don't really know her, say:
> "Hi, aren't you from my school?"[27]

Peck goes on to discuss the appropriate facial expression to use (friendly and casual), the sort of mental notes to take (remember everything you can), proper responses to questions one is likely to be asked (answer any question and then ask a question of your own), and then advises:

> At every change, throw the conversational ball back to *them*, so that at the end of your first talk with them, they've said lots of things *to you*. This leaves a better first impression than if they've been talked at *by you*. After all, who are *you*, at this moment, as far as they're concerned? A new Candystriper who doesn't know her way around. They *do* know their way around. So let them talk and you just be appreciative. If they aren't talking that much, ask them questions. But keep the focus on *them*; it's flattering to them and they'll like you for it.[28]

The intimate relationship of manipulativeness with phoniness should be obvious from such material; in fact, every put-on is potentially a set-up.

The irony of such guides to fakery is illustrated by this classic from Peck's pen (in discussing the sort of "tests" that neophyte group members can expect):

> Pass the second type of test by knowing what's in the news and what's what around school. You should know what songs are on the charts, who sings them, what films are around, who your class officers are, and so on. *Never fake.* Example: "Don't you think the new singer Simon Croon is the greatest?" somebody asks. (You've never heard of him.) Don't agree, "Yes, he's the greatest." Just possibly, no such person exists!
>
> The right response in this case is, "Gee, is he new, or have I been missing something?" Ask questions after you answer them, remember? This gives somebody a chance to say, "Oh, he's nobody important, really."[29]

A translation of the essential message here might read, "While being faked by the faker you are trying to fake your way into, don't *compound* the fakery!"

In *The Cosmo Girl's Guide to the New Etiquette* a similar message is conveyed: "Men say they *hate* false eyelashes . . . that means your fake eyelashes shouldn't *look* false. Avoid a gummy glue line or exaggerated spikes. Apply liner carefully to bridge any gap between the real lash and the fake" (italics in original).[30]

Peck really comes into her own when discussing the classic backstage fakery that goes with creating a facade of "prettiness":

> Now, let's make it clear that the girls in Sheila's crowd aren't automatically of a different *breed* from Marge. Marie, in fact, is the only 'natural' beauty in the group, and she illustrates my point exactly, by the way. Marie has rather limited interests and no originality, but she is *pretty*. And since the business of a crowd of teen girls is to attract boys, Marie is desirable as a crowd member.[31]

But Peck notes that the other girls have had to *work* at their looks. For example, Sheila, who has a problem with broad shoulders, flat chest, and chubby round face, uses a straight fall, two shades of foundation, sweaters with raglan sleeves, thin lamb's wool pullovers, and a crepe-set pre-shaped bra (by Peter Pan, of course). She admits all this. "My figure is so *fake*," she laughed once after class. "Latex, fiber-fill—the works."[32]

Regarding Irene's problem with a 'big nose,' Peck tells us that she solved the problem by "really playing up her eyes." Her morning ritual involved the "blending, blending, blending" of white eye-shadow, cake type taupe eye liner, liquid black eye liner, two coats of black mascara, and false lashes, "meticulously" applied.[33] At this point, one begins to wonder whether the girls in Peck's stable have any time left for front-stage fakery!

The *Cosmo Girl's Guide*, which might be regarded as the post-graduate course for Peck's teen-age set, has probably the most detailed catalogue of fakery published anywhere. Under the general heading of "Your Beautiful Body" we get, for example:

Beauty-to-Go

Bibi is a model who works out at my gym and cleverly carries the ingredients of her fresh, 'natural' beauty in a gigantic fishing-tackle box. For portable grooming, you need a carrier too—something more practical, I hope. Keep one of every beauty aid you need in your office and a second, smaller, survival kit in a zipper vinyl cosmetic bag you carry in your purse. I keep a third one-of-everything packed in an overnight case for out-of-town trips. If you have to pack quickly, you're liable to forget *something*.[34]

Following a listing of 64 items for the "at home survival kit," 16 for the "office survival kit," and 17 for the "travel survival kit," the *Guide* goes on:

Think about what you *do* with your hands—the gestures (gentle, restrained, non-distracting), the movements (holding a champagne glass, pouring a cup of soothing Earl Grey tea), the loving touches. Hands ought to be silky soft, groomed, and move with feminine grace. . . .

You *do* smell good. You take a long, hot relaxing bath, or a quick refreshing shower daily—or both! You really lather your body with a good soap, brush your teeth, even carry a tiny spray flacon of mouthwash in your purse for garlic crises at lunch. . . .

Perfume conveys a message . . . are you woodsy, slinky, petulant, sophisticated, a tigress or a pussycat . . . . Find the scent that is *you*. Make it your signal, so a man smelling that scent in a crowded room when you are *not* there will think of you. Use it at pulse points. Spray all over your body and hair. Try Helen Gurley Brown's favorite scentism—douse a bit of cotton, place a second cotton in front to protect your clothes and tuck it into your bra . . . it lasts and lasts. In these braless times, you may have to tape it to your chestbone.[35]

Females, of course, don't have a monopoly on the basic techniques of phoniness. Ellis and Conway's *The Art of Erotic Seduction* starts the seducers off with the same basic type of lessons that Peck's teenyboppers receive:

Attract favorable attention

Before you can seduce or have an ongoing relationship with a woman, you must be attractive or have something to "sell" or offer to her. Since all of us are stuck with our looks, and few of us are rich or notably witty, we can't go too far with these kinds of attractions. But there are certain things you can do to attract favorable attention from the great majority of women; and one of these is to become something of a master of the social graces. . . .

The social graces often pay direct erotic dividends. They lull mothers into thinking you are a highly desirable and safe escort for their daughters. They enable you to get dates with girls who tend to relax their guard. They sometimes earn you special privileges, such as staying out later than the girl normally would. They don't usually vault you directly into milady's bed; but they often allow you to get so close that only a little extra hop will put you there.[36]

Noting that young men should attempt to "beat women at their own games," Ellis and Conway describe some of the techniques:

The usual gambit you'll encounter from a female is, "Now tell me about yourself," or "What do you do in life, and what do you want to do with the rest of your days?" Be prepared to answer, at least for a starter, with a brief—yes, BRIEF—response. For she often isn't interested, really, in the story of your life; and certainly not in many of its deadly details. She's either sitting on "ready" waiting to tell the story of *her* life; or she's nervous, uncomfortable, and doesn't know what to say. Therefore, she wants you to start the ball rolling and take her off the hook. . . .

Should you give her a "line"? *No, not too much of one.* You don't know how much you will be seeing her in the future, and any real line that you give will have too much exaggeration and falsehood in it, which she will eventually see through. So let your sins largely be those of omission rather than commission. Leave out the dull parts of your past and present doings, and spotlight the adventurous, romantic, and unusual parts (italics added).[37]

The art of phoniness reaches its height in this sage counsel from Ellis and Conway:

Do you need practice in talking to girls about sex and related subjects? You certainly do! You weren't born to speak dispassionately about passion; and you generally have to learn to do so. Stand in front of a mirror, if necessary, and practice asking questions like, "When you took World History in high school, what was your grade?" You know damned well she took World History and made *some* grade. There is nothing exciting or unusual in this. Now that you have mastered that kind of question, go on—still in front of the mirror—to sexually intimate questions, to see if you can ask them in exactly the same tone of voice and with the same calm inflection. "When you went with your last boyfriend, how did you feel about heavy petting?" Got it now?[38]

Ellis and Conway then provide intricate details for practicing with a "real live girl," interspersed with sessions at the tape recorder. From here, anything further would be downhill, so let's take our programmed phonies, plug them in, and let them start their machiavellian machinations.

PUT-OFFS: "YOU CAN'T PIN ME DOWN"

The simplest put-offs involve direct evasion of one's partner in interaction, and are illustrated by such one-liners as, "Sorry, wrong number," "Saturday night? Sorry, I'm busy," "Not tonight dear, I'm having my period." The game of frigidity is the classic simple put-off carried to the logical extreme.[39] More complex put-offs involve third parties, and have to do with the evasion of the partners from the third party, i.e., in conspiring to keep the truth about their activities from a mate, parent or friend. Such complex evasions are of course grist for the mill of the "how-to-do-it" pornographies (just as they are for the pornographic television program "Love American Style." The use of the word "love" in the title of this program has got to be one of the all-time bastardizations of the English language).

Peck devotes several pages to such complex evasions in her instructions on how to play the "communications game" with parents. Again, the principle of faking fakery so it doesn't appear fake is evident as she cautions the girls to "paint pictures" that aren't a "complete fiction." She points out that there is a difference between concealing a few facts which might be misinterpreted by parents and being completely dishonest. The distinction becomes a bit blurred in this example, however:

> One time, after some heavy making-out, a girl I know didn't feel like following her usual ritual of talking to her mother. Besides, she was too rumpled to be looked at closely just then. She solved the problem by pausing briefly at the living-room door and saying, "Mom, it finally happened! He kissed me!" She then swept upstairs to bed, having won her privacy for the evening *and* having managed to give her mother the impression she was sharing things with her. Even though, this time, she really wasn't.
>
> If your parents are restrictive rather than understanding, use the same formula: candid comment, then neutral comments. In your case, these neutral comments will really act as a kind of "smoke screen" to becloud anything you *don't* want to talk about.[40]

The justification for all of this is provided in the classic, "you *have* to make this effort to build a smoke screen in order to at least create the *impression* that they know what's going on."[41]

Evasion finds its Bosworth, though, in Gael Greene's advice to the Cosmo girls. The full treatment is anticipated in this advice under the heading, "Two For the Road":

> *Question: "I get so nervous when I check into a hotel out of town with my lover. We're both married to other people and I can't believe we can get away with this much longer. What to do to ease my anxiety?"*
>
> Answer: Take two single rooms . . . not adjoining, under two different names, preferably your own. It is easier to explain what you are doing in a single under your own name than in a double under a fictitious one. *If caught, lie well.* The extra $10 or $20 this costs will be more effective than $20 worth of tranquilizers (italics added).[42]

Under "A Philosophy of Considerate Adultery" Greene artfully combines phoniness, manipulativeness and evasion in these memorable words:

> The unbreakable rule is . . . discretion. . . .
>
> The ideal extramarital adventure—in terms of potential for discretion—is the visiting author-lecturer who is leaving next week or the man from Omaha you met during a convention. Or a cabana boy at a club to which you don't belong. Or your minister or analyst—someone with *more* to lose from exposure than you. Alas, lust is not always thoughtfully disciplined or disciplinable. . . .
>
> If you love your husband and hope to keep him, you'll want him to benefit from your revived lust . . . your beautiful new confidence . . . and new sexual expertise. Be subtle and understated about the latter, though. Bring it home to bed with a kind of ad-lib spirit . . . as if you just thought it up. Or read it in a book. Your husband is *not* a dummy![43]

But the zenith (or nadir) comes in this advice: *"If asked, lie. If caught, lie. Never admit anything. Never accept exposure. Lie, embroider, improvise, deny. Be convincing."* No faking the fakery here!

SET-UPS: THE ART OF SEDUCTION

In the set-up, the full richness of a machiavellian orientation comes into its own. The essence of the set-up is manipulation; further, the game itself is at least as satisfying as a winning score.

In *The Art of Erotic Seduction* we get an extended treatment of this game; in fact, the authors start with a conceptual analysis of the difference between seduction and "modified seduction"!

Whereas seduction is simply the art of being so persuasive that you induce an initially unwilling girl to "have sex" with you, modified seduction

> includes the goal of your giving pleasure to your partner, of providing her with sexual satisfaction even at some temporary cost to you. It involves your finding an unwilling female and then doing your best to provide *her* with so much satisfaction that both this time and the next she becomes more willing. Where, in unadulterated seduction, you strive for a series of unrelated incidents, and make the conquests themselves all-important, in modified seduction you still have such incidents from time to time, but you also strive for a continuing relationship with at least a minority (or even the majority) of the females with whom you have these incidents.[44]

This conceptual distinction appears to us to be analogous to the earlier distinctions we noted between fakery and faked fakery or lying and concealment. Such distinctions undoubtedly serve an important function as rationalizations for machiavellians (and their pornographers), but Ellis and Conway leave little room for doubt about the true nature of the game in the remainder of the book. In discussing the "ethics" of erotic seduction, for example, they say:

> But isn't this a bit unfair? it may be asked. Is it right for you, who may be bright, informed, and a sweet-mouthed talker, to persuade a delectable young thing, who may be much less bright, informed and silver-tongued, to do something which she may be unenthusiastic about doing with you at the time, and even more dim-viewed about later? Should your natural superiority in certain respects enable you to have your way with her, even to her current or subsequent detriment?
>
> The answer to these questions is: *Who said the world is, or even should be, fair?* Let's suppose, for the sake of discussion,

that the girl really doesn't want to go to bed with you, and that later she regrets doing so; and suppose that she only does so because any of your arguments are intrinsically good. Even so, how is your "taking advantage" of her in this respect any different from your taking your brains and your loquacity to become a top man in your class at school, to be elected head of your fraternity, to become vice president of your company in record time, or to win out in many other competitive ventures that you are bound to pursue in life (unless, of course, you neurotically withdraw from all competition entirely, because you are scared witless of failing)?

Competitiveness, the use of brains, and verbal and physical persuasiveness, in other words, seem to be inherent components of human endeavor . . . (italics added).[45]

Ellis and Conway note that the usual first act in seduction is to "establish a kissing relationship." After enumerating six "original strategies" for copping the first kiss,[46] they get down to serious business under the rather ludicrous heading of "subsequent kisses":

Try to control the sound of your breathing while kissing—preferably keep it silent. Learn the technique of "leashed intensity." In using this method, you want to create the illusion of hugging her intensely but actually being gentle. You can do this by gripping her back with your fingers, keep your forearm muscles tense, but letting your biceps remain loose. That is, you do not actually squeeze her; but your fingers and forearms give the illusion of a powerful grasp.[47]

Probably the *most* ludicrous passage in Ellis and Conway's book is in the chapter on light petting (necking) under the heading "manual breast contact":

Get yourself a leather pillow and borrow a girl's bra. Fasten the bra and slip it over the pillow. With one hand hold the snap tight against the pillow and practice unfastening the bra with your other hand. Practice in the dark or with your eyes closed. Become equally skillful with *either* hand; so that, in a sense, your left hand *does* know what your right hand is doing! Be able to unfasten a bra from the top or from the bottom.

Go to department stores and study the construction of bras. Some fasten in the center, some to the left of center, and some to the right. Study bras with straps as well as the strapless kind. Put a pillow slip over the bra you are practicing with and learn to find the snap from the outside by lightly running your fingers over your girl's back. Locate the snap exactly and learn to find it on the inside the first time you reach for it.

If you keep practicing along these lines, you should soon become so skillful that you may be able to unfasten a bra and not even have the girl suspect that you are working to do so. The unsnapping process may take place during either a tickling or caressing routine or during a "passionate hug" while you are kissing (italics in original).[48]

One can hardly avoid reflecting on the ludicrousness of literature such as this. Morbid humor is one of the last defenses in a machiavellian society. The thought of a person practicing on a leather pillow, of studying bra construction in a department store (without getting arrested)—these things are tragi-comic in themselves. But even more tragi-comic is the alienation of the authors who use terms such as "tickling or caressing routine" and place "passionate hug" in quotation marks (indicating that it's a technique discussed under that heading in another part of the book). The robot and his programmers are indistinguishable.

Of course, the object of the seduction game is also viewed in alienated terms. Consider Ellis and Conway's view of women, for instance, expressed under the heading of "a dress, sweater, or blouse that zips or buttons in the front"(!):

Oral techniques with the nipple include: (a) brushing the tip of the nipple with the tip of your tongue; (b) brushing the shafts of the nipples with your parted lips; (c) licking the nipple; (d) gently nibbling the nipple; (e) gently sucking the nipple; (f) a full-scale mouth sucking and tonguing of the nipple, sometimes including restrained use of your teeth.

There are a few women but not enough to be significant who

are completely ready at this point and will eagerly have intercourse. They are often discernible by their reaction when your
mouth touches their nipples. They show a sudden, sharp intake of
breath, and they "freeze." *Some of them go into what is
practically a state of coma.* In such a case, it is wisest to keep your
mouth on the woman's nipple and unhurriedly but efficiently
raise her dress, pull her pants down a few inches, arrange her in
some comfortable position, and have intercourse. *Only after penis
entry has been effected should you remove your mouth from her
breasts* (italics added).[49]

Or again, under "light petting positions":

An alternate position is to slide slightly to the right of the
steering wheel and ask the girl to lie across your chest. Get her
right arm behind your back (*thus eliminating it*), and put your left
arm around her and hold her left hand. Now your *right* hand is
free. This is a good position for manual and oral breast manip-
ulating and for other forms of light petting. It is an inferior
position for intercourse itself, because you must move her to
effect coitus. But for nights when you are working her up to the
point where she will later engage in heavy petting or intercourse,
it's an excellent position (italics added).[50]

By the time Ellis and Conway get to "Heavy Petting," they've
gone about as far as they can go. They start the discussion with the
profound observation that there are two main directions in which
one can approach the female genitals, (a) from above, and (b) from
below. They divide their discussion of petting techniques accordingly: 1. Petting from above (fingers below wrist). (a) The general
tickle approach. (b) The tummy rub approach. (c) The skirt-wad
approach (wadding up the girl's skirt while massaging her hip with
"feigned, but controlled intensity"). 2. Petting from the bottom
(fingers above wrist). (a) The thigh-tickle approach. (b) The approach of last resort (reaching the hand under the dress and onto her
genitals all in one single motion).

Two final lists provide us with the last of Ellis and Conway's
materials to be considered here. The first is titled "heavy petting in
spite of clothing" and discusses the "problem of clothes" under the

subheadings of "rubber pants," "girdle with a crotch," "girdle that is open-ended," "light underpants" and "leotard-type underpants." The basic message is "get those goddam pants off!"[51]

The second list is a catalog of clitoral stimulation techniques which might well have inspired the authors of the more recent "sensuality manuals."[52] The list includes the "eraser," the "doodle bug," the "banjo string," the "globe master," the "pin-point" and the "teaser." The switch has been located, and now we have six ways to turn it on!

Consistent with our earlier statement about the focus on seduction, we find that Ellis and Conway devote only 15 pages of their 154 page book to "Giving Full Satisfaction" (intercourse). That's the goal, but in best machiavellian style, the means are given much more attention—and Ellis and Conway have served their purpose.

Interestingly, *The Cosmo Girl's Guide* includes almost nothing on set-ups. Apparently, the phony facade of the put-on is considered sufficient ammunition for the female seductress. In the section titled "The Matinee," though, under the general heading of "Office Romance," the setting for seduction is described as:

> *Where* is this affair conducted? If he is rich, a small *pied-a-terre* or a permanent suite at a hotel affords discreet anonymity. For a single girl, there is your apartment, of course . . . always neat, the bed immaculate, curtains drawn to filter the light slightly, martinis chilling in the refrigerator, and the makings of a light, fast lunch all ready. (When two people return to their respective offices from a two-hour lunch with stomachs rumbling, frayed tempers and possible disaster may result).[53]

THE SET-UP/PUT-OFF: FLIRTATION

The final game type to be considered in this analysis is the complex game of flirtation.[54] Flirtation may be "mild," but it is not simple! The essential elements in flirtation are a come-on followed by a put-off. The game is only successful when the player *eludes* the victim. A flirter who goes "all the way" with the object of flirtation can be said to have been "had" by the victim, who ends up as the ultimate winner. This game, it seems to us, is closest to the kind of pornography Michelson is concerned with.[55] Given the subtleties of flirtation coupled with the double sexual standard, it is not surprising that our examples of flirtation are found in *How to Get a Teenage Boy*. While one might expect to also find examples in *Cosmo Girl*, Greene is concerned with being nearer to where the action is for big girls today. After all, big sister has grown up and become "liberated." Like her male counterpart, she doesn't waste her time with flirtation but goes straight into swinging.

Peck's book is a veritable source-book for flirtation. The obscenity here is not in the sexuality, but rather in the *relative lack of it*. Peck extends the American standard of packaged, fluffed, sexy, sexless, look-but-don't-touch, I-may-be-available-someday virginal American girlhood to the logical limit. These girls *may* have vaginas but we're never quite sure of it (except in reference to a few comments about menstruation and one injunction that "modified making out is better than going all the way"). This latter is virtually the only explicitly sexual advice in the entire book; given that "modified making out" is never defined it could hardly be said to be meaningful.

But Peck knows her stuff on flirtation. Regarding Irene, the girl with the big nose who spends each morning in front of her mirror making up her eyes, Peck provides this commentary on her backstage preparations:

> After all, she figures, what's more important than lashes? They're just about the Number-1 weapon in the arsenal of female flirtation. Mention the word "flirt." Don't you think of fluttering *lashes*? When you're wide-eyed, it's the *lashes* that frame that look of raptured interest. The come-on glance is given by lowering the *lashes*. And what about the split-second, almost-not-there *wink*?[56]

Now for front-stage. Irene also goes to school, which "is a social place as well as a learning place" and, says Peck:

> Flirting in the classroom is a matter of paying attention to these five things:
> 1. Appearance.
> 2. The attitude you project.

3. Your position in the classroom.

4. Nonverbal contacts during class.

5. Conversation before and after class.

Your *appearance* is OK. You've read Chapter 1. Today, you have on either your swashy pirate outfit or that black-and-white Glen-plaid knit. Nothing wrong with either of those! You look so good that you just *feel* like flirting.

What *attitude* are you projecting? It's the basic "I'm great" attitude we talked about in Chapter 3, but it's tailored to fit geography class. The I'm-great attitude is terrific for the corridors on the first floor and for the world at large, and you never lose it; *but*—what are the boys like in *this class*? Even more specifically, what is *Greg* like?

Is Greg the intellectual type and fascinated by geography? Then, you're going to have to look at least *interested* in it. Your attitude is, "*I'm great; thoughtful, too.*" If Greg, though, is the comic or activities major, busy planning for after class and indifferent to mean annual rainfalls, your attitude is, "*I'm great. Casual about this class, but great.*" And, if Greg's attention is on girls as often as it is on the lecture, you meet this attitude with, "*I'm great. Also attractive and a bit sexy.*"[57]

After detailing the "poses" which will convey such attitudes, and presenting an elaborate seating chart accompanied by a detailed analysis of where the flirt should establish a base of operations, Peck then provides one of our favorite examples of machiavellianism in these next instructions, which even go so far as to indicate the *number of seconds* of eye contact which will be effective in flirtation:

A certain kind of sidelong glance is what you'll use. A glance that says "Hi, there, I'm aware of you." Or "Hi, there; *you're* much more interesting than all *this*. . . . "

Remember that the sidelong glance is just that: a *glance*. It's not anything that's going to take your mind off your work even. It's too brief. It's just a little signal that you cast toward Greg because he's there, and he's a boy and you're a girl. Since it's a signal, it's sometimes going to get an answer, in the form of a return glance. But not always. Don't expect it to. And don't prolong your glance hoping it *will*. Glance at Greg. Glance away. That's it. The whole thing takes two seconds. *If* Greg doesn't get the signal. Glance at Greg. If he *does* catch your eye, smile slightly. Lower your eyelashes and turn away. This takes something between two and four seconds. No longer or he'll get uncomfortable. . . . How often to use the sidelong glance? Four tries per class is the upper limit.[58]

Not surprisingly, Peck's catalog for flirtatiousness is expanded considerably in the chapter on "partygoing." In the following gambit, Peck nicely illustrates the complexity of flirtation, involving as it does both come-on and put-off:

If the boy you're talking to has any sense of fun at all, this technique should work beautifully; so let the talk about whatever-it-is you're asking for continue until it either loses momentum or gets too suggestive. Example:

Neil: I've got to go downtown tomorrow.

You: Hmm, you'll have to call off your plans to go to the perfume department at Macy's. It's been crowded all week with free-sample-seekers. You won't be able to get near it.

Neil: Oh? Was I planning to?

You: Oh . . . well, weren't you going to buy me perfume?

Neil: Now, why should I buy you perfume?

You: Well, I love perfume . . . do you like what I'm wearing, by the way? It's my own blend of Chanel No. 5 and. . . .

Neil: Yeah, now that you mention it . . .

You: . . . and I just thought that, as a symbol of your lasting devotion, you might want to buy me some perfume . . .

Neil: Now, just what have you done to earn my lasting devotion? Or perfume, for that matter?

You: Well, it's not a question of earning, exactly. I mean if I want something, can't I have it?

Neil: I don't know. Can I have anything I want?

You: (Shake your head "No" and change the subject NOW. Ask for something *else* and make *this* your new talk topic.) . . . but I'll tell you what else I'd like from downtown—a Tech student, male—to do my term paper for me.

and the topic is changed to term papers for the time being. Flirtation Accomplished![59]

Peck manages to come pretty close to seduction in the latter stages of the party:

> When you *do* see him later, resume flirting.
>
> And, since it's later in the evening now, let's get a bit more serious about it.
>
> The most serious flirtation is physical. . . .
>
> Tell him his shoulders look tense. . . . And to relax his shoulders he should move them in a circle—forward, then up, then back, then down. You demonstrate this, of course, because when your shoulders are back, your chest looks good. . . .
>
> This is known, in popular parlance, as giving a guy the come-on. And he nearly always does.
>
> Where is all this leading? Maybe to choosing partners and making-out. Let's face facts. At some parties, this is what happens. And whether or not it does is something you really have no control over. We've been assuming, however, that you go along with the idea. . . .[60]

But she catches herself and remembers the decorum of her young neophyte at the last moment:

> By the way, other people are going to glance your way at odd moments. Even if you're 100 percent for this sporting scene, can you be a little aware of how you look to *them*? You don't want Frank's last impression of you this evening to be of you in an uncharming *sprawl*, do you?[61]

Leaving our young party-girl in an uncharming sprawl on the floor is probably as good a place as any to take our exit from Peck's book.

SEXUAL GAME PLAYING AND SELF-ACTUALIZATION

In this chapter we have argued that obscenity involves anything that degrades the essential humanity of human beings. Soft-core pornography is one example of such obscenity; the prostituted life-styles modelled upon such literature are another example. The basic clarification of these ideas is contained in the concept of self-actualization.

As Abraham Maslow makes clear, self-actualization represents the fulfillment of the individual's highest potential, his *becoming* everything he has the capacity to become.[62] Carl Rogers has identified the conditions under which relationships can be self-actualizing.[63] These include trust, risk-taking, true intimacy and caring. Only when people are willing to face the vulnerability of genuine relationships—to put away the guns, masks and facades—are they able to experience the knowledge of self and others which can lead to self-actualization. If they approach others with distrust or threat orientations, they must construct a complex but shaky edifice of poses which keep them from knowing themselves or others, which operate as a form of self-fulfilling prophecy, and which fixate growth at a level far short of self-actualization. That is an obscene thing to do to oneself or another.

We believe that contemporary American societal forces have created a nation of permanent adolescents. There is insufficient space in this chapter to adequately develop the argument, but in addition to the values and social processes already mentioned, one doesn't have to look much beyond the force of *competition* in American society to locate the source of game-playing. Americans are so oriented toward success striving, toward successful manipulation of objects, that little room is left for the development of person-oriented values. Instead, the person himself becomes an object: the man a "prize" to be snatched away from the competition, the woman a status symbol to be dangled on the arm of the man, the child a possession to be paraded in front of relatives and friends. We have become as plastic dolls, responding virtually devoid of empathy or fellow-feeling.

While the counter-culture can be viewed as attempting to change some of these pornographic aspects of American social and sexual life, several caveats are in order. First, the counter-culture is still a relatively small minority, and an apparently dwindling one. Second, the system has shown a remarkable ability to co-opt the counter-culture and convert its symbols into new styles and fashions of the game-players. Third, the counter-culture shares, along with the general culture, in many aspects of a "fun morality" which can be viewed as counterpoint to the pressures of competitive striving. Such a hedonism can hardly be viewed as providing a basis for self-actualization in the fullest sense. The lack of commitment to permanent relationships is an important concomitant of this pattern. Finally, in our view, many aspects of the counter-culture are themselves pornographic. "Free love" in return for a "stash of pot," for example, may be more *honest* than some of the middle-class games, but it can hardly be said to be less prostituting or more self-actualizing. It's still "Love American style."

NOTES

1. For a general statement of the relationship between society and thought, see any monograph or textbook on the sociology of knowledge; Werner Stark, *The Sociology of Knowledge* (London: Routledge & Kegan Paul, 1958) is representative. For a parallel perspective relating societal development to achievement themes in children's literature, see David C. McClelland *The Achieving Society* (Princeton: Van Nostrand, 1961).

2. Cf. Richard L. Means, *The Ethical Imperative* (New York: Doubleday, 1969).

3. Albert Ellis and Roger Conway, *The Art of Erotic Seduction* (New York: Ace Publishing, 1967).

4. Helen Gurley Brown, *Sex and the Single Girl* (New York: Geis, 1962).

5. For a similar view, see Ned Polsky, "On the Sociology of Pornography," in *Hustlers, Beats, and Others* (New York: Doubleday-Anchor, 1969), pp. 183-200.

6. Concerning both of the above aspects of hard-core pornography, see The Presidential Commission on Obscenity and Pornography, *The Report of the Commission on Obscenity and Pornography* (Washington, D.C.: U.S. Government Printing Office, 1970); portions are reprinted in this volume.

7. Ellen Peck, *How To Get A Teenage Boy and What To Do With Him When You Get Him* (New York: Avon Books, 1969), pp. 223-24.

8. George Steiner, "Night Words: High Pornography and Human Privacy," in *Language and Silence: Essays on Language Literature, and the Inhuman* (New York: Atheneum Press, 1967), pp. 76-77; reprinted in this volume. All page numbers in references to other articles in this volume refer to the pagination in the original source rather than to the present volume.

9. In this regard, see the definition of obscenity in Fr. Harold Gardiner, "Moral Principles Toward a Definition of the Obscene," *Law and Contemporary Problems*, vol. 20 (Fall 1955): 560-71, reprinted in this volume.

10. Niccolo Machiavelli, *The Prince* written 1513 (New York: Collier, 1938). The modern American prototype is Dale Carnegie, *How to Win Friends and Influence People* (New York: Simon and Schuster, 1936). While Carnegie's book differs greatly in intent from either *The Prince* or *Playboy*, the emphasis on "winning and influencing" others is still the very essence of machiavellianism.

11. Peter Michelson, "The Pleasures of Commodity or How to Make the

World Safe for Pornography," *The Antioch Review*, vol. 24 (Spring, 1969): 84; reprinted in this volume.

12. For definitions and discussion of these value orientations as sources of alienation in American society, see John MacGregor, "Western Beliefs and Values and the Quality of American Life," in *Proceedings of the Second Annual Congress on the Quality of American Life* (Chicago: American Medical Association, in press).

13. The original statement of this view is in Willard Waller, "The Rating and Dating Complex," *American Sociological Review*, vol. 2 (October 1937): 727-34.

14. See Richard Christie, and Florence L. Geis, *Studies in Machiavellianism* (New York and London: Academic Press, 1970); and Stanley S. Guterman, *The Machiavellians: A Social-Psychological Study of Moral Character and Organizational Milieu* (Lincoln: University of Nebraska Press, 1970).

15. Ibid.

16. Christie, *Studies in Machiavellianism*, pp. 173, 209, 235, 311, 358, 371, 375. The game playing and duplicity are particularly important and receive extended attention below.

17. See Martin Buber, *I and Thou*, trans. Walter Kauffman (New York: Scribners, 1970).

18. See especially, Erving Goffman, *The Presentation of Self in Everyday Life* (New York: Doubleday Anchor, 1959); *Behavior in Public Places* (New York: Free Press, 1963); and *Interaction Ritual* (New York: Doubleday Anchor, 1967).

19. Goffman, *Presentation of Self*, Ch. 3.

20. See Steiner, "Night Words," for a similar view.

21. Gael Greene, *The Cosmo Girl's Guide to the New Etiquette* (New York: Special Projects Division, Cosmopolitan, 1971).

22. Peck, *How To Get a Teenage Boy*.

23. Ellis and Conway, *The Art of Erotic Seduction*.

24. Or see Walter M. Gerson, and Sander H. Lund, "Playboy Magazine: Sophisticated Smut or Social Revolution?" *Journal of Popular Culture*, vol. 2 (Winter 1967): 218-27; or Michelson, "The Pleasures of Commodity."

25. Cf. William Iversen, *The Pious Pornographers* (New York: Morrow, 1963); and David Sonenschein, "Love and Sex in the Romance Magazines," *Journal of Popular Culture*, vol. 4 (Fall 1970), for analyses of the pornographic themes in popular women's magazines somewhat parallel to our own.

26. The classification scheme is our own, but it is not unlike others in common usage. For present purposes, it is intended primarily as a convenience in classifying games, rather than as an analytical tool. On the other hand, note that the basic games tend to develop in the sequence we have listed them, i.e., first the phony pose is assumed, then evasions are engaged in in order to maintain the pose, then the "patsy" is set up and finally—when he no longer serves a purpose—the patsy is put down.

27. Peck, *How To Get a Teenage Boy*, p. 21.

28. Ibid, p. 22.

29. Ibid, pp. 28-29.

30. Greene, *The Cosmo Girl's Guide*, p. 8.

31. Peck, *How To Get a Teenage Boy*, p. 44.

32. Ibid, p. 45.

33. Ibid, p. 47.

34. Greene, *The Cosmo Girl's Guide*, p. 8.

35. Ibid, pp. 10-11. This last statement provides its own vivid illustration of how ludicrous the life of a phony can be. By the way, you might try reading some of these passages aloud to friends in *your* favorite put-on voice to participate fully in the message of phoniness that's being communicated here. Try this one for instance, which is Greene's advice to the Cosmo girl on how to "date inexpensively":

> Have an orgy of old movies all day on the *telly*, nibbling imported goodies out of cans (your treat) . . . smoked mussels, Greek olives, pickled eggplant, artichoke hearts, quail eggs, truffled foie gras, babas au rhum . . . fresh, strong espresso brewed in your tiny Neopolitan coffee pot. Ibid, p. 23.

36. Ellis and Conway, *The Art of Erotic Seduction*, pp. 19, 21.

37. Ibid, p. 23.

38. Ibid, pp. 27-28.

39. This can involve put-down too, where it's meant to psychologically castrate the male partner, as in some current variations of "women's lib."

40. Peck, *How To Get a Teenage Boy*, pp. 262-63.

41. Ibid, p. 263.

42. Greene, *The Cosmo Girl's Guide*, p. 33.

43. Ibid, pp. 47-48.

44. Ellis and Conway, *The Art of Erotic Seduction*, p. 53.

45. Ibid, p. 13.

46. These originally appeared in Albert Ellis, *Sex and the Single Man* (New York: Lyle Stuart, 1963).

47. Ellis and Conway, *The Art of Erotic Seduction*, p. 69.

48. Ibid, pp. 83-84.

49. Ibid, p. 86.

50. Ibid, p. 87.

51. Ibid, p. 50.

52. Cf., for example, "J", *The Sensuous Woman* (New York: Dell Publishing, 1969); Wendy Bradley, *How to be Sensual . . . (and Drive Him Wild)* (New York: Modern Literary Editions, 1970); "M", *The Sensuous Man* (New York: Dell Publishing, 1971); and Robert Chartham, *The Sensuous Couple* (New York: Penthouse/Ballantine, 1971).

53. Greene, *The Cosmo Girl's Guide*, p. 25.

54. The put-down and its derivative, the set-up/put-down are not considered here since there are virtually no examples of them in soft-core pornography. While there are several reasons for this, the most important is that put-downs simply don't fit the repertoire of a machiavellian, given the

ends. The put-down is a way of *ending* an unsatisfactory relationship, not a way of "baiting and trapping a live one." Only in the relatively rare situation of a highly masochistic victim would a put-down be the appropriate come-on. Finally, as Eric Berne points out in his classic work on games, *Games People Play* (New York: Grove Press, 1964), put-downs are primarily unconscious games of which the players themselves are unaware. Machiavellians, in contrast, are deliberate game players, or "con-men." They are much too calculating to use put-downs. See Everett Shostrom, *Man the Manipulator* (Nashville, Tenn.: Abingdon Press, 1964), for more on the distinction between conscious and unconscious games.

55. Michelson, "The Pleasures of Commodity." Flirtation is the pattern of the "sexual sell" used by American business firms, who appear to offer sex along with the product, but who always fail to deliver the goods. In our view, the come-on/put-off image of many female bank tellers joins the issues of money and sex about as closely as can be done without going into actual seduction or literal prostitution.

56. Peck, *How To Catch a Teenage Boy*, p. 47.

57. Ibid, pp. 123-24.

58. Ibid, p. 134.

59. Ibid, pp. 224-25.

60. Ibid, pp. 227-29.

61. Ibid, p. 229.

62. See Abraham Maslow, *Toward a Psychology of Being*, 2nd ed. (New York: Van Nostrand, 1968). Maslow and a number of his contemporaries have, we believe, provided enough evidence from the clinician's standpoint to leave no question about the objective status of self-actualization, its parameters, and the conditions under which it is blocked or flourishes.

63. See Carl Rogers, *On Becoming a Person* (Boston: Houghton-Mifflin, 1961).

Night Words: High Pornography and Human Privacy

George Steiner

Is there any science-fiction pornography? I mean something *new*, an invention by the human imagination of new sexual experience? Science fiction alters at will the coordinates of space and time; it can set effect before cause; it works within a logic of total potentiality— "all that can be imagined can happen." But has it added a single item to the repertoire of the erotic? I understand that in a forthcoming novel the terrestrial hero and explorer indulges in mutual masturbation with a bizarre, interplanetary creature. But there is no real novelty in that. Presumably one can use anything from seaweed to accordions, from meteorites to lunar pumice. A galactic monster would make no essential difference to the act; it would not extend in any real sense the range of our sexual being.

The point is crucial. Despite all the lyric or obsessed cant about the boundless varieties and dynamics of sex, the actual sum of possible gestures, consummations and imaginings is drastically limited. There are probably more foods, more undiscovered eventualities of gastronomic enjoyment or revulsion, than there have been sexual inventions since the Empress Theodora resolved "to

From *Language and Silence: Essays on Language, Literature, and the Inhuman*, by George Steiner. Copyright ©1965 by George Steiner. Reprinted by permission of the author and Atheneum Publishers.

satisfy all amorous orifices of the human body to the full and at the same time." There just aren't that many orifices. The mechanics of orgasm imply fairly rapid exhaustion and frequent intermission. The nervous system is so organized that responses to simultaneous stimuli at different points of the body tend to yield a single, somewhat blurred sensation. The notion (fundamental to de Sade and much pornographic art) that one can double one's ecstasy by engaging in coitus while being at the same time deftly sodomized is sheer nonsense. In short: given the physiological and nervous complexion of the human body, the number of ways in which orgasm can be achieved or arrested, the total modes of intercourse, are fundamentally finite. The mathematics of sex stop somewhere in the region of *soixante-neuf*; there are no transcendental series.

This is the logic behind de Sade's *120 Days*. With the pedantic frenzy of a man trying to carry pi to its final decimal, he labored to imagine and present the sum total of erotic combinations and variants. He pictured a small group of human bodies and tried to narrate every mode of sexual pleasure and pain to which they could be subject. The variables are surprisingly few. Once all possible positions of the body have been tried—the law of gravity does interfere—once the maximum number of erogenous zones of the maximum number of participants have been brought into contact— abrasive, frictional, or intrusive—there is not much left to do or imagine. One can whip or be whipped; one can eat excrement or quaff urine; mouth and private part can meet in this or that commerce. After which there is the gray of morning and the sour knowledge that things have remained fairly generally the same since man first met goat and woman.

This is the obvious, necessary reason for the inescapable monotony of pornographic writing, for the fact well known to all haunters of Charing Cross Road or pre-Gaullist bookstalls that dirty books are maddeningly the same. The trappings change. Once it was the Victorian nanny in high-button shoes birching the master, or the vicar peering over the edge of the boys' lavatory. The Spanish Civil War brought a plethora of raped nuns, of buttocks on bayonets. At present, specialized dealers report a steady demand for "WS" (stories of wife-swapping, usually in a suburban or honeymoon resort setting). But the fathomless tide of straight trash has never varied much. It operates within highly conventionalized formulas of lowgrade sadism, excremental drollery and banal fantasies of phallic prowess or feminine responsiveness. In its own way, the stuff is as predictable as a Boy Scout manual.

Above the pulp line—but the exact boundaries are impossible to draw—lies the world of erotica, of sexual writing with literary pretensions or genuine claims. This world is much larger than is commonly realized. It goes back to Egyptian literary papyri. At certain moments in Western society, the amount of "high pornography" being produced may have equaled, if not surpassed, ordinary *belles-lettres*. I suspect that this was the case in Roman Alexandria, in France during the *Régence*, perhaps in London around the 1890s. Much of this subterranean literature is bound to disappear. But anyone who has been allowed access to the Kinsey library in Bloomington, Indiana, and has been lucky enough to have John Gagnon as his guide, is made aware of the profoundly revealing, striking fact that there is hardly a major writer of the nineteenth or twentieth century who has not, at some point in his career, be it in earnest or in the deeper earnest of jest, produced a pornographic work. Likewise there are remarkably few painters, from the eighteenth century to post-Impressionism, who have not produced at least one set of pornographic plates or sketches. (Would one of the definitions of abstract, nonobjective art be that it cannot be pornographic?)

Obviously a certain proportion of this vast body of writing has literary power and significance. Where a Diderot, a Crébillon *fils*, a Verlaine, a Swinburne or an Appollinaire write erotica, the result will have some of the qualities which distinguish their more public works. Figures such as Beardsley and Pierre Louÿs are minor, but their lubricities have a period charm. Nevertheless, with very few exceptions, "high pornography" is not of pre-eminent literary importance. It is simply not true that the locked cabinets of great libraries or private collections contain masterpieces of poetry or fiction which hypocrisy and censorship banish from the light. (Certain eighteenth-century drawings and certain Japanese prints suggest that the case of graphic art may be different; here there seems to be work of the first quality which is not generally available.) What emerges when one reads some of the classics of erotica is the fact that they too are intensely conventionalized, that their repertoire of fantasy is limited, and that it merges, almost imperceptibly, into the dream-trash of straight, mass-produced pornography.

In other words: the line between, say, *Thérèse Philosophe* or *Lesbia Brandon*, on the one hand, and *Sweet Lash* or *The Silken Thighs*, on the other, is easily blurred. What distinguishes the "forbidden classic" from under-the-counter delights on Frith Street is, essentially, a matter of semantics, of the level of vocabulary and rhetorical device used to provoke erection. It is not fundamental. Take the masturbating housemaid in a very recent example of the Great American Novel, and the housemaid similarly engaged in *They Called Her Dolly* (n.d., price six shillings). From the point of view of erotic stimulus, the difference is one of language, or more exactly— as verbal precisions now appear in high literature as well—the difference is one of narrative sophistication. Neither piece of writing adds anything new to the potential of human emotion; both add to the waste.

Genuine additions are, in fact, very rare. The list of writers who have had the genius to enlarge our actual compass of sexual awareness, who have given the erotic play of the mind a novel focus, an area of recognition previously unknown or fallow, is very small. It would, I think, include Sappho, in whose verse the Western ear caught, perhaps for the first time, the shrill, nerve-rending note of sterile sexuality, of a libido necessarily, deliberately, in excess of any assuagement. Catullus seems to have added something, though it is at this historical distance nearly impossible to identify that which startled in his vision, which caused so real a shock of consciousness. The close, delicately plotted concordance between orgasm and death in Baroque and Metaphysical poetry and art clearly enriched our legacy of excitement, as had the earlier focus on virginity. The development in Dostoevsky, Proust and Mann of the correlations between nervous infirmity, the psychopathology of the organism, and a special erotic vulnerability, is probably new. De Sade and Sacher-Masoch codified, found a dramatic syntax for, areas of arousal previously diffuse or less explicitly realized. In *Lolita* there is a genuine enrichment of our common stock of temptations. It is as if Vladimir Nabokov had brought into our field of vision what lay at the far edge—in Balzac's *La Rabouilleuse*, for instance, or what had been kept carefully implausible through disproportion (*Alice in Wonderland*). But such annexations of insight are rare.

The plain truth is that, in literary erotica as well as in the great mass of "dirty books," the same stimuli, the same contortions and fantasies, occur over and over with unutterable monotony. In most erotic writing, as in man's wet dreams, the imagination turns, time and time again, inside the bounded circle of what the body can experience. The actions of the mind when we masturbate are not a dance; they are a treadmill.

Maurice Girodias would riposte that this is not the issue, that the interminable succession of fornications, flagellations, onanisms, masochistic fantasies and homosexual punch-ups which fill his *Olympia Reader* are inseparable from its literary excellence, from the artistic originality and integrity of the books he published at the Olympia Press in Paris. He would say that several of the books he championed, and from which he has now selected representative passages, stand in the vanguard of modern sensibility, that they are classics of post-war literature. If they are so largely concerned with sexual experience, the reason is that the modern writer has recognized in sexuality the last open frontier, the terrain on which his talent must, if it is to be pertinent and honest, engage the stress of our culture. The pages of the *Reader* are strewn with four-letter words, with detailed accounts of intimate and specialized sexual acts, precisely because the writer has had to complete the campaign of liberation initiated by Freud, because he has had to overcome the verbal taboos, the hypocrisies of imagination in which former generations labored when alluding to the most vital, complex part of man's being.

Writing dirty books was a necessary participation in the common fight against the Square World . . . an act of duty.

Girodias has a case. His reminiscences and polemics make sour reading (he tends to whine); but his actual publishing record shows nerve and brilliance. The writings of Henry Miller matter to the history of American pose and self-definition. Samuel Beckett's *Watt* appeared with Olympia, as did some writings of Jean Genêt, though not the plays or the best prose. *Fanny Hill* and, to a lesser degree, *Candy*, are mock-epics of orgasm, books in which any sane man will take delight. Lawrence Durrell's *Black Book* seems to me grossly overrated, but it has its serious defenders. Girodias himself would

probably regard *Naked Lunch* as his crowning discernment. I don't
see it. The book strikes me as a strident bore, illiterate and
self-satisfied right to its heart of pulp. Its repute is important only
for what it tells us of the currents of homosexuality, camp and
modish brutality which dominate present "sophisticated" literacy.
Burroughs indicts his readers, but not in the brave, prophetic sense
argued by Girodias. Nevertheless, there can be no doubt of the
genuineness of Girodias' commitment or of the risks he took.

Moreover, two novels on his list *are* classics, books whose genius
he recognized and with which his own name will remain proudly
linked: *Lolita* and *The Ginger Man*. It is a piece of bleak irony—
beautifully appropriate to the entire "dirty book" industry—that a
subsequent disagreement with Nabokov now prevents Girodias from
including anything of *Lolita* in his anthology. To all who first met
Humbert Humbert in *The Traveller's Companion Series*, a green
cover and the Olympia Press's somewhat mannered typography will
remain a part of one of the high moments of contemporary
literature. This alone should have spared Mr. Girodias the legal and
financial harryings by which Gaullist Victorianism hounded him out
of business.

But the best of what Olympia published is now available on every
drugstore counter—this being the very mark of Girodias' foresight.
The *Olympia Reader* must be judged by what it actually contains.
And far too much of it is tawdry stuff, "doing dirt on life," with
only the faintest pretensions to literary merit or adult intelligence.

It is almost impossible to get through the book at all. Pick it up at
various points and the sense of *déja-vu* is inescapable ("This is one
stag movie I've seen before"). Whether a naked woman gets tor-
mented in de Sade's dungeons (*Justine*), during Spartacus' revolt
(Marcus Van Heller: *Roman Orgy*), in a kinky French château (*The
Story of O*), or in an Arab house (*Kama Houri* by one Ataullah
Mordaan) makes damn little difference. Fellatio and buggery seem
fairly repetitive joys, whether enacted between Paris hooligans in
Genêt's *Thief's Journal*, between small-time hustlers and ex-prize
fighters (*The Gaudy Image*), or between lordly youths by Edwardian
gaslight in *Teleny*, a silly piece attributed to Oscar Wilde.

After 50 pages of "hardening nipples," "softly opening thighs,"
and "hot rivers" flowing in and out of the ecstatic anatomy, the
spirit cries out, not in hypocritical outrage, not because I am a poor

Square throttling my libido, but in pure, nauseous boredom. Even fornication can't be as dull, as hopelessly predictable, as all that.

Of course, there are moments which excite. *Sin for Breakfast* ends on a subtle, comic note of lewdness. *The Woman Thing* uses all the four-letter words and anatomical exactitudes with real force; it exhibits a fine ear for the way in which sexual heat compresses and erodes our uses of language. Those, and I imagine it includes most men, who use the motif of female ononism in their own fantasy life will find a vivid patch. There may be other nuggets. But who can get through the thing? For my money, there is one sublime moment in the *Reader*. It comes in an extract (possibly spurious?) from Frank Harris' *Life and Loves*. Coiling and uncoiling in diverse postures with two naked Oriental nymphets and their British procuress, Harris is suddenly struck with the revelation that "there indeed is evidence to prove the weakness of so much of the thought of Karl Marx. It is only the bohemian who can be free, not the proletarian." The image of Frank Harris, all limbs and propensities ecstatically engaged, suddenly disproving *Das Kapital*, is worth the price of admission.

But not really. For that price is much higher than Girodias, Mary McCarthy, Wayland Young and other advocates of total frankness seem to realize. It is a price which cuts deep, not only into the true liberty of the writer, but also into the diminishing reserves of feeling and imaginative response in our society.

The preface to the *Olympia Reader* ends in triumph:

> Moral censorship was an inheritance from the past, deriving from centuries of domination by the Christian clergy. Now that it is practically over, we may expect literature to be transformed by the advent of freedom. Not freedom in its negative aspects, but as the means of exploring all the positive aspects of the human mind, which are all more or less related to, or generated by, sex.

This last proposition is almost unbelievably silly. What needs a serious inquiry is the assertion about freedom, about a new and transforming liberation of literature through the abolition of verbal and imaginative taboos.

Since the *Lady Chatterly* case and the defeat of a number of attempts to suppress books by Henry Miller, the sluice gates stand open. De Sade, the homosexual elaborations of Genêt and Burroughs, *Candy, Sexus, The Story of O,* are freely available. No censorship would choose to make itself ridiculous by challenging the sadistic eroticism, the minutiae of sodomy (smell and all) which grace Mailer's *American Dream.* This is an excellent thing. But let us be perfectly clear why. Censorship is stupid and repugnant for two empirical reasons: censors are men no better than ourselves, their judgments are no less fallible or open to dishonesty. Secondly, the thing won't work: those who really want to get hold of a book will do so somehow. This is an entirely different argument from saying that pornography doesn't in fact deprave the mind of the reader, or incite to wasteful or criminal gestures. *It may, or it may not.* We simply do not have enough evidence either way. The question is far more intricate than many of our literary champions of total freedom would allow. But to say that censorship won't work and should not be asked to is *not* to say that there has been a liberation of literature, that the writer is, in any genuine sense, freer.

On the contrary. The sensibility of the writer is free where it is most humane, where it seeks to apprehend and re-enact the marvelous variety, complication and resilience of life by means of words as scrupulous, as personal, as brimful of the mystery of human communication, as the language can yield. The very opposite of freedom is cliché, and nothing is less free, more inert with convention and hollow brutality, than a row of four-letter words. Literature is a living dialogue between writer and reader, only if the writer shows a twofold respect: for the imaginative maturity of his reader, and, in a very complex but central way, for the wholeness, for the independence and core of life, in the personages he creates.

Respect for the reader signifies that the poet or novelist invites the consciousness of the reader to collaborate with his own in the act of presentment. He does not tell all because his work is not a primer for children or the retarded. He does not exhaust the possible responses of his reader's own imaginings, but delights in the fact that we will fill in from our own lives, from resources of memory and desire proper to ourselves, the contours he has drawn. Tolstoy is infinitely freer, infinitely more exciting, than the new eroticists when he arrests his narrative at the door of the Karenins' bedroom, when he merely initiates, through the simile of a dying flame, of ash cooling in the grate, a perception of sexual defeat which each of us can re-live or detail for himself. George Eliot is free, and treats her readers as free, adult human beings, when she conveys, through inflection of style and mood, the truth about the Casaubon honeymoon in *Middlemarch*, when she makes us imagine for ourselves how Dorothea has been violated by some essential obtuseness. These are profoundly exciting scenes, they enrich and complicate our sexual awareness, far beyond the douchebag idylls of the contemporary "free" novel. There is no real freedom whatever in the compulsive physiological exactitudes of present day "high pornography," because there is no respect for the reader, whose imaginative means are set at nil.

And there is none for the sanctity of autonomous life in the characters of the novel, for that tenacious integrity of existence which makes a Stendhal, a Tolstoy, a Henry James tread warily around their own creations. The novels being produced under the new code of total statement shout at their personages: strip, fornicate, perform this or that act of sexual perversion. So did the S.S. guards at rows of living men and women. The total attitudes are not, I think, entirely distinct. There may be deeper affinities than we as yet understand between the "total freedom" of the uncensored erotic imagination and the total freedom of the sadist. That these two freedoms have emerged in close historical proximity may not be coincidence. Both are exercised at the expense of someone else's humanity, of someone else's most precious right—the right to a private life of feeling.

This is the most dangerous aspect of all. Future historians may come to characterize the present era in the West as one of a massive onslaught on human privacy, on the delicate processes by which we seek to become our own singular selves, to hear the echo of our specific being. This onslaught is being pressed by the very conditions of an urban mass technocracy, by the necessary uniformities of our economic and political choices, by the new electronic media of communication and persuasion, by the ever-increasing exposure of our thoughts and actions to sociological, psychological and material intrusions and controls. Increasingly, we come to know real privacy, real space in which to experiment with our sensibility, only in extreme guises: nervous breakdown, addiction, economic failure. Hence the appalling monotony and *publicity*—in the full sense of the word—of so many outwardly prosperous lives. Hence, also, the need for nervous stimuli of an unprecedented brutality and technical authority.

Sexual relations are, or should be, one of the citadels of privacy, the night place where we must be allowed to gather the splintered, harried elements of our consciousness to some kind of inviolate order and repose. It is in sexual experience that a human being alone, and two human beings in that attempt at total communication which is also communion, can discover the unique bent of their identity. There we may find for ourselves, through imperfect striving and repeated failure, the words, the gestures, the mental images which set the blood to racing. In that dark and wonder ever renewed both the fumblings and the light must be our own.

The new pornographers subvert this last, vital privacy; they do our imagining for us. They take away the words that were of the night and shout them over the rooftops, making them hollow. The images of our lovemaking, the stammerings we resort to in intimacy, come prepackaged. From the rituals of adolescent petting to the recent university experiment in which faculty wives agreed to practice onanism in front of the researchers' cameras, sexual life, particularly in America, is passing more and more into the public domain. This is a profoundly ugly and demeaning thing whose effects on our identity and resources of feeling we understand as little as we do the impact on our nerves of the perpetual "suberoticism" and sexual suggestion of modern advertisement. Natural selection tells of limbs and functions which atrophy through lack of use; the power to feel, to experience and realize the precarious uniqueness of each other's being, can also wither in a society. And it is no mere accident (as Orwell knew) that the standardization of sexual life, either through controlled license or compelled puritanism, should accompany totalitarian politics.

Thus the present danger to the freedom of literature and to the inward freedom of our society is not censorship or verbal reticence. The danger lies in the facile contempt which the erotic novelist exhibits for his readers, for his personages and for the language. Our dreams are marketed wholesale.

Because there were words it did not use, situations it did not represent graphically, because it demanded from the reader not obeisance but live echo, much of Western poetry and fiction has been a school to the imagination, an exercise in making one's awareness more exact, more humane. My true quarrel with the *Olympia Reader* and the genre it embodies is not that so much of the stuff is boring and abjectly written. It is that these books leave a man less free, less himself, than they found him; that they leave language poorer, less endowed with a capacity for fresh discrimination and excitement. It is not a new freedom that they bring, but a new servitude. In the name of human privacy, enough!

PORNOGRAPHY
AND
SOCIAL SCIENCE RESEARCH

The Effects of Explicit Sexual Materials

The Report of the Commission on Obscenity and Pornography

The Effects Panel of the Commission undertook to develop a program of research designed to provide information on the kinds of effects which result from exposure to sexually explicit materials and the conditions under which these effects occur.[1] The research program embraced both inquiries into public and professional belief regarding the effects of such materials, and empirical research bearing on the actual occurrence and condition of the effects. The areas of potential effect to which the research was addressed included sexual arousal, emotions, attitudes, overt sexual behavior, moral character and criminal and other antisocial behavior related to sex.

Research procedures included: (1) surveys employing national probability samples of adults and young persons; (2) quasi-experimental studies of selected populations; (3) controlled experimental studies; and (4) studies of rates and incidence of sex offenses and illegitimacy at the national level. A major study, which is cited frequently in these pages, was a national survey of American adults and youth which involved face-to-face interviews with a random

Reprinted from *The Report of the Commission on Obscenity and Pornography*. (Washington, D.C.: United States Government Printing Office, 1970). pp. 23-27.

probability sample of 2,486 adults and 769 young persons between the ages of 15 and 20 in the continental United States.[2]

The strengths and weaknesses of the various research methods utilized are discussed in Section A of the Report of the Effects Panel of the Commission.[3] That Report is based upon the many technical studies which generated the data from which the Panel's conclusions were derived.

OPINION CONCERNING EFFECTS OF SEXUAL MATERIALS

There is no consensus among Americans regarding what they consider to be the effects of viewing or reading explicit sexual materials. A diverse and perhaps inconsistent set of beliefs concerning the effects of sexual materials is held by large and necessarily overlapping portions of American men and women. Between 40 percent and 60 percent believe that sexual materials provide information about sex, provide entertainment, lead to moral breakdown, improve sexual relationships of married couples, lead people to commit rape, produce boredom with sexual materials, encourage innovation in marital sexual technique and lead people to lose respect for women. Some of these presumed effects are obviously socially undesirable, while others may be regarded as socially neutral or desirable. When questioned about effects, persons were more likely to report having personally experienced desirable than undesirable ones. Among those who believed undesirable effects had occurred, there was a greater likelihood of attributing their occurrences to others than to self. But mostly, the undesirable effects were just believed to have happened without reference to self or personal acquaintances.

Surveys of psychiatrists, psychologists, sex educators, social workers, counselors and similar professional workers reveal that large majorities of such groups believe that sexual materials do not have harmful effects on either adults or adolescents. On the other hand, a survey of police chiefs found that 58 percent believed that "obscene" books played a significant role in causing juvenile delinquency.

EMPIRICAL EVIDENCE CONCERNING EFFECTS

A number of empirical studies conducted recently by psychiatrists, psychologists and sociologists attempted to assess the effects of exposure to explicit sexual materials. This body of research includes several study designs, a wide range of subjects and respondents and a variety of effect indicators. Some questions in this area are not answered by the existing research, some are answered more fully than others and many questions have yet to be asked. Continued research efforts which embrace both replicative studies and inquiries into areas not yet investigated are needed to extend and clarify existing findings and to specify more concretely the conditions under which specific effects occur. The findings of available research are summarized below.

Psychosexual Stimulation

Experimental and survey studies show that exposure to erotic stimuli produces sexual arousal in substantial portions of both males and females. Arousal is dependent on both characteristics of the stimulus and characteristics of the viewer or user.

Recent research casts doubt on the common belief that women are vastly less aroused by erotic stimuli than are men. The supposed lack of female response may well be due to social and cultural inhibitions against reporting such arousal and to the fact that erotic material is generally oriented to a male audience. When viewing erotic stimuli, more women report the physiological sensations that are associated with sexual arousal than directly report being sexually aroused.

Research also shows that young persons are more likely to be aroused by erotica than are older persons. Persons who are college educated, religiously inactive and sexually experienced are more likely to report arousal than persons who are less educated, religiously active and sexually inexperienced.

Several studies show that depictions of conventional sexual behavior are generally regarded as more stimulating than depictions of less conventional activity. Heterosexual themes elicit more frequent and stronger arousal responses than depictions of homosexual activity; petting and coitus themes elicit greater arousal than oral sexuality, which in turn elicits more than sadomasochistic themes.

Satiation

The only experimental study on the subject to date found that continued or repeated exposure to erotic stimuli over 15 days resulted in satiation (marked diminution) of sexual arousal and interest in such material. In this experiment, the introduction of novel sex stimuli partially rejuvenated satiated interest, but only briefly. There was also partial recovery of interest after two months of nonexposure.

Effects Upon Sexual Behavior

When people are exposed to erotic materials, some persons increase masturbatory or coital behavior, a smaller proportion decrease it, but the majority of persons report no change in these behaviors. Increases in either of these behaviors are short-lived and generally disappear within 48 hours. When masturbation follows exposure, it tends to occur among individuals with established masturbatory patterns or among persons with established but un-available sexual partners. When coital frequences increase following exposure to sex stimuli, such activation generally occurs among sexually experienced persons with established and available sexual partners. In one study, middle-aged married couples reported in-creases in both the frequency and variety of coital performance during the 24 hours after the couples viewed erotic films.

In general, established patterns of sexual behavior were found to be very stable and not altered substantially by exposure to erotica. When sexual activity occurred following the viewing or reading of these materials, it constituted a temporary activation of individuals' pre-existing patterns of sexual behavior.

Other common consequences of exposure to erotic stimuli are increased frequences of erotic dreams, sexual fantasy and conversa-tion about sexual matters. These responses occur among both males and females. Sexual dreaming and fantasy occur as a result of exposure more often among unmarried than married persons, but conversation about sex occurs among both married and unmarried persons. Two studies found that a substantial number of married couples reported more agreeable and enhanced marital communication and an increased willingness to discuss sexual matters with each other after exposure to erotic stimuli.

Attitudinal Responses

Exposure to erotic stimuli appears to have little or no effect on already established attitudinal commitments regarding either sexuality or sexual morality. A series of four studies employing a large array of indicators found practically no significant differences in such attitudes before and after single or repeated exposures to erotica. One study did find that, after exposure, persons became more tolerant in reference to other persons' sexual activities, although their own sexual standards did not change. One study reported that some persons' attitudes toward premarital intercourse became more liberal after exposure, while other persons' attitudes became more conservative, but another study found no changes in this regard. The overall picture is almost completely a tableau of no significant change.

Several surveys suggest that there is a correlation between experience with erotic materials and general attitudes about sex: those who have more tolerant or liberal sexual attitudes tend also to have greater experience with sexual materials. Taken together, experimental and survey studies suggest that persons who are more sexually tolerant are also less rejecting of sexual material. Several studies show that after experience with erotic material, persons become less fearful of possible detrimental effects of exposure.

Emotional and Judgmental Responses

Several studies show that persons who are unfamiliar with erotic materials may experience strong and conflicting emotional reactions when first exposed to sexual stimuli. Multiple responses, such as attraction and repulsion to an unfamiliar object, are commonly observed in the research literature on psychosensory stimulation from a variety of nonsexual as well as sexual stimuli. These emotional responses are short-lived and, as with psychosexual stimulation, do not persist long after removal of the stimulus.

Extremely varied responses to erotic stimuli occur in the judgmental realm, as, for example, in the labeling of material as obscene or pornographic. Characteristics of both the viewer and the stimulus influence the response: for any given stimulus, some persons are more likely to judge it "obscene" than are others; and for persons of a given psychological or social type, some erotic themes are more likely to be judged "obscene" than are others. In general, persons who are older, less educated, religiously active, less experienced with erotic materials or feel sexually guilty, are most likely to judge a given erotic stimulus "obscene." There is some indication that stimuli may have to evoke both positive responses (interesting or stimulating), and negative responses (offensive or unpleasant), before they are judged obscene or pornographic.

Criminal and Delinquent Behavior

Delinquent and nondelinquent youth report generally similar experiences with explicit sexual materials. Exposure to sexual materials is widespread among both groups. The age of first exposure, the kinds of materials to which they are exposed, the amount of their exposure, the circumstances of exposure and their reactions to erotic stimuli are essentially the same, particularly when family and neighborhood backgrounds are held constant. There is some evidence that peer group pressure accounts for both sexual experience and exposure to erotic materials among youth. A study of a heterogeneous group of young people found that exposure to erotica had no impact upon moral character over and above that of a generally deviant background.

Statistical studies of the relationship between availability of erotic materials and the rates of sex crimes in Denmark indicate that the increased availability of explicit sexual materials has been accompanied by a decrease in the incidence of sexual crime. Analysis of police records of the same types of sex crimes in Copenhagen during the past 12 years revealed that a dramatic decrease in reported sex crimes occurred during this period and that the decrease coincided with changes in Danish law which permitted wider availability of explicit sexual materials. Other research showed that the decrease in reported sexual offenses cannot be attributed to concurrent changes in the social and legal definitions of sex crimes or in public attitudes toward reporting such crimes to the police, or in police reporting procedures.

Statistical studies of the relationship between the availability of erotic material and the rates of sex crimes in the United States presents a more complex picture. During the period in which there has been a marked increase in the availability of erotic materials, some specific rates of arrest for sex crimes have increased (e.g., forcible rape) and others have declined (e.g., overall juvenile rates). For juveniles, the overall rate of arrests for sex crimes decreased even though arrests for nonsexual crimes increased by more than 100 percent. For adults, arrests for sex offenses increased slightly more than did arrests for nonsex offenses. The conclusion is that, for America, the relationship between the availability of erotica and changes in sex crime rates neither proves nor disproves the possibility that availability of erotica leads to crime, but the massive overall increases in sex crimes that have been alleged do not seem to have occurred.

Available research indicates that sex offenders have had less adolescent experience with erotica than other adults. They do not differ significantly from other adults in relation to adult experience with erotica, in relation to reported arousal or in relation to the likelihood of engaging in sexual behavior during or following exposure. Available evidence suggests that sex offenders' early inexperience with erotic material is a reflection of their more generally deprived sexual environment. The relative absence of experience appears to constitute another indicator of atypical and inadequate sexual socialization.

In sum, empirical research designed to clarify the question has found no evidence to date that exposure to explicit sexual materials plays a significant role in the causation of delinquent or criminal behavior among youth or adults.[4] The Commission cannot conclude that exposure to erotic materials is a factor in the causation of sex crime or sex delinquency.

NOTES

1. The Report of the Effects Panel of the Commission provides a more thorough discussion and documentation of this overview.

2. The study was conducted by Response Analysis Corporation of Princeton, New Jersey, and the Institute of Survey Research of Temple University, Philadelphia, Pennsylvania.

3. See also the Preface of the Commission's Report.

4. Commissioners G. William Jones, Joseph T. Klapper and Morris A. Lipton believe "that in the interest of precision a distinction should be made between two types of statements which occur in this Report. One type, to which we subscribe, is that research to date does not indicate that a causal relationship exists between exposure to erotica and the various social ills to which the research has been addressed. There are, however, also statements to the effect that 'no evidence' exists, and we believe these should more accurately read 'no reliable evidence.' Occasional aberrant findings, some of very doubtful validity, are noted and discussed in the Report of the Effects Panel. In our opinion, none of these, either individually or in sum, are of sufficient merit to constitute reliable evidence or to alter the summary conclusion that the research to date does not indicate a causal relationship."

Violence, Pornography and Social Science

James Q. Wilson

To the extent that it has a philosophical basis, the case against censorship—at least in this country—typically rests on a utilitarian argument. Indeed, it is a leading utilitarian—John Stuart Mill—who is often cited in opposition to censorship in any form. Though Mill, in his essay *On Liberty*, wrote chiefly of the censorship of political and religious speaking and writing, his position can easily—I should say, must inevitably—be extended to the arts and amusements. "The only purpose for which power can be rightfully exercised over any member of a civilized community, against his will," Mill wrote, "is to prevent harm to others." This principle applies not only to freedom of expression, but also to "liberty of tastes and pursuits." In this latter realm, Oliver Wendell Holmes gave the utilitarian position its most memorable practical expression: "No woman was ever seduced by a book." Though many people echo this as an article of faith, it is of course an empirical statement. The truth or falsity of such factual, consequential statements is the ultimate basis of the utilitarian argument.

If the question of censorship rests on the appraisal of such consequences, then one might suppose that social science should be

Reprinted with permission from the *Public Interest*, No. 22, (Winter 1971). Copyright ©National Affairs, Inc. 1971.

an important source of information about what public policies are necessary and defensible. Careful research might, in principle, reveal the effect of the dissemination of certain images or words; if harm is to be the criterion, then a showing of such an effect would be a necessary—but not sufficient—condition for justifying the exercise of some form of legal restraint. (It is an important but little-remarked feature of utilitarianism that it can as easily justify the most extreme form of social control as it can justify the most perfect liberty; everything depends on consequences.) Of course, disutility is not the only grounds one can imagine for censorship; but in the United States, at least (and perhaps in most Western nations), it is almost invariably the only one employed—or, more accurately, the claim that no positive harm will flow from the free circulation of any visual or written material is the most common argument made *against* censorship.

Such, at least, are the philosophical premises of two presidential commissions, each of which has relied on extensive social science research to support quite different positions on the restraint of free communication. One, the National Commission on the Causes and Prevention of Violence, found that "the preponderance of available research evidence strongly suggests ... that violence in television programs can and does have adverse effects upon audiences—particularly child audiences." The other, the Commission on Obscenity and Pornography, found that "extensive empirical investigation ... provides no evidence that exposure to or use of explicit sexual materials plays a significant role in the causation of social or individual harms such as crime, delinquency, sexual or nonsexual deviancy or severe disturbances."

On the basis of these findings, the two Commissions naturally made very different policy recommendations. The Violence Commission recommended that television broadcasters abandon "children's cartoons containing serious, non-comic violence," that the time devoted to broadcasting programs containing violent episodes be reduced, that the "basic context in which violence is presented" be altered, that there be more support for educational television, that the "validity" of the motion picture rating system ("G," "X," etc.) be evaluated as it applies to violent films; and that there be "further research."[2] In contrast, the Obscenity Commission argued that the "spirit and letter of our Constitution tells us that Government should not interfere with these rights [for each individual to decide for himself what to see or to read] unless a clear threat of harm makes that course imperative." Accordingly, the Commission recommends that "federal, state and local legislation prohibiting the sale, exhibition or distribution of sexual materials to consenting adults be repealed," but that legislation preventing the "commercial distribution or display for sale" of certain sexual materials to young persons and prohibiting the "public display of sexually explicit pictorial materials" be enacted. Finally, it, too, called for more research.

"VIOLENCE" AND "SEXUALITY"

The quite different recommendations of the two commissions—one calling for more restraint (which, if taken seriously by the FCC, can only mean more constraint), the other calling for less—might be the result, not of different empirical findings, but of different judgments about similar findings. One might argue that even a slight chance of people becoming more violent as a result of television warrants restraint, whereas even a significant chance of people becoming more "sexual" as a result of looking at obscene books warrants no restraint. Violence is harmful; sexuality is not; therefore, media that might encourage the former should be regulated, whereas media that certainly encourage the latter should not.

But saying that violence is harmful and sexuality is not assumes a clear understanding of what we mean by "violence" and "sexuality." Neither Commission displayed such clarity on this score. War is violent, but the Violence Commission did not call for abandoning news programs about Vietnam. Football and hockey not only appear violent to the viewer, they are in fact violent for the participant; in contrast to westerns, people actually get hurt in televised sports programs, and the hurt cannot even be justified by a higher cause (he was a "bad guy" or he "did it for his country"). By some standards (not mine), this is the most shocking form of violence, done merely for sport or fun. Yet the Commission passed it by without censure.

As for sexuality, it cannot be utterly benign, for the Obscenity Commission wants to make it illegal for young persons to purchase pornography. On the one hand, the Commission found "no evidence" that exposure to erotica "adversely affects character or moral attitudes"; on the other hand, the Commission recommends legislation that will "aid parents in controlling the access of their children to [sexual] materials during their formative years." (Two Commission members—interestingly, the only two sociologists on it—were at least consistent: they wanted no legal restrictions at all, whether for juveniles or adults.)

Moreover, some erotic materials are violent and some forms of violence are sexual. In these cases, which element is to be decisive? The Violence Commission would presumably discourage the explicit portrayal of a rape in a film because it is violent, while the Obscenity Commission would presumably permit it because it is sexual. And what of "violence" that the recipient finds not only bearable but even enjoyable? Are sado masochistic acts violent or nonviolent?

FROM HYPOTHESES TO CONCLUSIONS

Clarity on these and other matters was not enhanced by the kind of social science research with which the Commissions supplied themselves or the uses to which they put it. In both cases, the central defect was the failure or inability to select an appropriate definition of the kind of effects either violence or erotica in the media might produce.

The great bulk of the research relied upon by the Violence Commission consisted of laboratory studies, usually involving young children or college students, in which "aggression" or "violence" was defined: (in the case of the young children) as a willingness to engage in harmless play activities involving physical force used on inanimate objects, or (in the case of the college students) as a greater willingness to administer ostensible electric shocks to other subjects under circumstances such that the student had no choice about *whether* to administer the "shocks" but only how many or with what severity.

On the basis of these laboratory experiments, plus a few other studies of lesser significance, the Task Force on Mass Media and Violence concluded:

Persons who have been effectively socialized into the norms for violence contained in the television world of violence would behave in the following manner:

a) They would probably resolve conflict by the use of violence.

b) They would probably use violence as a means to obtain desired ends.

c) They would probably passively observe violence between others.

d) They would not be likely to sanction or punish other's use of violence.

e) They would probably use a weapon when engaging in violence.

f) If they were policemen, they would be likely to meet violence with violence, often escalating its level.

To be sure, the Task Force does not say any of this has been proved; these are described as "hypotheses," but ones which are "clearly consistent with and suggested by established research findings and by the most informed social science thinking about the long-run effects of exposure to mass media portrayals of violence." And as for short-run effects, the Task Force is prepared to assert conclusions, not merely hypotheses:

Audiences who have learned violent behavior from the media are likely to exhibit that learning (i.e., engage in acts of violence) if they encounter a situation similar to the portrayal situation, expect to be rewarded for violent behavior, or do not observe disapproving reactions to the portrayed aggression from another person in the viewing situation.

The Violence Commission as a whole put the matter in simpler language: "Violence in television programs can and does have adverse effects upon audiences—particularly child audiences."

The blunt truth is there is almost no scientific evidence whatsoever to support the conclusions of either the Task Force or the Commission. Neither the Task Force nor the Commission gathered any evidence about whether children learn, in the short run or the long run, "violent behavior"—*unless what one means by "violent behavior" is a willingness to engage in certain forms of harmless play.*

BOBO DOLLS AND ELECTRIC SHOCKS

Consider what is perhaps the largest single series of experimental studies, those done by Professor Albert Bandura of Stanford University. One experiment is typical. Nursery school children watched an adult, sometimes in person, sometimes on film, hit and kick a large inflated ("Bobo") doll. Afterwards, the children were subjected to mild forms of frustration (e.g., having favored toys taken away from them). Then they were observed at play in a room filled with toys, among them Bobo Dolls. Children who had previously watched the adult hit or kick the doll were more likely to hit and kick their Bobo Dolls.

Now, if it were in the public interest to protect Bobo Dolls from being hit by children encouraged to play with them, and if hitting Bobo Dolls were a regular feature of television, then admonishing the media to refrain from such features might be in order. Of course this is not what the Commission had in mind. But what evidence is there from the Bandura experiments that aggression against dolls is ever transferred into aggression against people, or even that the children in the experiments define hitting a doll as "aggression"? In the Bandura experiments, there is no evidence at all on either score. Richard Goranson, a consultant to the Task Force, faced up to this problem in his essay. He noted that the definition of "aggression" is crucial to the meaning of the experiments. For some, aggression means "the intentional inflicting of pain or injury on another person." Clearly the Bandura experiments do not measure aggression, thus defined. Indeed, it is not even necessary to have laboratory experiments to induce in children the kind of "aggression" Bandura observed—all that is necessary is to give them a football on a Saturday afternoon in October and they will supply plenty of "aggression." Bandura argues that his definition of "aggression"—performing certain kinds of physical acts, such as hitting or kicking—is appropriate even though it is directed at nonhuman objects, but it is hard to imagine why it *should* be appropriate unless one can show that harmless play activity will later be transferred to interpersonal situations. And this is precisely what has not been shown.

The experiments that do seem to measure aggression, in the sense of intentionally harming others, are those of Leonard Berkowitz and R.H. Walters, using electric shocks. The experiments vary in their conduct and the results are not entirely consistent, but one, by Walters, suggests the general idea. Subjects were told they were participating in a study of how learning was affected by punishment. Each was told to give "electric shocks" at whatever level he wished to another subject (in reality, a confederate of the experimenter who only simulated the effects of shock, every time the "learner" made a mistake. Then the subjects were shown either a film of a knife fight (taken from *West Side Story*) or a nonviolent film. The "learning" experiment was then repeated. This time, subjects who had watched the fight scene gave slightly stronger shocks (about half a setting higher) than those who had watched the nonviolent film. Here, one might argue, is a clear case of media-induced "aggression." But there are at least two caveats: it is by no means clear that the subjects defined what they were doing as "violent"; they were told, after all, they were trying to make people learn better by punishing them for wrong answers (a not uncommon pedagogical technique), and that it was legitimate to do so. Furthermore, no subject could decide (unless he wanted to drop out of the experiment) not to give any shocks; he could only decide with what level of severity to administer them.

Very few studies have attempted to measure the incidence of genuinely aggressive behavior among persons in real-life settings and to estimate the association, if any, with exposure to media violence. The obstacles in the way of such a study are obvious—the lack of an opportunity for constant observation, the inability to control the viewing habits of respondents, and so forth. At least one such study has been done, however. Seymour Feschbach of the University of California at Los Angeles found an opportunity to use laboratory-like controls in a real-world situation. Boys attending seven residential schools in California were divided into two groups—one was allowed to watch in their cottages only television programs drawn from a list of those featuring violence (cowboy, spy, detective, police and war shows), while the other was allowed to watch only programs on a list containing nonviolent programs. They were all required to watch a minimum of six to fourteen hours of television a week for six weeks. The boys were told that the purpose was to get their ratings of the programs. Personality tests were administered before and after viewing. In addition, the teachers and cottage supervisors filled out daily reports on the boys' behavior at play and in class. Boys who had watched a steady diet of "violent" television displayed no more signs of violent or aggressive behavior than those who had watched only nonviolent programs. On only one measure did a difference appear—boys watching nonviolent programs, when asked to make up stories, made up fewer stories in which fighting took place.

Feschback has been identified with the so-called "catharsis" hypothesis—i.e., that observing media violence enables a person to discharge or vicariously satisfy whatever violent tendencies he may have. Much of the laboratory experimentation and a good deal of critical commentary has been devoted to disproving this hypothesis, and any fair summary of the state of the art would have to conclude that there is as little evidence that media violence exercises a cathartic effect as there is that it exercises an arousal effect. But the criticisms of the catharsis view have tended to neglect the larger findings of the Feschback studies—namely, that the media's power to induce aggression, reasonably defined, is unproved.

BEGGING THE QUESTIONS

A short review cannot treat all the issues raised by the Violence Commission's hasty and unsupported acceptance of the most far-fetched interpretations of the aggression experiments. Perhaps the most distressing aspect of the entire enterprise is the tone of advocacy that pervades some of the chapters written by social scientists who seem more interested in finding any data, however badly interpreted, that will support their policy conclusions. Critics of these studies are dismissed in one place as "apologists for the media." Interlaced between paragraphs recounting experiments are ones of pure polemic in which the substantive arguments are advanced by asking rhetorical questions. For example, an account of a child who hanged himself apparently trying to imitate Batman leaping through the air moves Professor Alberta Seigel of Stanford to ask, "In what sense is television 'responsible' for this child's violent death?" No answer is offered to this rhetorical question, nor is any indication given of what one would do with any conceivable answer (perhaps ban costumed figures, from Peter Pan to Superman, from flying on television?).

Repeatedly the argument is made that television "teaches," and that to ignore this fact is perilous. After all, advertisers do spend millions on soap commercials because they hope viewers will buy more of their soap; broadcasters spend millions on violent television programs, apparently because they think violence also "sells." If viewers "learn" to buy Oxydol, why shouldn't we expect them to "learn" violence, as well?

But rhetorical queries and easy analogies beg all the interesting questions. There can be little doubt that television has a profound influence on our life and that we learn much, for better or for worse, from it. The crucial question is to specify the conditions under which something is learned and that "something" is then acted upon. It is interesting that neither the Violence Commission, nor the Kerner Commission before it, tried seriously to answer the question of whether broadcasts of an urban riot stimulated persons in the same city to join in, and aroused persons in other cities to start riots of their own. (Indeed, the Kerner Commission dodged the question, even though it was explicitly put to it by the President of the United States.) I do not pretend to know the answer to the question, though a plausible conjecture is that portraying in exciting terms actions by real people who are described as outraged by their grievances is more likely to effect behavior than fictional portrayals of imaginary events or obviously staged games. All the interesting variables—the degree of legitimacy attached to the act, the reward or penalty that might be expected from committing it, the opportunity for becoming a participant, the subjective definition of the act itself—are precisely the ones that most of the laboratory studies leave out. They cannot be brought back into account with analogies between selling soap and selling violence.[2]

EROTIC EFFECTS

The Commission on Obscenity, in finding that obscenity had no adverse effects on users, did not rely (as did the Violence Commission) on existing research; instead, it contracted for its own—ten volumes worth. These volumes (the "Technical Reports") are not yet available to the public, and thus a review of these studies must depend for now on the summary of them given in the Commission report itself, and especially in the report of the "Effects Panel" to the Commission. Perhaps because the Commission fostered new research, perhaps because the Effects Panel included two respected sociologists, the central question of how one defines and measures "effects" was given more serious and thoughtful attention by the Obscenity Commission than by the Violence Commission. Three kinds of effects of erotica were examined—on the incidence of sex offenses in the nation as a whole, on the difference (if any) between sex offenders and non-offenders in their consumption of erotica, and on the attitudes and behavior of persons exposed to erotica in experimental or laboratory situations.

The research methods employed included opinion surveys that asked people to recall their exposure to erotica and to report on their sexual behavior and attitudes; comparisons of sex offenders and "matched" groups of non-offenders with respect to their use of erotica; and controlled experiments in which volunteers, usually college students or married couples, were asked to peruse erotic books and films for periods ranging from a single hour-long session to daily sessions of 90 minutes for three weeks. There was little use of clinical studies (e.g., the psychoanalysts' reports) or police and probation officer experiences (e.g., the frequency with which erotic materials are found in the possession of persons arrested for sexual or violent offenses). No studies were done of children.

By these methods, the Commission concluded that exposure to erotica does produce sexual arousal in varying degrees among both men and women, especially among younger, college-educated persons who are nonreligious and sexually experienced; that some persons briefly change their sexual behavior after exposure to erotica, but that most do not; that attitudes toward sex and morality do not change significantly after experimental exposure to erotica; that delinquent and nondelinquent youth have been exposed about equally to erotica; that reported sex offenses in Copenhagen decreased coincident with the repeal of anti-obscenity statutes; and that recent changes in arrests for sex offenses in the United States show no clear pattern—some, as for forcible rape, have gone up, while others have gone down, at a time when obscenity has become much more readily available.

The Effects Panel acknowledges that there are limitations to these findings. Three are of special importance—long-term effects could not be investigated by a Commission with only a two-year existence; there were almost no studies of the effects on children; and the behavior of volunteer (i.e., self-selected) subjects in experiments cannot be generalized to any known population. Despite these limitations, however, the Effects Panel felt confident in concluding that if a case against pornography is to be made, "it will have to be made on grounds other than demonstrated effects of a damaging personal or social nature." Taking the findings as a whole, "no dangerous effects have been demonstrated on any of the populations which were studied."

Dissents to these findings were filed by three commission members. Two commissioners wrote a detailed critique questioning the reliability and interpretation of the empirical studies; unfortunately, the issues raised cannot be resolved until the full Technical Reports become publicly available. One dissent, by Charles H. Keating, Jr., the head of Citizens for a Decent Literature, Inc., and the sole appointee of President Nixon to the Commission, is an intemperate, unpleasantly ad hominem creed in which interesting and perhaps important objections are frequently obscured by a ranting tone.

AN UNSETTLED MATTER

For many persons, the social science findings endorsed by a majority of the Commission's members will settle the matter, especially since any effort to maintain even the much-weakened anti-obscenity statutes that now survive requires one to support the proposition, abhorrent to many, that the law may rightly proscribe the distribution of certain kinds of books and pictures. Perhaps it is this that leads some to adopt apparently different standards by which to evaluate the effects of obscenity, as opposed to violence. Professor Otto Larsen, for example, served as a member of both the Obscenity Commission and as a consultant to the Media Task Force of the Violence Commission. In his former capacity, he finds no justification for any restriction whatsoever on the sale or display of obscenity to adults or to children, even though the Technical Reports contain almost no experimental or clinical studies of the effects of obscenity on children, and despite the fact that most Americans no doubt find the display of obscenity in public places to unwitting parties quite objectionable. In his latter capacity, he submitted a paper to the Violence Commission which concluded that laboratory research "mounts a strong indictment of media performance" with respect to the portrayal of violence and that, while the present state of knowledge leaves something to be desired, "enough is known" to be sure that we are running "grave risks" in a policy of the "indiscriminate use of violence." And this despite the largely irrelevant, sometimes trivial findings of the research on media violence. The reason for the apparently different standards of judgment may be that, to control obscenity "books" must be "censored," while to control violence it is only necessary that the "media" be "regulated." (Professors publish books; they rarely own television stations.) Or perhaps the argument is that, while the contemplation of the obscene may produce many effects, they are not particularly harmful, whereas exposure to portrayals of violence may produce a few effects which are very harmful. Stated another way, the expected disutility of even a slight risk of a great harm (watching violence) is more serious than a substantial risk of a trivial harm (reading obscenity).

The question, then, is whether the harm from obscenity is trivial or great. On this question, the findings of the Commission are not nearly so conclusive as they are made out to be—provided one adopts a proper measure of "harm." If by harm one means the probability of committing a rape, then it is not surprising that exposure to erotica does not "cause" the act. Criminal actions generally, as the Effects Panel points out, are the product of many influences—social class, peer group relationships, intelligence, early family experiences and the like. As for national rates of sex crimes, these vary enormously with the changing propensity to report sexual assaults and provide no reliable measure of an "effect" which can be correlated with the availability of erotica, even assuming that such availability could itself be measured. (The majority of the Commission believe that the study of sex crimes in Copenhagen satisfactorily controlled for the propensity to report, but the minority interprets the same data as showing that certain kinds of crimes did not decrease at all with the legalization of obscenity, and that changes in other crime rates can be explained by a decreased willingness to call the police. Not having the Copenhagen study available, I can offer no judgment as to who is correct in this case.)

The laboratory experiments provide perhaps the weakest evidence. Though such experiments have on occasion provided revealing insights into human behavior, the rigor with which they are conducted is purchased at the price of unreality. One cannot simulate in the laboratory the existence or nonexistence of a life-long exposure to or preoccupation with obscenity, any more than one can simulate a life-long exposure to racist or radical opinions. Imagine what one would think of an experiment in which volunteer college students were exposed, for an hour a day for three weeks, to the *Protocols of the Elders of Zion, Mein Kampf* and an apology for slavery. No one would suppose that more than small and transient changes—or no changes at all—in behavior towards Jews and blacks, would occur. Similarly, we should not be surprised that no enduring changes in sexual behavior and attitudes result from equivalent exposure to erotica, any more than we should have been surprised to learn from Professor Feschback that exposure to television violence for a few weeks caused no important changes in the behavior of young boys.

A more revealing experiment would be to compare the attitudes and behavior of a group of children, reared in a community with easy and frequent access to erotica (or media violence, or whatever) to those of a group, carefully matched in all other respects, reared in a community with no access, or only occasional and furtive access, to the obscene (or the violent). Obviously, such an experiment would have to last over many years—perhaps two generations, in order to control for prior parental attitudes—and the subjects would have to be carefully monitored to insure that experimental conditions were not violated by, for example, moving to another town or taking frequent trips to New York City to patronize the book stores on 42nd Street. Just as obviously, such an experiment is utterly absurd even to contemplate; no one, fortunately, can control human lives to that degree in this society or perhaps in any other.

The nearest approximation to such a study would be a comparison of various cultures, some of which maintain a taboo against written and pictorial erotica and some of which do not, to discover what differences, if any, are thereby produced in the moral capacity, social vitality and political stability of the societies. But even here inferences would be hard to draw—societies differing in one respect are likely to differ in many others as well, and settling upon some measure of effect (what is "moral capacity" anyway?) would be at best controversial, and at worst impossible. It is interesting, however, to note that scholars whose job it is to compare cultures appear more willing than other social scientists to support the prohibition against obscenity (Arnold Toynbee, J.D. Unwin and Pitirim Sorokin have been cited in this connection).

THE LIMITS OF SOCIAL SCIENCE

In short, social science probably cannot answer the questions put to it by those who wish to rest the case for or against censorship on the proved effects of exposure to obscenity, media violence, scurrilous political literature or whatever. In a society in which the obscene or the violent is not part of the regular literary diet of the young, the furtive or occasional consumption of such material may have little effect, or be at best "one factor among many." In a society in which the obscene or the violent is everywhere on display, whether any given individual is or is not exposed to, say, a dirty book may be less important than the perceptions of life and morality he draws from a community obsessed with the carnal or bestial. In either case, there is not likely to be a significant correlation between *individual* exposure and *individual* attitudes or behavior. Even where the obscene is commonplace, there are likely to be important differences attributable to social class, intelligence and family structure, in the extent to which individuals display a preoccupation with that which is base or ignoble; and thus a social scientific study of the sources of antisocial behavior would probably conclude that these differences in class or family, being the correlates of behavior, were thus the "causes" of such behavior. It would have been as difficult for a social scientist in Nero's Rome to prove that a person who himself did not read erotic stone tablets was thereby benefited as it would have been for a social scientist in Cromwell's London to prove that a person who did read dirty books was thereby harmed; yet most historians would agree that the different attitudes toward public obscenity in Nero's Rome and

Cromwell's London are not irrelevant to understanding these two very different societies.

Social science at its best seeks to show a relationship among two or more variables that cannot be attributed to chance or to intervening variables. Showing such relationships persuasively is easiest when the variables can be unambiguously defined (e.g., voting for a Democrat or Republican for president, or earning over $10,000 a year), and when the variables believed to have causal power are not highly intercorrelated with other variables (e.g., physical height tends to be independent of intelligence or social class, but education tends to be covariant with income, occupation and race). When social scientists are asked to measure consequences in terms of a badly conceptualized or hard-to-measure "effect" of one among many highly interrelated "causes," all of which operate (if at all) over long periods of time, they tend to discover that there is no relationship, or at best, a weak and contingent one. This is one of the reasons, for example, for the controversy over human intelligence—the measures of intelligence are much disputed and the correlates of intelligence (race, class, family status, diet or whatever), are themselves so intercorrelated as to make it hazardous to guess which one or which few variables, and in what temporal sequence, account for changes in I.Q. Or, another example—social science studies of the effects of governmental interventions of a broad and diffuse nature (building "better schools," running a "community action program" or enrolling students in Project Head Start) on various vague social objectives (improving education or strengthening the sense of community) are usually inconclusive and controversial.

The irony is that social science may be weakest in detecting the broadest and most fundamental changes in social values, precisely because they *are* broad and fundamental. Intuitively, it seems plausible that the media and other forces have contributed powerfully over the last generation to changes in popular attitudes about sexuality, political action and perhaps even violence. But, for lack of a control group, it is unlikely that this will ever be proved scientifically. Social science may be better at showing the effects of various forces on relatively small and specially selected populations— for example, the effects of prison or childhood experiences on delinquents, or the effects of various stimuli (including the media) on phobic persons.

If, by its nature, social science can be of little help on policy questions of the broader sort, to what mode of inquiry should a reasonable man turn to decide on the issue of censorship (or "regulation")? Reo Christenson has suggested that, if social science cannot settle the matter on the grounds of consequences, the average American cannot be blamed for concluding that the views of the majority should prevail—and the majority clearly wants some form of restriction. A person who interprets the First Amendment solely by applying the "clear and present danger" test would, of course, find a majoritarian solution unacceptable; but it is by no means obvious that a showing of clear and present danger should be the test for all forms of writing and speech—the test was devised for gauging the reasonableness of limitations on *political* writing and speech.

Even the Obscenity Commission, despite its claim that it rests its recommendation for the abolition of restrictions on the distribution of obscenity to adults on the showing of no adverse effect, is not prepared to accept the full implications of that position. In the section immediately following that concerning effects, the Commission writes:

> Regardless of the effects of exposure, there is still a considerable amount of uneasiness about explicit sexual materials and their pervasiveness in our society. . . . [But] it is often overlooked that legal control on the availability of explicit sexual materials is not the only, or necessarily the most effective, method of dealing with these materials.

The Commission goes on to note, in general approving tones, these other ways of "dealing" with erotica, such as industry self-regulation (among comic book publishers and broadcasters, for example), and the possibility of effective citizen action groups at the community level. But if obscenity is not harmful, on what grounds are such informal—and, no doubt, effective—controls over what we may read or see to be condoned? If no harm ensues, should not this extra-legal form of censorship be sharply criticized? Clearly, the commission here—as with the issues of public display of erotica and the circulation of such material among juveniles—is deferring, not to social science, but to popular feelings.

THE ULTIMATE CRITERIA

It would be easy to dismiss deference to popular feelings by either proponents or opponents of censorship as an unworthy catering to mere prejudice or shallow opinion. And surely in the area of free speech properly conceived—as it relates to argument and instruction, rather than simply entertainment—no one (especially no professor) would want to take the popular feelings at any given moment as a decisive guide to what should be permissible. But, in the absence of social science evidence that is conclusive, and confining our attention to matters of popular amusement, the deeply held convictions of citizens about the relationship between amusement and morality are by no means irrelevant or trivial. As Harry M. Clor writes, in *Obscenity and Public Morality*:

> People are influenced by what they think others believe and particularly by what they think are the common standards of the community. There are few individuals among us whose basic beliefs are the result of their own reasoning and whose moral opinions do not require the support of some stable public opinion. The free circulation of obscenity can, in time, lead many to the conclusion that there is nothing wrong with the values implicit in it—since their open promulgation is tolerated by the public. They will come to the conclusion that public standards have changed—or that there are no public standards. Private standards are hard put to withstand the effects of such an opinion.

I do not know whether the consequences for private standards of changed public standards will be as Clor predicts. I do know that I have seen no evidence to disprove his view, and that many public policies—such as those against racial or sexual discrimination—are based in part precisely on the presumed educative force of law.

I happen to think (though I cannot prove it) that certain kinds of political speeches and writings do inestimable harm to our society—but I also believe that no one should be trusted with the power to decide which speeches and writings those are, and thus which should or should not be allowed. I also think, as a parent whose children watch Saturday morning cartoons and Sunday afternoon football on television, that they are not in the slightest harmed by what they see; I cannot prove it, and I may be quite naïve, but I cannot conceive of a study on this subject that I would find more persuasive than my own knowledge of my children's attitudes and behavior. I also do not want my children to be exposed to sex by way of easily available materials that portray what should be tender and private as base and brutal. I further confess to being quite uncertain as to what forms of legal restraint, if any, this requires. I know that they will encounter prurient materials furtively, and that does not trouble me. Perhaps it should; or perhaps I should be worried that I cannot "prove" my belief that human character is, in the long run, affected not by occasional, furtive experiences but by whether society does or does not state that there is an important difference between the loathsome and the decent. I would, for example, want my government to say that race is not to be used as a basis for granting or denying access to public facilities, even if social science could not show that such racial restrictions harm individual Negroes—indeed, even if social science could show that such restrictions *benefit* Negroes. A public commitment to equal opportunity and public opposition to disgusting racial distinctions should be made as a matter of right and propriety, whatever the immediate effects; I would also imagine that, over the long term, such public commitments would play a part in shaping individual attitudes in what I take to be a desirable direction.

The failure of the Violence Commission is that it relied, in the case of its task force on the media, on bad (or badly interpreted) social science; the weakness of the Obscenity Commission is that it relied too exclusively on social science research, even though that research, within the limited framework of each study, was on the whole quite unexceptionable. The general circumstances under which public decisions can be made—or should be made—on the basis of social scientific findings, is by no means clear. It is not hard to imagine issues on which such research could have depositive if not determinative weight, and others on which it should have little or no weight. Regrettably, there has been of late a growing unwillingness to make such distinctions, but this may reflect not so much on excessive enthusiasm with the policy value of social science as a general inability to make distinctions of any kind.

In the cases of violence and obscenity, it is unlikely that social science can either show harmful effects or prove that there are no harmful effects. It is unlikely, in short, that considerations of utility or disutility can be governing. These are moral issues and ultimately all judgments about the acceptability of restrictions on the various media will have to rest on political and philosophical considerations.

NOTES

1. Lest one assume that the verbal urgings of the Violence Commission to the television industry bear no taint of censorship, bear in mind that television (unlike the publishing of books, pure or impure) is a governmentally licensed and regulated industry. Were the Federal Communications Commission to indicate that the renewal of these licenses was dependent on the broadcaster's progress in changing television programs to reduce "violence," you can be certain there would be less violence on television. Without new legislation of any kind, the federal government today can exercise, should it act on the views of the Violence Commission, a "chilling effect" on the content of television programs. It already exercises that chilling effect with respect to many other matters—the "fairness doctrine," for example, imposes heavy costs on broadcasters who give over programs to one side of a controversial issue, by requiring them to provide equivalent time to the other side. (No magazine, book or film, by contrast, is under any such obligation to be "fair.") Nor is the FCC the only potential source of constraint. Recently the Foundation to Improve Television brought suit to prevent a Washington station from broadcasting "The Wild, Wild West" before 10 P.M., on the grounds that the evidence of the harmful effects of violence meant that the program "violates the constitutional rights of child viewers."

2. For a comprehensive and dispassionate review of studies of media effects, see the chapter by Walter Weiss in *The Handbook of Social Psychology*, 2nd ed., vol. 5, ed. George Lindzey (Reading, Mass.: Addison–Wesley 1968).

14 Polity, Politics and Social Research: A Study in the Relationship of Federal Commissions and Social Science

Ray C. Rist

Although both presidential and congressional commissions have been a part of the American political scene for some decades, they have been especially numerous in recent years. During his first two years as president, Richard Nixon appointed more than 50 commissions, ranging from those concerned with federal statistics and oil import quotas to those concerned with campus unrest and drug abuse. As Daniel Bell has suggested, the increasing use of federal commissions may indicate a new trend by which national policy will come to be formulated.[1] Bell speaks of "governance by commission" as a response to the growing isolation of the public from the decision-making processes at the federal level. Policy generated by commissions will become more important, Bell avers, due to the slippage of initiative legislation away from the legislative branch and over to the executive branch. As a consequence of this slippage, elected representatives will be less able to respond to the needs of their constituents in the face of enhanced executive power. Federal commissions may become a significant structure for mediating between the drive toward centralized executive power and the need for citizen participation.

Reprinted with permission of The Society For the Study of Social Problems. *Social Problems*, vol. 21, no. 1 (Summer 1973).

The events related to federal commissions in the seven years since Bell's assessment indicate that he was overly optimistic and benign. The impetus for many recent commissions has not been a desire by federal officials for citizen input in decision-making, so much as an attempt by both the executive and legislative branches to respond in a politically "safe" fashion to a "problem" or "crisis." When a politically delicate issue has emerged—such as black revolt in the cities, student protest, political assassinations, large-scale use of marijuana or the proliferation of sexually explicit materials—a federal commission has been created, as a convenient mechanism by which the federal system could avoid immediately confronting the issue while still giving public evidence of its concern. As W.T. Johnson notes: "It is useful for government to demonstrate interest in these issues by appointing blue ribbon panels to study them, and, of course, to be able to postpone action until the panel has filed its report."[2] Michael Lipsky and David Olson suggest much the same analysis in their critique of the National Commission on Civil Disorders.[3]

If these authors are correct in their assertion that federal commissions serve an important function in "cooling out" demands for federal response to sensitive and volatile social issues, why the active participation of so many of the nation's leading academic, corporate and legal experts? How are they co-opted into serving the political motives of others? Warren Lehman suggests:

A Presidential commission (one is tempted to generalize) is a pride of domesticated intellectuals and leading intellectuals and leading citizens willing to sacrifice disagreements in hope of drinking at the springs of power. This hope is a snare and a delusion: the commissarial lions jump to the whip of the politician. And it is the lion tamer whose reputation is enhanced by the lions, not vice versa.[4]

Recently, however, four prominent federal commissions organized to study a social "problem" have had their report and recommendations rejected outright by either the President, the Congress, or both. Whether or not one wishes to attribute the rejection of the reports of the National Advisory Commission on Civil Disorders (1968), the National Commission of the Causes and

Prevention of Violence (1969), the President's Commission on Campus Unrest (1970) and the Commission on Obscenity and Pornography (1970) to the fact that all four relied extensively on social science methodology and analysis, the recommendations were not endorsed by the President in office at the time. The various reports were not found unacceptable for the nature and analysis of their data, but rather for pragmatic political contingencies. For example, Lyndon Johnson did not wish to acknowledge the impact of "white racism" as a factor contributing to black violence and Richard Nixon did not, at the time of an upcoming election, wish to identify himself with recommendations for the liberalization of legal statutes permitting the sale of sexually explicit material to adults.

KNOWLEDGE FOR WHAT?

When politicians choose to create federal commissions as a response to pressing social issues, perhaps of "crisis" proportions, those social scientists who choose to participate in the commission create for themselves an acute dilemma. The dilemma emerges because politicians and social scientists have differing motivations for dealing with the issue at hand. For the former, it is an opportunity to generate potential political resources; for the latter, it is an opportunity to engage in scholarly investigation in an area of public concern. As a result, the research carried out by social scientists is vulnerable to reinterpretation by the politician so as to legitimate his posture. At times of national concern, the political response does not rest upon limitations in data, but upon limitations in political feasibility. Therefore, social scientists engaged in commission research face the reality that the criteria for reliable knowledge used by scholars are different from those used by politicians.

This situation presents the individual researcher with an ethical decision: does one or does one not maintain scholarly integrity with respect to recommendations derived from research data, when acceptance or rejection of the recommendations ultimately rests on non-scholarly criteria? The temptation to "drink at the springs of power," as Lehman phrases it, presents a very real opportunity for the transformation of analytic data into acceptable political data.

Parenthetically, he suggests that such temptations are not reserved only for those involved with data, but may also influence the final recommendations of an entire commission. This is precisely what happened, he argues, with the report of the President's Commission on Law Enforcement and the Administration of Justice, released in 1967.[5]

Commissions created for political reasons discover that their final reports regarding sensitive social problems will be accepted or rejected in such a manner so as to maximize the political benefits of the recipient, especially if he is the President. If the President accepts the recommendations of a report, it will lend weight and prestige to ensuing legislative proposals. A report can also enchance the President's position by presenting him with a tailor-made legislative program which has been developed and refined by a panel of distinguished "experts." Unlike the President, individual congressmen or even congressional committees do not always have the staff, time, money or expertise to take advantage of commission reports and create a continuous stream of proposals in socially vital areas.

When they do not find a commission's final report acceptable, the President and Congress have not necessarily lost political points. Through a variety of techniques, the executive or the legislative branch can minimize adverse publicity generated by the recommendations and even turn the rejection to political advantage. By decrying the "unbalanced" composition of the commission, points can be made with groups not represented; by suggesting the commission is the responsibility of a previous administration, uncomfortable implications of the report can be deflected; or by resorting to the reiteration of "traditional American values," recommendations advocating specific social changes can be made to appear "un-American." Whatever the technique, the aim is the political enhancement of the recipient.

KNOWLEDGE FOR WHOM?

The policy research conducted under the auspices of a federal commission presents social scientists with a distinct set of conditions. First, commission research has a particular social structure. When commissions are created, they are given directives from the authorizing agent to deal, often within a predefined cultural or ideological context, with a particular issue, and are expected to orient their research efforts to generate specific recommendations which can be accomplished through executive or legislative authority. Furthermore, such recommendations are to be accompanied by an extended rationale as to why these recommendations are appropriate. The goal is less one of fact finding than of case building.

A commission report is the end product of efforts by a three-level organizational structure: the research staff, the executive staff and the commission members. As Lipsky and Olson have noted, all three groups may not share a similar perspective on the tasks, methods or even goals of the commission. The most publicized instance of internal commission/staff tension occurred with the National Advisory Commission on Civil Disorders. Lipsky and Olson write:

> The ... tension revolved around the rejection of a document entitled, "The Harvest of American Racism" drafted by social scientists employed by the Kerner Commission. From all indications, it appears that this draft was rejected for inclusion in the final report not only because its conclusions were radical, but also because documentation for its underlying theory of riot causation was lacking. There was also a problem of communication within the commission. The social scientists were shocked to find the document that they considered only a draft treated as a final product. ... Very shortly after the "Harvest" draft was rejected, the commission changed its timetable to eliminate the interim report and released most of the staff, about 100 people.[6]

A second set of circumstances surrounding research for federal commissions involves its public or quasi-public nature. Inasmuch as a commission may produce a highly viable report, the incorporated research results are vulnerable to distortion and misinterpretation for political purposes. At present, researchers are at a disadvantage when seeking to refute the distortions of their findings; social scientists' access to the mass media is still rather minimal.[7]

But there is another side to the issue of the public nature of commission research and reports. Though they may not accept the research and the conclusions derived from it, the president or

Congress must at least acknowledge the existence of the research, if only to decry and distort it. Distinct from private contractual policy research, the public nature of the commission does allow social scientists to force a wedge into the purely political construction and definition of reality. Their research, however battered through its publicity in the mass media, does represent an alternative to the politicians' pragmatic definitions of situations.

Another aspect of the public nature of commission reports centers around their use by citizens to demand greater accountability from politicians. One may not necessarily agree with the Kerner Commission or the one on campus unrest, but their recommendations for change provide a basis on which groups can call politicians to task and can inquire about the constructive action which can or should be undertaken. While politicians might hope the length of time necessary for the commission's investigation is sufficient to defuse public interest, the final report justifies the position of those persons who do not believe the crisis has been resolved merely by the passage of time.

The means by which federal commissions make known their findings provides a third distinct aspect of this kind of research. Commissions ordinarily present their findings in a single document made visible through legislative or executive sponsorship. Together with task force and technical reports, the final report makes public significant amounts of the pertinent research. (The Commission on Obscenity and Pornography released ten volumes of research findings in conjunction with its final report.) Such extensive publication and exposure of research findings are not available to private contracted research, even if desired. Furthermore, private research is often Balkanized and presents only the distillation of a variety of research findings.

A final aspect of the special circumstances surrounding research from federal commissions relates to their origins. Many commissions are created as political responses to perceptions of crisis in the social fabric. Consequently the research conducted is related directly to the anxieties and discomforts experienced by large numbers of citizens—otherwise, it is doubtful whether commissions dealing with social problems would even be created. As Lehman has observed, social scientists find themselves in a pivotal position to address the major social issues and to offer interpretations of them.[8]

What follows is an attempt to assess the political and cultural influences upon a specific commission, the Commission on Obscenity and Pornography, which responded to a subject about which the American public was both "anxious and ill-informed." Within the context of a natural history of the Commission, I shall examine the cumulative political response to the final Commission report. The aim is not an appraisal of the findings themselves; such an evaluation has already been undertaken.[9] Rather, within the framework of a single case study, I will seek to elucidate the public and political nature of commission-type policy research and decision-making.

"A MATTER OF NATIONAL CONCERN"

Prior to the passage of legislation creating the Commission on Obscenity and Pornography in October 1967, various bills calling for the creation of a commission to suggest policy recommendations in the area of sexually explicit materials had been pending in congressional committees for at least five years. The aim of those bills was to develop means by which to suppress and eliminate such material, as their titles would indicate: the "Commission for the Elimination of Pornographic Materials," and the "Commission for the Elimination of Lewd and Obscene Materials." Increasingly, Congress was being prodded to "do something" about sexually explicit material, but found itself without a consensus on how to proceed, since there had existed a long-term deadlock between the civil libertarians and those who viewed sexual materials as a moral menace.

In the prior attempts to create a commission, and in the initial bill which resulted in the 1967 Commission, there was no mention of interest in the study of "effects" of sexually explicit material. It was not until hearings were held on the proposed commission in April of 1967 that the issue of effects was first raised. In the words of Senator Mundt, "a great deal of work has been done by sociologists and others in this field [study of effects] and I would hope that with adequate staffing the Commission would come up with a consensus of the findings on this problem."[10] Inasmuch as

Mundt was a major advocate of "doing something" about sexually explicit material, his request was incorporated into the legislation. The inclusion of the study of effects represented a shift from earlier bills and was indicative of the search by Congress for new sources of information. Senator Miller of Iowa stated, "I do not claim to have the answer [to the effect of sexual material]. Nor do I think anyone of us in this room today is confident that he or she has the answer. And for that reason, I advocate that a commission be formed to develop solutions."[11]

A second consequence of the shift towards an interest in effects was evident in the composition of the Commission. While early legislative attempts had stipulated that members were to come from the Federal Bureau of Investigation, the Department of Justice, the Department of Defense, the Post Office Department and the Bureau of Customs, the approved measure clearly stipulated that representatives from the fields of psychiatry, sociology, psychology, criminology, religion, communications and the judiciary were to be included. A reading of the congressional testimony on the proposed commission indicates that members of Congress who testified believed that there were negative effects from sexually explicit materials. They appeared uncertain only as to the intensity and scope of such effects. As several members implied, inclusion of members of the scientific community on the Commission would provide the "evidence" necessary to warrant a large-scale attempt at control and eradication. The thrust for the creation of the Commission came from the conservative element in Congress, and during the hearings, there were repeated references to "corruption," "filth," "moral slime" and the like. But in order to placate liberals and simultaneously legitimize eventual stringent control of the material, the issue of effects became a mechanism by which "scientific evidence" could provide the means for political response. As the opening sentences of the legislation stated:

The Congress finds that the traffic in obscenity and pornography is a matter of national concern. The problem, however, is not one which can be solved at any one level of government. The Federal government has the responsibility to investigate the gravity of this situation and to determine whether such materials are harmful to the public, and particularly to minors, and whether more effective methods should be devised to control the transmission of such materials.[12]

Again, the impetus appears more one of case building than fact finding.

Bell, Lehman and Johnson have all noted that the kind of appointments to federal commissions indicate the end product desired by the authorizing agent. These writers have also suggested that the appointments, by taking account of various constituencies or interest groups, serve important functions in legitimizing the final report. "Constituent elites" are appointed to demonstrate that the issue has been dealt with by "responsible" representatives of the concerned groups. Through collective participation, they are expected to come to a consensus as to the most appropriate policy recommendations. Unanimity in diversity is the basis for authority. Johnson avers, however, that the Commission on Obscenity and Pornography diverged somewhat from this established pattern:

> The composition of the Commission on Obscenity and Pornography was conspicuous in not reflecting the usual number of represented constituencies in accordance with the dictates of "interest group liberalism." Power, wealth and influence were notably absent from the roster of seven university professors, five lawyers, three clergymen, one non-academic sociologist, one clinical psychiatrist and one retired vice-president of a publishing house. Although some have argued that vested interests were represented by the four commissioners affiliated with publishing, television and motion pictures, the constituencies of the professors (law, English, communications, sociology, psychiatry, library science) and the two psychiatrists are less obvious. Only in the case of two commissioners, each affiliated with organized antipornography citizen groups, are the represented constituency and vested interest immediately apparent. But the pre-existing commitment of the commissioners generally more closely resembled *disinterest* than anything else [emphasis in the original].[13]

Though Johnson may be correct in asserting "power, wealth, and

influence were notably absent," representatives of various constituencies were not. Using the six lawyers as an example, one finds: the
Dean of the Law School at the University of Minnesota, the
President of Atlanta News Agency Inc., the Chief Juvenile Judge for
the State of Connecticut, the President of Citizens for Decent
Literature, Inc., the Attorney General of California and the Deputy
Attorney of the Motion Picture Association of America. Rather than
indicating "disinterest," the affiliations of these six commissioners
suggest that all would have had more than merely passing interest in
the recommendations of the Commission.

The Commission, when created by Congress, was directed to
undertake investigation and subsequently develop recommendations
in four substantive areas. They were:

1) with the aid of leading constitutional law authorities, to
analyze the laws pertaining to the control of obscenity and
pornography; and to evaluate and recommend definitions of
obscenity and pornography;

2) to ascertain the methods employed in the distribution of
obscene and pornographic materials and to explore the nature and
volume of traffic in such materials;

3) to study the effect of obscenity and pornography upon the
public, and particularly minors, and its relationship to crime and
other antisocial behavior; and

4) to recommend such legislative, administrative, or other
advisable and appropriate action as the Commission deems
necessary to regulate effectively the flow of such traffic without
in any way interfering with constitutional rights.[14]

Utilizing these congressional directives as guidelines, the Commission organized a study panel for each of the four broad areas
outlined in the legislation. Chairmen for each of these four panels
were selected at the first meeting of the Commission and they in
turn had major responsibility for securing research staff, most of
whom were hired within three months.

One aspect of the Commission's staff deserves special mention.
This was the first Commission to deal with a socially sensitive area,
which was directed by someone other than a "White House man." It

was the policy of President Johnson (and Nixon) to appoint a close political associate (usually a lawyer) as the executive director, so the President could be kept informed of the Commission's activities. The Commission on Obscenity and Pornography was allowed to choose its own executive director, and chose a social scientist, who could double as research director.

THE LOW PROFILE

The legislation creating the Commission on Obscenity and Pornography was passed by Congress and signed by the president in October of 1967. Commission members were appointed in January of 1968. Funds were not approved by Congress, however, until July of 1968, at which time Congress also extended the life of the Commission for two years. The Commission was funded during its first year with $643,000, and with $1,100,000 during its second.

At the Commission's first meeting several policy decisions were made which were to become the sources of internal dispute. The Commission decided not to hold public hearings until there had been sufficient time for the development and implementation of various research endeavors. The general consensus of six Commission members interviewed by the author was that hearings were most appropriate near the end of the research collection, but before the writing of the final report.[15] As Skolnick has noted, the members appeared to recognize full well that "Hearings are a form of theater."[16] Therefore, a deliberate attempt was made to avoid early hearings, both to protect the ongoing research and to minimize the politicization of the Commission's deliberations.

A second policy decision made by the Commission was to retain as confidential all discussion and minutes of Commission meetings. It was assumed that this confidentiality would encourage dialogue among Commission members. It was also agreed that the Commission chairman, William Lockhart, would serve as the spokesman to the media; individual members would not be at liberty to discuss findings or release research materials to anyone not connected with the Commission.

From July of 1968 until July of 1969, the Commission held bi-monthly meetings, and the various panel groups were periodically called into session by the chairmen. There was little publicity this first year, for which at least one member was grateful:

> There is no doubt but that we were engaged in some "sensitive" research that may have had to be modified or canceled all together if it were widely known, especially in the Congress. By keeping a "low profile," we were able to go about the activities we felt necessary without interference.

At the end of the first year, the Commission released its brief Progress Report, the introduction to which reflected the generally cautious wording throughout.[17] Any clues of becoming a "permissive" commission might have threatened funding for the second year, prompted public explanations of the orientation of the Commission and created a defensive climate for the deliberations of the members.

The Progress Report itself is only nine pages in length, followed by a "Tentative Draft of Statute Regulating Unsolicited Mailings of Potentially Offensive Materials." (This proposed statute is quite similar to the one actually passed by the Congress in September of 1970.) In retrospect, the inclusion of this proposed statute, whether intended or not, was an important political maneuver. As Lipsky and Olson note, progress reports are often "scrambled" so as to maintain the widest number of options for the orientation of the final report.[18] By presenting material so as not to arouse antagonism from the authorizing agent, the Commission protected itself from early criticism.

Additional political points were made by the Commission for including the proposed statute, since it closely resembled one submitted to the Congress only two months earlier by President Nixon in his message of May 2, 1969. In his legislative request, Nixon asked for controls on the sending of "offensive sex materials" to any individual under the age of 18; controls on the "sending of advertising designed to appeal to a prurient interest"; and finally, provision of "additional protection from the kind of smut advertising now being mailed, unsolicited, into so many homes." The proposed statute in the Progress Report of the Commission included the second and third of Nixon's proposals.

The final six pages of the Progress Report contain "separate remarks" by Commissioner Hill, and a rebuttal by the remaining 16 members. Hill argued that the Commission was too strongly oriented towards the study of "effects," to the detriment of other issues, particularly those related to the regulation of sexually explicit material. Foreshadowing what was to become the basis for much of his dissent to the Final Report released one year later, Hill asserted:

> it is difficult to see how the Commission, under its present leadership, can produce the results Congress intended. If the Commission continues in the direction in which it is now moving, it will simply propose laws on pandering, invasion of privacy and sales to minors. Congress does not need a Commission to recommend legislation of this sort. Such limited proposals will not "regulate effectively the flow of such traffic."[19]

Prophetically, Commissioner Hill was correct in the three restrictive recommendations the Commission would make in its Final Report.

INTO THE PUBLIC ARENA

In the time between the release of the Progress Report and the Final Report, the Commission found it increasingly difficult to avoid media exposure. A number of events occurred during the second year which had a cumulative effect on publicity. (The crescendo was reached during the 1970 fall political campaigns.) The following, listed in sequential order, are those events:

1. Richard Nixon appointed his first and only member to the Commission. Charles Keating, president of Citizens for Decent Literature, assumed the Commission position held by Kenneth Keating, who resigned to become Ambassador to India. C. Keating attended three meetings during the remaining life of the Commission, announced that he would not abide by the agreement of confidentiality for both research and Commission member discussions, and was subsequently denied access to research reports until such reports were in the final stages of preparations.
2. Commissioners Hill and Link on their own initiative conducted public hearings in eight cities across the nation. Packard

termed them "runaway hearings,"[20] for they were neither sanctioned nor endorsed by the Commission as an official act of the Commission. The hearings made front-page headlines in several of the cities where they were held. Their aim appeared to be to build political support for a "control" orientation to the upcoming recommendations of the Commission. As both Commissioners noted in their dissent to the Final Report, "Twenty-six of twenty-seven witnesses at the hearings in New York City expressed concern and asked for remedial measures."[21]

3. At the time the Commission itself held public hearings in Washington, D.C., front-page headlines were again made, but this time because the hearings became a forum for public theater. Commissioner Larsen was hit in the face with a pie thrown by a member of an underground press organization who accused the Commission of conducting a "witchhunt" and holding "McCarthy-like hearings" in an attempt to suppress freedom of the press. The Washington media apparently was tipped in advance, and the event was widely reported.

4. Commission research findings were leaked to Jack Anderson, who reported them in his syndicated column. This research involved a study made at the University of North Carolina to measure the effects of satiation by repeated exposure to sexually explicit material. One part of the research involved the use of a plethysmograph (a device attached to the penis to measure various changes over time) on a sample of college males who were exposed to the material for 90 minutes per day for three weeks.

5. The leaking of research materials by various Commission members became so frequent as the date for publication drew closer that on August 11, 1970, Congressman Robert Nix called the Subcommittee on Postal Operations into session, to hear testimony from various persons on a report which was not yet public. Nix early identified himself as one who favored a "control" approach in dealing with sexually explicit materials. The hearings held by his Subcommittee were oriented towards delegitimating the forthcoming report and the research contained within it. These hearings constituted

the first attempt by a politician to gain political advantage by denouncing the Final Report.

The people called to testify before the Subcommittee attempted to evaluate the Report and its research from only selectively leaked material. The semantic acrobatics were evident.[22] When a witness was asked if he had read the Commission Report or any actual research findings, the comments ranged from "I have closely followed newspaper accounts," to "I don't have those studies funded by the Commission which are cited and used in part as evidence in coming to many of their conclusions. I do have a number of studies, but not those which the Commission had funded."

In addition to the academicians and politicians who testified against the anticipated Report, the researchers from the University of North Carolina who had conducted the research with the plethysmograph were called in front of the Subcommittee. The questions directed to these researchers focused on their salaries, the amount of research funding they received from the Commission, whether any North Carolina state funds were used, whether parental consent was sought for the sample, and whether they believed their research was "moral." Several of the Subcommittee members commented how "thankful" they were that such research had not been conducted in their home state and that none of their state tax money was involved. The Commission was coming to serve as a convenient dragon that politicians could attempt to slay as they fought for "public morality."

6. Shortly before the release of the Final Report of the Commission, Stein and Day Publishing Co. released a small paperback entitled, *The Obscenity Report*. This book was advertised as the final report of the Commission and carried an unsigned letter to the President indicating the Commission understood the Stein and Day publication was so politically volatile it could not be mentioned in the "final" report of the Commission, nor publicly acknowledged by the Commission members who dissented. The book resembled much of the campaign rhetoric of those politicians who were striving to preserve the "threatened American culture" and to warn against "permissiveness."

7. On September 9, 21 days before the date set for the release of the Final Report, Commissioner C. Keating sought and received a court injunction barring publication of the Final Report until he had had time to prepare an "effective response" against the majority recommendations. A week later, Chairman Lockhart and Keating agreed out of court to give Keating until the day before the release date to prepare his dissent, the final length of which was 117 pages. The temporary injunction was lifted by the District Court in Washington, D.C., and Keating submitted his dissent on the 29th of September. (Presses ran all night at the Department of Defense, and the Report was released on the morning of the 30th.)

POLITICIANS AND PORNOGRAPHY

If commissions are political offspring, it is natural that their efforts should be scrutinized by those who created them. So it was with the Commission on Obscenity and Pornography and its Final Report. In a well-orchestrated fashion, members of the Nixon administration began to denounce the findings of the Commission even before they were released. The press secretary for the president told reporters, one week prior to the release of the Report, that the views of the Commission were not those of the President, and that its recommendations should be interpreted in light of the fact that the appointments to the Commission were made by the previous Democratic administration. Two days before release of the Report, the Postmaster General stated in a campaign speech, "If I read the President correctly, this administration is not going to legalize pornography."

On the day of the release of the Commission Report, September 30, Vice-President Spiro Agnew, campaigning in the state of Utah, delivered an evening speech to a large contingent of Utah Republicans. His remarks constituted the administration's first formal renunciation of the findings after the Report became public. His pertinent comments about the Commission were as follows:

Just today, the lame duck Commission on Obscenity and

Pornography weighed in with its final report. Its views do not represent the thinking of the Nixon Administration. This Commission was not named by President Nixon. No sir, your honor, it's not our baby.

Credit, or culpability, for that Commission, rests with those who embrace its conclusions—and, as far as Laurence Burton [Utah Senatorial candidate], the President and I are concerned— the radical liberals can have it, free of charge. The only Nixon appointee on that Commission submitted the kind of blistering dissent you would expect from a man concerned about decency in America.

We often speak about the quality of life in America. But that quality will only be degraded if the floodgates are further opened and more of this garbage is dumped into the mainstream of American communications. As long as Richard Nixon is President, Main Street is not going to be turned into Smut Alley.[23]

Two days later, on October 2, 1970, Robert Finch, who served as Counsellor to the President, objected—by means of a press release issued at the White House—to the Commission findings. After noting that the Commission was appointed by President Johnson, he indicated he was speaking as a "parent and private citizen, and as an official of the Federal Government." Finch stressed what he believed to be the negative effects of pornography on the young and asserted, "They [the Commission members] invoke the name of freedom to condone utter license in the area of such behavior and morality. I reject this approach totally. It reduces morality to the lowest common denominator of a passing fad."[24]

Though the Nixon Administration was most persistent in its rejection of the Commission's findings and labeled them the product of Democratic "radical-liberals," the political points to be made by denouncing the Report were not lost on members of Congress. On October 13, three weeks before the fall elections, Senator John McClellan from Arkansas introduced a resolution insisting, "that the Senate reject the findings and recommendations of the Commission on Obscenity and Pornography." The essence of Senate Resolution 477 was contained in two statements:

The Senate declares that—

1. Generally the findings and recommendations are not sup-

ported by the evidence considered by or available to the Commission.

2. The Commission has not properly performed its statutory duties nor has it complied with the mandates of Congress.

In the ensuing 30 minutes of discussion of the resolution on the Senate floor, various criticisms were set forth. For example, Senator John McClellan stated, "I fear that if we allow and encourage the flow of obscene material, there will be no stopping these sex offenders. This filth is stimulating to them, they feed on it, and the Commission would guarantee that they have their fill." Senator Robert Griffin put the matter as follows: "The Commission's report should be tossed into the trash can along with all the foul and corrupting pornographic material that it would make available to the public."

The only opponent of the resolution who spoke about it on the Senate floor was Walter Mondale, from Minnesota. He indicated he believed himself called upon to defend William Lockhart, the Chairman of the Commission and Dean of the School of Law at the University of Minnesota. At the end of the 30-minute discussion, the vote on the resolution was 60 in favor and five against. The five Senators voting against were Case, Javits, McGovern, Mondale and Young of Ohio.

On October 24, a week before the election, President Nixon issued his statement rejecting the findings and recommendations of the Commission. This statement included the following excerpts:

I have evaluated that report and categorically reject its morally bankrupt conclusions and major recommendations.

So long as I am in the White House, there will be no relaxation of the national effort to control and eliminate smut from our national life.

The Commission contends that the proliferation of filthy books and plays has no lasting harmful effect on a man's character. If that were true, it must also be true that great books, great paintings and great plays have no ennobling effect on man's conduct. Centuries of civilization and ten minutes of common sense tell us otherwise.

The Commission calls for the repeal of laws controlling smut for adults—while recommending continued restrictions on smut for children. In an open society, this proposal is untenable. If the level of filth rises in the adult community, the young people in our society cannot help but also be inundated by the flood.[25]

Nixon went on to state that smut should be outlawed in every state in the union. In his view, the Commission on Pornography and Obscenity had performed a major disservice.

Though, metaphorically, one might suggest that the high tide of criticism against the Commission Report came with its rejection by the president, the waters receded only slowly, even after the November 3, 1970, election. Congressman Nix, on November 17 and 18, again called into session his Subcommittee on Postal Operations to hear further testimony on the Commission Report. As with the hearings Congressman Nix had held three months earlier, these later hearings were largely devoted to refuting the Commission's findings and recommendations.

What had begun in the Congress more than two years earlier, as the result of a political impasse over what policy decisions could or should be made regarding the presence of sexually explicit materials in American society, concluded with the impasse unresolved and the concern of large segments of citizens undiminished. The use of the Commission Report during the campaign of 1970 to fuel the fires of political piety quickly left the sense and intent of the recommendations blurred and distorted. The use of the Report as fodder in the campaign only served to exacerbate the anxieties and dilemmas which had first precipitated the formation of the Commission.

REALITIES, POLICIES AND PUBLICS

As is evident from an examination of the reception given the Report of the Commission on Obscenity and Pornography, the accuracy, validity and generalizability of the social science data had little to do with the acceptance or rejection of the Report. A federal commission represents a situation in which any number of competing systems of reality are operant and striving to have their conception of "the way things are" become the official conception. Those who bring a social science orientation to commission endeavors, and who seek to address themselves to the issues within such an analytical framework, confront others who do not accept the social science approach as appropriate. Those members of the Obscenity Commission who argued that the debate over sexually explicit material was not one of utility, but one of philosophy and ethics, illustrate this point: from the perspective of an alternative social reality, "mere facts" about the effects of sexually explicit material are irrelevant to the issue.

In a social setting with alternative realities, what roles or functions are open to the social scientist who strives to participate in the process of formulating public policy? Federal commissions represent a situation of contending multiple realities and any commission-sanctioned research will necessarily be scrutinized from these various perspectives. Etzioni argues that the decision-making aspect of policy formation is not necessarily "value-free," for there is a necessity to choose among alternative goals and priorities.[26] Consequently, those who advocate a particular position will want to present findings in such a fashion as to strengthen their own goals and refute those of others. Again, where does the social scientist stand amid all this? There appear to be two complementary strategies available—one with respect to the process of policy-making, and the second with respect to the publics for whom the policies are enacted.

Policy-making involves both methodological and epistemological components. Seeking some end condition or set of circumstances, the policy-maker necessarily utilizes knowledge about the causal relations among variables in order to achieve the desired goal. Katz has provided a succinct statement on the role of the social scientist in clarifying the causal analysis used in policy decision-making.

Although social scientists are still circumscribed by their limited ability to explain causal sequences or the relationships between social events or phenomena, the "logic of social inquiry" enables them to demonstrate the inadequacy of explanations offered to support outmoded public policies by disclosing the inadequacies or insufficiencies in method, looseness in reasoning, or paucity of evidence relied upon to construct the causal model upon which the policy rest.[27]

Such a stance as that suggested by Katz may well be most

effective for the social scientist in a situation of contending multiple realities. By noting "inadequacies or insufficiencies," the issues are not only clarified, but those who would benefit from less precise findings must also contend with "facts" which do not necessarily fit in with their position. Alternatively stated, the role of the social scientist with respect to policy-making is to remain rigorous in analysis, forcing others to sharpen and perhaps re-examine their views on the causal sequences involved. Realistically, there does not appear to be much more the social scientist can do to try and be convincing in the "correctness" of his "reality." Ironically, even if his position is accepted as the most accurate assessment of the causal model and is consequently endorsed by the policy-maker, the basis for that endorsement may not relate to the "scientific" aspects of the data, but rather to their political utility.

If political acceptability and scientific acceptability are not to be equated and if, in fact, they exist on different planes of evaluation, then social science research conducted for federal commissions will necessarily be evaluated on political, as well as scholarly, criteria. Consequently, the data will inevitably be politicized, as a result of its undergoing scrutiny for political ends, regardless of the intent of the investigator. It is this politicization of one's findings which shapes the response and strategy of the social scientist to the publics for whom ultimately the decisions are to be made. Thus, in his response to the politicization of his work, it is encumbent upon the social scientist to become truly "political," not in the sense of becoming partisan or an advocate for a particular interpretation, but rather in the generic sense—by fusing his response as scholar and citizen. The social scientific endeavor becomes as much a choice of how one lives as of how one works. As C. Wright Mills observed:

What he ought to do for the individual is to turn personal troubles and concerns into social issues and problems open to reason—his aim is to help the individual become a self-educating man, who only then would be reasonable and free. What he ought to do for the society is to combat all those forces which are destroying genuine publics and creating a mass society—or put as a positive goal, his aim is to help build and to strengthen self-cultivating publics. Only then might society be reasonable and free.[28]

Forsaking any notion of maintaining a "value-free" posture in the face of the politicization of one's research, the social scientist can assume an advocacy role in creating dialogue and political discussion in the public arena of this society. As now, when the public places are threatened,[29] the imperative is greater, so the forces "which are destroying genuine publics and creating a mass society" are combatted. *Put positively, the social scientist must become political in a manner not typical of current politicians. By so doing, the social scientist engaged in policy research unifies both his methodological approach to causal analysis and his political response to publics.* For the manner in which the social scientist assigns cause to certain actors or events ultimately exhibits a political point of view. As Howard Becker and Irving Louis Horowitz have noted:

When sociologists, in their investigation of causes, implicitly or explicitly assign blame for events and when they suggest what must be done to cause meaningful social change, they speak of matters that are also the subject of political analyses. Their analyses can be judged to be radical, liberal, or conservative by the same criteria used to judge political analyses.[30]

In opposition to this perspective, Daniel Moynihan suggests that "the role of social science lies, not in the formulation of social policy, but in the measurement of its results."[31] This misses the mark. If the social scientist is to be more than a plumber who identifies policy leaks and seals them accordingly, he must involve himself in an analysis through which he presents alternatives to existing programs. With federal commission research, specifically, there are pressures to legitimate any number of "commonsense" notions held by people in high places.

Evaluated in light of the above, the Report of the Commission on Obscenity and Pornography fares well. The research conducted for the Commission forced a wedge into the political constructions of definitions of sexually explicit materials. Although many politicians denounced the Commission's findings and its recommendations, the Report, however briefly, opened a public debate over the issue of "effects" and its relation to the science-vs.-morals debate. And surely an unanticipated consequence of the publicity given the

Commission and its Report has been the greater discussion of sexual values and attitudes in American society. Given the fact that a commission created by the Congress and its members appointed by the president openly discussed sexually explicit materials, the topic gained a legitimacy otherwise difficult to achieve.

Yet, in one important respect, the Report does not fare well, for it tends to provide a conventional response to a conventional "problem." The Report noted that "much of the 'problem' regarding materials which depict explicit sexual activity stems from the inability or reluctance of people in our society to be open and direct in dealing with sexual matters."[32] This insight is not pursued or systematically confronted, though it provides the basis for a re-interpretation of the cause-effect relationship between sexually explicit material and action. To couch the research in terms of effects of the materials leads one in quite different directions than does the counteranalysis revolving around the question of what societal forces generate the effect of the presence of sexually explicit material. That is, might not the analysis of the "inability or reluctance of people in our society" to deal with sexual matters create the conditions for an examination and discussion about ourselves as a society, rather than for a focus upon qualities of pictures, books and films? The Report does not assist the individual in "self-education," nor does it provide the means by which personal troubles can be transformed into social issues. Consequently, both the personal troubles and the social issues remain—unconnected and unresolved. But, given the multiple realities, the political origins, the distortions of findings for political gain and the hints in the Report about the "problem" in American society, can we fairly expect a federal commission to make the leap between troubles and issues that social science itself persistently fails to do?

NOTES

1. Daniel Bell, "Government by Commission," *The Public Interest*, no. 3 (Spring 1966).
2. W.T. Johnson, "The Pornography Report: Epistemology, Methodology, and Ideology," *Duquesne Law Review*, vol. 10 (Winter 1971): 191.
3. Michael Lipsky and David Olson, "Riot Commission Politics," *Trans-action* (now *Society*), vol. 6, no. 9 (July/August 1969): 21.
4. Warren Lehman, "Crime, the Public, and the Crime Commission: A

Critical Review of the Challenge of Crime in a Free Society," *Michigan Law Review*, vol. 66, no. 7 (May 1968): 1489.

5. Ibid., p. 1538.

6. Lipsky and Olson, "Riot Commission Politics," pp. 15-16.

7. Such circumstances would allow for an important contribution by professional organizations both in securing wider media coverage of the rebuttal as well as in providing a channel through which the researcher could present his position in detail to others in the organization.

8. Lehman, "Crime, the Public, and the Crime Commission," p. 1491.

9. cf. Leonard Berkowitz, "Sex and Violence: We Can't Have it Both Ways," *Psychology Today*, vol. 5 (December 1971): 14-23; Harry Clor, "Science, Eros, and the Law: A Critique of the Obscenity Commission Report," *Duquesne Law Review*, vol. 10 (Fall 1971): 63-76; Weldon Johnson, "The Pornography Report," pp. 190-219; Herbert Packer, "The Pornography Caper," *Commentary*, vol. 51, no. 2 (February 1971): 72-76; Ray C. Rist, "The Dilemmas of Obscenity in American Society," *The Cresset*, vol. 35, no. 1 (November 1971): 8-13; and James Q. Wilson, "Violence, Pornography and Social Science," *The Public Interest*, no. 22 (Winter 1971): 45-61.

10. cf. Statement by Senator Karl E. Mundt, Hearings before the Select Subcommittee on Education, House of Representatives (H.R. 2525 at 14, 1967).

11. cf. Statement by Senator Jack Miller, Hearings before the Select Subcommittee on Education, House of Representatives (H.R. 2525 at 15, 1967).

12. cf. Public Law 90-100, 90th Congress, S. 188.

13. Johnson, "The Pornography Report," pp. 214-15.

14. Public Law 90-100.

15. Commission members interviewed by the author were Edward Greenwood, Otto Larsen, Irving Lehrman, Freedman Lewis, William Lockhart and Barbara Scott. Paul Bender, legal counselor to the Commission, was also interviewed. Commissioner Hill refused to be interviewed and Commissioner Charles Keating did not respond to several inquiries. Time, lack of funds and location did not allow the opportunity to interview other Commission members.

16. Jerome Skolnick, "Violence Commission Violence," *Trans*action, vol. 7, no. 12 (October 1970): 36.

17. Commission on Obscenity and Pornography, *Progress Report*, (Washington, D.C.: U.S. Government Printing Office, 1969), p. 1.

18. Lipsky and Olson, "Riot Commission Politics," p. 18.

19. *Progress Report*, p. 24.

20. Packer, "The Pornography Caper," p. 73.

21. Commission on Obscenity and Pornography, *Report of the Commission on Obscenity and Pornography*, (Washington, D.C.: U.S. Government Printing Office, 1970), p. 387.

22. cf. Hearings before the Subcommittee on Postal Operations, House of Representatives (H.R. 19541, 1970).

23. Spiro Agnew, Prepared remarks, Salt Lake City, Utah, September 30, 1970.

24. Robert Finch, Statement released at the White House, October 2, 1970.

25. Richard Nixon, Statement released at the White House, October 24, 1970.

26. Amitai Etzioni, "Policy Research," *The American Sociologist*, vol. 6, Supplementary Issue, (June 1971): 8-12.

27. Michael Katz, "The Unmasking of Dishonest Pretensions: Towards an Interpretation of the Role of Social Science in Constitutional Litigation," *The American Sociologist*, vol. 6, Supplementary Issue, (June 1971): 56.

28. C. Wright Mills, *The Sociological Imagination* (New York: Oxford University Press, 1959), p. 186.

29. cf. The discussion by Hannah Arendt, *On Revolution* (New York: Viking Press, 1965).

30. Howard S. Becker and Irving Louis Horowitz, "Radical Politics and Sociological Research," *American Journal of Sociology*, vol. 78, no. 1, (July 1972): 58.

31. Daniel Patrick Moynihan, *Maximum Feasible Misunderstanding* (New York: The Free Press, 1969), p. 193.

32. Commission on Obscenity and Pornography, p. 47.

Bibliography

GENERAL

Berns, Walter. *Freedom, Virtue and the First Amendment*. Chicago: Henry Regnery, 1965.

Elliott, George. "Against Pornography," *Harper's Magazine*. March (1965).

Ellis, Albert. *The American Sexual Tragedy*. New York: Grove Press, 1962.

Gerber, Albert. *Sex, Pornography and Justice*. New York: Lyle Stuart, 1965.

Hughes, Douglas A. *Perspectives on Pornography*. New York: St. Martin's Press, 1970.

Jahoda, Marie. *The Impact of Literature: A Psychological Discussion of Some Assumptions in the Censorship Debate*. New York: Research Center for Human Relations, New York University, 1954.

Marcus, Steven. *The Other Victorians: A Study of Sexuality and Pornography in Mid-Nineteenth Century England*. New York: Bantam Books, 1967.

"Obscenity and the Arts," a symposium appearing in *Law and Contemporary Problems*. Vol. 20, no. 4. (1955).

Rolph, C.H. (ed.) *Does Pornography Matter?* London: Routledge & Kegan Paul, 1961.

Sorokin, Pitirim. *The American Sex Revolution*. Boston: P. Sargeant, 1956.

PORNOGRAPHY AND ISSUES OF LAW

Bender, Paul. "Technical Report, The Definition of 'Obscene' Under Existing Law." Commission on Obscenity and Pornography. Washington, D.C., 1970.

———. "The Obscenity Muddle," *Harpers*. Vol. 246, no. 1473 (February 1973).

Cairns, Robert, James Paul and Julius Wishner, "Sex Censorship: The Assumptions of Anti-Obscenity Laws and the Empirical Evidence." *Minnesota Law Review*. Vol. 46 (1962).

Clor, Harry, (ed.) *Censorship and Freedom of Expression*. Chicago: Rand McNally, 1971.

Comment, "Obscenity: The Pig in the Parlor," *Santa Clara Law*. Vol. 10 (1970).

Day, J. Edward. "Mailing Lists and Pornography," *American Bar Association Journal*, Vol. 52, no. 12. (December 1966).

Ernast, Morris L. and Alan U. Schwartz. *Censorship: The Search for the Obscene*. New York: MacMillan, 1964.

Gellhorn, Walter. *Individual Freedom and Governmental Restraints*. Baton Rouge: Louisiana State University Press, 1956.

Henriques, Fernando. "Perils of Pornography," *Twentieth Century*. No. 171 (Summer 1962).

Kalven, Harry. "The Metaphysics of the Law of Obscenity." *1960 Supreme Court Review*, Ed. P. Kurland. Chicago: University of Chicago Press, 1960.

Kilpatrick, James J. *The Smut Peddlers*. New York: Avon, 1960.

Kuh, Richard H. *Foolish Figleaves*. New York: MacMillan, 1967.

Krause, Marshall, "The Court and Obscenity," *This World*, Supplement to *San Francisco Chronicle*, (October 8, 1972).

Kronhausen, Eberhard and Phyllis. *Pornography and the Law*. New York: Ballantine Books, 1959.

Lewin, Nathan, "Sex at High Noon in Times Square," *The New Republic*, Vol. 168, no. 27 (July 1973).

Lockhart, William B. and R.C. McClure. "Censorship of Obscenity," *Minnesota Law Review*. Vol. 45 (1961).

Mead, Margaret. "Sex and Censorship in Contemporary Society," *New World Writing*. New York: The New American Library of World Literature, Third Mentor Selection, 1953.

Murphy, Terrence J. *Censorship: Government and Obscenity*. Baltimore: Garamond Press, 1963.

Paul, James and Murray L. Schwartz. *Federal Censorship? Obscenity in the Mail*. New York: The Free Press, 1961.

Randall, R.S. *Censorship of the Movies*. Madison: University of Wisconsin Press, 1968.

Seaton, Richard H. "Obscenity: The Search for a Standard," *Kansas Law Review*. Vol. 13 (1964-1965).

Semonche, Jone E. "Definitional and Contextual Obscenity," *UCLA Law Review*, Vol. 13, no. 5 (1966).

"The Scope of Supreme Court Review in Obscenity Cases," *Duke Law Journal*. Vol. 34 (1965).

PORNOGRAPHY AND ISSUES OF MORALITY

Burgess, A. "What is Pornography?" in Hughes, D.A. (ed.) *Perspectives on Pornography*. New York: St. Martin's Press, 1970.

Chandon, John (ed.) *To Deprave and Corrupt*. New York: Association Press, 1962.

Clor, Harry. *Obscenity and Public Morality*. Chicago: University of Chicago Press, 1969.

Cousins, Norman, "See Everything, Do Everything, Feel Nothing," *Saturday Review*. Vol. 54, no. 3 (January, 1971).

Devlin, Patrick. *The Enforcement of Morals*. London: Oxford University Press, 1965.

Dortmund, E.K., "Pornography: Why Did They Do It?" *Northwest Magazine*, Supplement to *The Oregonian* (October 8, 1972).

Gagnon, John, and William Simon, (eds.) *Sexual Deviance*. New York: Harper and Row, 1967.

Gardiner, Harold. *Catholic Viewpoint on Censorship*. Garden City, New York: Doubleday Image Books, 1961.

Glock, Charles and Start, R., *Religion and Society in Tension*. Chicago: Rand McNally, 1965.

Harris, Louis. *Time Morality Poll*. New York: Harris and Associates, 1969.

Hart, H., *Law, Liberty and Morality*. New York: Vintage Books, 1966.

Hoover, J.E., "The Fight Against Filth." Revised (1965) from an article appearing in *The American Legion Magazine*, (1961).

Hyman, S.E., "In Defense of Pornography." in Hughes, D.A. (ed.) *Perspectives on Pornography*. New York: St. Martin's Press, 1970.

Kyle-Keith, Richard. *The High Price of Pornography*. Washington, D.C.: Public Affairs Press, 1961.

Levitt, E.E., "Pornography: Some New Perspectives on an Old Problem," *The Journal of Sex Research*. Vol. 5 (1969).

Sonenschein, D., "Pornography: A False Issue," *Psychiatric Opinion*. Vol. 6 (1969).

Tynam, D. "Dirty Books Can Stay," in Hughes, D.A. (ed.) *Perspectives on Pornography*. New York: St. Martin's Press, 1970.

PORNOGRAPHY AND SOCIAL SCIENCE RESEARCH: THE COMMISSION ON OBSCENITY AND PORNOGRAPHY

Berkowitz, L. "Sex and Violence: We Can't Have It Both Ways," *Psychology Today*. Vol. 5 (December 1971).

Clor, H., "Science, Eros, and the Law: A Critique of the Obscenity Commission Report," *Duquesne Law Review*. Vol. 10 (Fall 1971).

Commission on Obscenity and Pornography. *Progress Report*. Washington, D.C.: U.S. Government Printing Office, 1969.
——. *Report of the Commission on Obscenity and Pornography*. Washington, D.C.: U.S. Government Printing Office, 1970.
——. *Technical Reports*. Washington, D.C.: U.S. Government Printing Office, 1970.

Johnson, W.T., "The Pornography Report: Epistemology, Methodology and Ideology," *Duquesne Law Review*. Vol. 10 (Winter 1971).

Larsen, Otto, "The Commission on Obscenity and Pornography: Form, Function, and Failure," paper presented to American Sociological Association, New York, August 1973.

Packer, H., "The Pornography Caper," *Commentary*. Vol. 51, no. 2 (February 1971).

Polsky, Ned, "On the Sociology of Pornography." *Hustlers, Beats, and Others*. New York: Doubleday Anchor Books, 1969.

Rist, R.C., "The Dilemmas of Obscenity in American Society," *The Cresset*. Vol. 35, no. 1 (November 1971).

————. "The Politics of Pornography: A Study of the Natural History of the Commission on Obscenity and Pornography," unpublished.

Contributors

Walter Berns is a professor of political science at the University of Toronto.

John H. Gagnon is an associate professor of sociology at the State University of New York at Stony Brook. He is both author and editor of books in the areas of sex education and sexual behavior. He is co-editor of *The Sexual Scene* published by Transaction Books.

Harold Gardiner is the literary editor of *America*, a national Catholic weekly.

Abraham Kaplan is a professor of philosophy at the University of Michigan. He is the author of numerous works including *The Conduct of Inquiry*, a philosophical study of behavioral science methodology.

John MacGregor is an associate professor of sociology at Western Washington State College. His current research centers on the means by which one can trace out how new concepts become institutionalized and accepted in various academic disciplines.

Peter Michelson is a professor of English at the University of Notre Dame and a frequent contributor to both periodicals and academic journals.

Ray C. Rist is senior policy analyst, National Institute of Education, Department of Health, Education and Welfare, Washington, D.C. His most recent book is *The Urban School: A Factory for Failure*. He is also the editor of *Restructuring American Education*, published by Transaction Books.

William Simon is program supervisor in sociology and anthropology at the Institute for Juvenile Research in Chicago. He is the author and editor of books and articles in the area of sex education and sexual behavior. He is co-editor with John H. Gagnon of *The Sexual Scene*.

Joseph Slade is an assistant professor of English at Long Island University in Brooklyn and the editor of *Markham Review*. He has written a biography of Edwin Markham, the radical American poet.

George Steiner is fellow and director of English studies at Churchill College, Cambridge University. He is the author of many articles and books including *Tolstoy or Dostoevsky* and *Language and Silence*.

Earl Warren, Jr., is a judge in the Municipal Court of Sacramento, California. He has been a member of the California State Board of Control and the Governor's Advisory Board on Mental Health.

James Q. Wilson is a professor of government at Harvard University. He has written widely in the area of criminology and also urban problems. He is on the Publication Committee of *The Public Interest*.

INDEX